Regulations, Institutions, and Commitment assesses the impact of core political and social institutions on regulatory structures and performance in the telecommunications industry in Jamaica, the United Kingdom, Chile, Argentina, and the Philippines. These core institutions are shown to strongly influence the credibility and effectiveness of regulation, and thus its ability to encourage private investment and support efficiency. Currently, privatization and regulatory reform are viewed as the solution to the problem of poor performance by telecommunications and other public utilities. The contributors argue that these high expectations may not always be met because of the way a country's political and social institutions – its executive, legislative, and judicial systems, its informal norms of public behavior – interact with regulatory processes and economic conditions. In some environments, regulatory solutions run counter to the prevailing wisdom: achieving credible commitment may require an inflexible regulatory regime, and sometimes public ownership of utilities may be the only feasible alternative.

REGULATIONS, INSTITUTIONS, AND COMMITMENT

POLITICAL ECONOMY OF INSTITUTIONS AND DECISIONS

Editors
James E. Alt, *Harvard University*
Douglass C. North, *Washington University in St. Louis*

Other books in the series
Alberto Alesina and Howard Rosenthal, *Partisan Politics, Divided Government and the Economy*
Lee J. Alston, Thráinn Eggertsson, and Douglass C. North, eds., *Empirical Studies in Institutional Change*
James E. Alt and Kenneth Shepsle, eds., *Perspectives on Positive Political Economy*
Jeffrey S. Banks and Eric A. Hanushek, *Modern Political Economy: Old Topics, New Directions*
Yoram Barzel, *Economic Analysis of Property Rights*
Robert Bates, *Beyond the Miracle of the Market: The Political Economy of Agrarian Development in Kenya*
Peter Cowhey and Mathew McCubbins, eds., *Structure and Policy in Japan and the United States*
Gary W. Cox, *The Efficient Secret: The Cabinet and the Development of Political Parties in Victorian England*
Jean Ensminger, *Making a Market: The Institutional Transformation of an African Society*
Murray Horn, *The Political Economy of Public Administration: Institutional Choice in the Public Sector*
Jack Knight, *Institutions and Social Conflict*
Michael Laver and Kenneth Shepsle, *Making and Breaking Governments*
Michael Laver and Kenneth Shepsle, eds., *Cabinet Ministers and Parliamentary Government*
Leif Lewin, *Ideology and Strategy: A Century of Swedish Politics* (English Edition)
Gary Libecap, *Contracting for Property Rights*
Mathew D. McCubbins and Terry Sullivan, eds., *Congress: Structure and Policy*
Gary J. Miller, *Managerial Dilemmas: The Political Economy of Hierarchy*
Douglass C. North, *Institutions, Institutional Change, and Economic Performance*
Elinor Ostrom, *Governing the Commons: The Evolution of Institutions for Collective Action*
Mark Ramseyer and Frances Rosenbluth, *The Politics of Oligarchy: Institutional Choice in Imperial Japan*
Jean-Laurent Rosenthal, *The Fruits of Revolution: Property Rights, Litigation, and French Agriculture*
Charles Stewart III, *Budget Reform Politics: The Design of the Appropriations Process in the House of Representatives, 1865–1921*
John Waterbury, *Exposed to Innumerable Delusions: Public Enterprise and State Power in Egypt, India, Mexico, and Turkey*

REGULATIONS, INSTITUTIONS, AND COMMITMENT

Comparative studies of telecommunications

Edited by

BRIAN LEVY
The World Bank

and

PABLO T. SPILLER
University of California at Berkeley

CAMBRIDGE UNIVERSITY PRESS

Published by the Press Syndicate of the University of Cambridge
The Pitt Building, Trumpington Street, Cambridge CB2 1RP
40 West 20th Street, New York, NY 10011-4211, USA
10 Stamford Road, Oakleigh, Melbourne 3166, Australia

First published 1996

Printed in the United States of America

Library of Congress Cataloging-in-Publication Data

Regulations, institutions, and commitment : comparative studies of
telecommunications / Brian Levy & Pablo Spiller, editors.
    p. cm. – (Political economy of institutions and decisions)
    ISBN 0-521-55013-0 (hc). – ISBN 0-521-55996-0 (pbk.)
    1. Telecommunication policy – Cross-cultural studies.
    2. Telecommunication – Deregulation – Cross-cultural studies.
    3. Privatization – Cross-cultural studies.   4. Economic development –
Cross-cultural studies. I. Levy, Brian. II. Spiller, Pablo T.
(Pablo Tomas), 1951–   . III. Series.
HE7645.R43   1996
384 – dc20   95-47538
                                                             CIP

A catalog record for this book is available from the British Library.

ISBN 0–521–55013–0 hardback
ISBN 0–521–55996–0 paperback

Contents

v

Foreword

The new institutional economics is a way of reasoning and approaching political economic problems. Its objective is to broaden out and modify the microeconomic foundation of economic theory by taking into account the way in which institutions, political and economic, affect the performance of economics over time. It provides a far richer context because it explores the many other dimensions besides just price and quantity, the basis for the comparative model of economic theory that shape the performance of economics through time.

While the new institutional economics has developed a body of theory to analyze the way in which political and economic institutions evolve, it has been short on empirical content. This study is a major contribution to filling in that lacuna. It is a careful and thoughtful study of the institutional features of regulation over telecommunications in five different countries, and draws from that empirical material important implications for developing sound regulatory policy that will improve the performance of that industry.

The study makes clear that, in attempting to provide a regulatory framework for an industry of such dynamic technological change as that of telecommunications, intelligent regulatory policy must take into account the institutional foundations and endowments of a nation, and the way those can be extended and applied. The study speaks for itself in demonstrating unequivocally the power of the new institutional economics to provide a far deeper foundation for economic policymaking, analyzing, and modeling then we have had heretofore.

Douglass North
Washington University
St. Louis, Missouri

Series editor's preface

The Cambridge Series in the Political Economy of Institutions and Decisions is built around attempts to answer two central questions: How do institutions evolve in response to individual incentives, strategies, and choices; and how do institutions affect the performance of political and economic systems? The scope of the series is comparative and historical rather than international or specifically American, and the focus is positive rather than normative.

This volume, an outcome of a research project initiated by the World Bank, explores regulation of telecommunications in five countries. The editors' objective was to make a comparative assessment of the impact of core political and social institutions on regulatory structures and performance in order to derive some generalizations about what works and doesn't work in telecommunications regulation. The study is rich in original insights into the interplay between specific institutional endowments of a polity, governance structures, design characteristics, and consequent industry performance. More than anything else the study demonstrates the usefulness of the new institutional economics as a tool to analyze regulatory structures and aid in the development of sound regulatory practice.

Preface

This volume is the outcome of a research project initiated by the World Bank. In recent years, the Bank has been actively supporting efforts at privatization in developing countries. For utilities in particular, it has become clear that the regulatory framework was an important determinant of the success or failure of these efforts. Yet there were important gaps in knowledge as to appropriate regulatory design across different institutional settings. Consequently, a first objective of the research project was to learn from experience as to what worked in the regulation of telecommunications – and, by extension, in utility regulation more broadly.

A second objective of the research was to probe what might be the practical relevance for World Bank work of the "new institutional economics" (NIE). Many World Bank staff were intrigued by the conceptual advances and the empirical findings emerging from the NIE research agenda – but were unclear as to the concrete implications of the intellectual advances for policy design. Some key characteristics of utilities – important economies of scale and scope, assets which can be specific and nonredeployable in other uses, and the frequent politicization of utility pricing – are presently those which have received detailed attention in the NIE literature. Consequently, there was much background work on which an applied study of regulation of telecommunications could build.

The research project was designed from the start to be empirical and comparative. It examines in each of five countries the relation between the regulatory regime, utility performance, and the background political institutions – and probes comparatively for cross country patterns in the interrelations among these variables. Given the innovative character of the work, the project commenced with a study of one country (Jamaica). For the initial case, it was important to strike a balance between rigor and flexibility. As a prelude to the case, we developed an initial array of empirical hypotheses. Subsequently, we adapted and extended these hypotheses in response to lessons learned in the field. The results of that study provided a common basis for the design of the four subsequent studies. While the countries were too diverse for it to be productive to impose an identical research schema on all the studies, there was close and continuing collaboration among all the researchers.

The research benefited from a variety of support. The research was funded by the World Bank's research support budget. Intellectually, we were well served by our advisory group, which included Lee Alston, Matt McCubbins, Roger Noll, Douglass North, and Bjorn Wellenius. Draft papers were presented at a conference at the World Bank in April 1993. They benefited from comments by Robert Bates, Richard Gilbert, Leroy Jones, David Newbery, Anthony Churchill, Ricardo Halperin, Gregory Ingram, Ashoka Mody, and Peter Scherer. We are grateful to the many people who provided us with information in the field. And we would like to give special thanks to Mary Shirley who was the project sponsor at the World Bank, part of the formal advisory group, and a continuing source of encouragement and practical wisdom through the ups and downs of the research process.

Contributors

Manuel Angel Abdala has a Ph.D. in economics from Boston University. Currently, he is an independent consultant in Buenos Aries, Argentina.

Hadi Esfahani has a Ph.D. in economics from the University of California at Berkeley. He is Associate Professor of Economics at the University of Illinois at Urbana-Champagne.

Ahmed Galal has a Ph.D. in economics from Boston University. He is a Principal Economist in the Private Sector Development Department of the World Bank.

Alice Hill has a Ph.D. in business economics from Harvard University. She was an economist in the Policy Research Department of the World Bank at the time the project was undertaken. She currently is working at McKinsey & Company, Inc. in London, England.

Brian Levy has a Ph.D. in economics from Harvard University. He currently is a Principal Economist in the Southern African Department of the World Bank and was in the Policy Research Department at the time the project was undertaken.

Cezley I. Sampson is Professor of Business Administration at the University of West Indies.

Pablo T. Spiller has a Ph.D. in economics from the University of Chicago. He is Professor of Business and Public Policy at the Haas School of Business at the University of California at Berkeley.

Ingo Vogelsang is Professor of Economics at Boston University.

1

A framework for resolving the regulatory problem

BRIAN LEVY AND PABLO T. SPILLER

People the world over are calling for privatization and regulatory reform as the solution to the problem of poor performance by public utilities, and as the means to improved service and lower prices. In this book we argue that these expectations may not always be met because of the way a country's political and social institutions – its executive, legislative, its judicial systems, its informal norms of public behavior – interact with regulatory processes and economic conditions. By making administrative expropriation and manipulation of utilities more or less difficult in some settings than in others, a country's institutions influence the confidence of investors and the performance of privatized utilities. In particular, the analysis in this book looks at the problem of utilities regulation through the lens of the new institutional economics – with its microanalytical perspective and its view of regulation as a contracting problem – to offer insights into the performance of privatized telecommunications utilities in different political and social circumstances.

The book presents the results of a comparative assessment of the impact of core political and social institutions on regulatory structures and performance in the telecommunications industry in Jamaica, the United Kingdom, Chile, Argentina, and the Philippines.[1] We argue that the credibility and effectiveness of a regulatory framework, and so its ability to encourage private investment and support efficiency in the production and use of services, vary with a country's political and social institutions. Performance can be satisfactory under a wide range of regulatory procedures, so long as three complementary mechanisms are in place to restrain arbitrary administrative action: substantive restraints on discretionary actions by the regulator, formal or informal restraints on changing the regulatory system, and institutions to enforce the restraints.

In addition to influencing a regulatory system's ability to restrain administrative action, political and social institutions also have an independent effect on the type of regulation that can be implemented and there-

1

fore on the appropriate balance between commitment to a particular regulatory system and flexibility in response to technological change. Our evidence suggests that credible commitment to a regulatory regime can be cultivated even in what appears to be a problematic environment and that without that commitment long-term investment will not take place.

In some environments solutions run counter to the prevailing wisdom: achieving commitment may require an inflexible regulatory regime, and sometimes public ownership of utilities may be the only feasible alternative. For example, regulatory schemes designed to maximize efficiency (price caps, incentive schemes, competition) usually require substantial discretion for the regulator. But unless a country's institutions allow arbitrary behavior to be distinguished from useful regulatory discretion, a system that grants generous administrative discretion might not generate the high levels of investment and welfare expected from private ownership. Conversely, a regulatory regime that allows almost no flexibility, though it looks very inefficient, might still provide adequate incentives for investment if it fits the country's institutional endowments.

The analysis presented here is relevant for the design of regulatory policy wherever the lack of economic development is related to a generalized lack of administrative restraints, as in developing and newly industrialized countries or in socialist economies in transition.[2] But the results are also relevant for understanding the historical evolution of utilities regulation and ownership in industrialized countries. Indeed, the analysis of the British case suggests that restraint of regulatory discretion is behind the development of regulatory institutions in industrial countries as well.[3]

While we believe that our results provide strong support for some core propositions aligned with the new institutional economics, the spirit of this book is exploratory, as much an exercise in hypothesis formulation as in hypothesis testing. The need for detailed analyses of the political, social, and regulatory institutions of each country limited the number of cases that we were able to consider.[4] Consequently, we offer no formal statistical tests of our central propositions, providing instead an analytical framework and casual but systematically collected and researched evidence.

THE ANALYTICAL FRAMEWORK

Three characteristics of utilities provide the starting point for our analysis. First, their services have important economies of scale and scope. Second, most utilities' assets are specific and nonredeployable in other uses (although the extent of sunk investments varies with the application and the technology). And third, utility services typically have a broad range of domestic users, often as broad as the entire voting population of the country. Viewed through the lens of the new institutional economics, these characteristics create contracting problems that undercut the ability of ordinary market mechanisms to deliver first-best performance (Barzel 1989; Goldberg 1976; North 1990; Williamson 1988).

Economies of scale and scope imply that the number of providers of basic utility services is going to be small. Because a large proportion of a utility's assets are sunk, a utility will be willing to operate even if it cannot recover its sunk investments so long as it covers its operating costs.[5] The wide base of domestic consumers implies that utility pricing is always going to have a political component,[6] while the whiff of monopoly (particularly when ownership is concentrated in foreign hands) raises the stakes for political action.

The combination of large investments in durable, specific assets and strong politicization means that utilities are particularly vulnerable to administrative expropriation of their vast quasi-rents. The easiest form of administrative expropriation is to set utility prices below the company's long-run average costs. More subtle are specific requirements for investment, equipment purchase, or labor contracts that extract quasi-rents as well. Where the threat of administrative expropriation is strong, private investors will limit their exposure.[7] Countries that allow broad administrative discretion often end up with public ownership of utilities, because the hazards of direct private investment are so great.[8]

Technology interacts with politics to determine the potential for administrative expropriation. Industries with very small sunk investments or rapid asset depreciation will not be prime candidates for administrative expropriation.[9] Nor are companies likely to be affected in the short run where demand for utility services is growing rapidly, because the political costs of investment delays might be too high for opportunistic behavior to pay off. In the longer run, however, the fight for control over the institutions of government and the corresponding division of the spoils mean that utilities are never free of the threat of administrative or outright expropriation, even in rapidly growing economies.

Resolution of the regulatory problem: A framework for empirical analysis

A common framework incorporating regulatory design and a country's institutional endowment guides the empirical analysis of how – and how well – each country has resolved its regulatory problems. The analysis also explains why the resolution took the form it did and explicates the relation between regulatory outcomes and the performance of private utilities.

Governance and incentives in regulatory design. To understand countries' ability to commit to particular regulatory processes and institutions, we find it useful to look at regulation as a "design" problem with two components: regulatory governance and regulatory incentives. The governance structure incorporates the mechanisms a society uses to restrain the discretionary scope of regulators and to resolve the conflicts to which these restraints give rise.[10] The regulatory incentive structure comprises the rules governing pricing, subsidies, competition and entry, interconnection, and the like.

The structure of regulatory incentives has been the central preoccupation of virtually all theoretical work on regulation, to the neglect of regulatory governance. An important finding of this study is that the emphasis on incentives is inadequate. Though incentives do affect performance, their full impact occurs only if the proper regulatory governance structure is in place.[11]

Regulatory governance and incentives are choice variables for policymakers. The choices are constrained, however. Choices about regulatory governance are constrained by the specific institutional endowment of the nation, which determines the form and the severity of the country's regulatory problems and the range of options for resolving them. Choices about regulatory incentives are also constrained by institutional endowment and by the governance features built into the regulatory system.

Institutional endowment and regulatory governance. Following North and others we consider five elements of a nation's institutional endowment:

- Legislative and executive institutions – the formal mechanisms for appointing legislators and decision makers, for making and implementing laws and regulations, and for determining the relations between these two institutions
- Judicial institutions – the formal mechanisms for appointing judges and determining the internal structure of the judiciary and for impartially resolving disputes among private parties or between private parties and the state
- Custom and other informal but broadly accepted norms that tacitly restrain the actions of individuals or institutions
- The character of the contending social interests within a society and the balance between them, including the role of ideology
- The country's administrative capabilities

None of these elements is entirely static, though changes in a particular country are often slow. But to keep the discussion manageable, the analysis treats each element as exogenous – as the institutional endowment of a particular nation. The analysis focuses on the first two elements – a country's political and judicial institutions – and comments on the others occasionally.

The structure and organization of a country's legislative and executive institutions influence its regulatory options according to how well they restrain arbitrary government action. Formal institutional mechanisms for restraining government authority include explicit separation of legislative, executive, and judicial powers (Gely and Spiller 1990; McCubbins, Noll, and Weingast 1987, 1989); a written constitution limiting the legislative power of the executive and enforced by the courts; two legislative houses elected under different voting rules;[12] an electoral system calibrated to produce a proliferation of minority parties or a smaller set of parties with little disciplinary authority over their legislators;[13] and a federal structure of power, with strong decentralization even down to the local level (Weingast 1993).

Utility regulation is likely to be far more credible – and regulatory problems less severe – in countries with political systems that curb executive and legislative discretion. Credibility is often achieved at the expense of flexibility, however, since the same mechanisms that make it difficult to impose arbitrary changes in the rules may make it difficult to enact sensible rules in the first place or to adapt the rules as circumstances change. In countries with these types of political institutions, reform may have to await some shock to the political system.

Legislative and executive institutions may also limit a country's options for regulatory governance. In parliamentary systems, for example, the executive may have substantial control over the legislative agenda and outcomes.[14] If legislative and executive powers alternate between political parties with substantially different interests, regulatory legislation may not be considered an adequate safeguard against administrative discretion since a change in the government can mean a change in the law.[15] Similarly, administrative procedures and administrative law will not be able to restrain an executive with strong legislative powers since the executive will tend to dominate the judiciary in the interpretation of laws. In this case, administrative procedures require some base other than administrative law.

A strong and independent judiciary could serve this function by limiting administrative discretion. A well-established body of administrative law opens the governance option of using administrative procedures to curb discretion.[16] A tradition of upholding contracts and property rights opens the governance option of using formal regulatory contracts (licenses) to restrain discretion, a valuable option in countries where the executive holds sway over the legislative process. A tradition of judicial independence and efficiency opens the governance option of using administrative tribunals to resolve conflicts between the government and the utility within the confines of the existing regulatory system. It also provides assurances against government deviation from specific legislative or constitutional commitments that underpin the regulatory system. Though there are no simple ways of measuring judicial strength, two characteristics seem indicative: general perceptions about judicial probity and the courts' record in deciding against the government. A corrupt judiciary that attempts to be independent may find its corruption publicly exposed, followed by a clampdown, while a judiciary that seldom rules against the government, even on contract disputes, will not be regarded as strong.[17]

Institutional endowment and regulatory incentives. To promote welfare, the regulatory incentive structure should facilitate investment, allocatively efficient pricing, and the introduction of new services and technologies. But regulatory incentives are not implemented in an institutional vacuum. They are affected by a country's institutional endowment, its distributive politics, and the nature of its regulatory governance.

Consider, first, the constraints that the nation's institutional endowment imposes on the design of regulatory incentives. Administrative capabilities – the ability of the nation's professionals to handle complex regulatory concepts and processes smoothly and without triggering a proliferation of disputes and litigation – are particularly relevant for the implementation of complex regulatory designs. Regulatory systems that call for complex implementation will work poorly in countries with weak administrative capabilities.

Distributive politics can interfere with the allocative efficiency that can be achieved by regulatory incentives. The demand for cross-subsidization from businesses to residential users, a common feature of telecommunications policy in many countries, often translates into high prices for long-distance or international calls. Insistence on cross-subsidization limits the potential for exploiting the advantages of competition.

Finally, and perhaps most important, the institutional realities of regulatory governance in some countries might limit the range of regulatory incentives options to third- or even fourth-best. In some countries the only way to curb administrative arbitrariness may be to withdraw almost all administrative discretion. That would confine the choice of regulatory incentive designs to those with little built-in flexibility. In telecommunications, where technological change is rapid, the cost of this regulatory inflexibility is high – but so is the cost of failing to adequately curb arbitrary administrative action.

But even with these constraints, the country studies suggest that policymakers retain a broad range of discretion on the design of regulatory governance and incentive structures. Indeed, utility performance turns out to be best when countries have achieved a good fit between their institutions and their regulatory governance and incentive designs and worst when regulatory design proceeds without attention to institutional realities.

A decision tree

The decision tree in Figure 1.1 helps in mapping the choices involved in matching regulatory systems to a country's institutions and sets the stage for analysis of the case studies in a way that highlights the impact of a country's institutional endowment on its regulatory design.[18] The heavy lines in the figure represent paths for which our sample offers examples. Because our framework has implications for other institutional environments, we present the decision tree in its general formulation. We make four sets of distinctions.

The first distinction is between countries that have domestic institutions capable of credibly refraining from arbitrary administrative action and those that do not. Our framework suggests that an independent judiciary with a reputation for impartiality, and whose decisions are enforced, is a necessary condition for making credible commitments. Among the countries studied Chile, Jamaica, and the United Kingdom had in place a strong and independent judiciary, while Argentina and the Philippines did not. Countries lacking a well-functioning judiciary will have difficulty in the short term developing a regulatory system capable of sustaining efficient levels of private participation and investment, and there is little reason for them to devote substantial scarce resources to such an effort. Rather, alternative mechanisms for securing commitment (like international guarantees) will be called for.

Among countries able to use regulation to secure commitment, the second distinction is between those whose political institutions allow them to make credible regulatory commitments through legislation and those that can best achieve such commitment by embedding their regulatory systems in the operating licenses of private companies. As we discuss below, legislation may provide regulatory credibility in a political system that does not generate a unified government, such as presidential systems with multichamber legislatures and different electoral cycles. In addition, however, legislation needs to specify the process for making regulatory decisions. Otherwise, regulatory discretion will be unchecked. In two-party parliamentary systems, with parties that alternate in government, legislation will not confer regulatory credibility. In that case a solution may be to embed the regulatory process in contract law rather than

Figure 1.1 A decision tree for regulatory design.

administrative law.[19] Chile (and the United States) falls into the group of countries that can embed their regulatory systems in legislation, and Jamaica and the United Kingdom into the group that will find embedding it in contracts more successful.

The third distinction (not depicted in Figure 1.1) is between countries requiring specific, substantive rules to achieve credibility, and countries that can use flexible regulatory processes and still restrain arbitrary action. In general, the potential for flexibility in design will be highest in two sets of countries. One set comprises countries whose institutional endowment includes informal norms or bodies of administrative law that restrain the arbitrary use of government power even in the absence of explicit legal restraints. The other set includes countries in which an institutionalized process of argumentation and consensus formation sets de facto limits on the administrative expropriation to which a private utility can be subjected. Among the countries studied that cannot provide credibility through legislation, Jamaica is in the category requiring specific, substantive rules to achieve regulatory credibility, while the United Kingdom can achieve credibility with a more flexible regulatory process. Chile is among the countries that can use legislation as its regulatory instrument, but it also has the ability to achieve credibility with a more flexible regulatory framework.

Among countries requiring very specific, substantive rules to achieve credibility, the fourth distinction in Figure 1.1 is between countries with strong administrative capabilities and those without. Countries with strong administrative capabilities can set up a regulatory system based on specific, substantive rules that restrain arbitrary action and so can attract investment and promote efficiency and flexibility. Countries with weak capabilities may have to settle for less efficient rules if their regulatory system is to work. Among the countries studied, Chile is in the group of countries with strong administrative capabilities, and Jamaica is in the group without such capabilities.

Viewed from a different perspective, the decision tree identifies three complementary sets of mechanisms for restraining arbitrary action: substantive restraints on regulatory discretion, which can take the form of process regulation or specific substantive rules (distinctions 3 and 4); restraints, of either the legislative or licensing variety, on changing the regulatory system (distinction 2); and institutions for enforcing the substantive restraints and restraints on changing the system (distinction 1). A central hypothesis explored in the comparative country analysis is that all three mechanisms must be in place and properly aligned with the specific characteristics of a country's background institutions for private performance to be satisfactory.

Brian Levy and Pablo T. Spiller

In exploratory research of the kind described here, there is a risk of retrospective rationalization in interpreting the role of exogenous variables such as a country's institutional endowment.[20] To reduce this risk, we have anchored our characterizations of the institutions of the five countries in prior scholarly writings. Further, we alert the reader whenever we push our interpretation of the behavior of a country's institutions beyond previous bounds. We divide the countries into three groups: traditional parliamentary systems (Jamaica and the United Kingdom), the archetypal presidential system (Chile), and rent-seeking presidential systems (Argentina and the Philippines). Each group has distinct implications for the types of regulatory regimes that are workable. Chapters 2–6 probe each of these country cases in detail. Table 1.1 provides a snapshot of the main institutional characteristics of the five countries and relates them to the potential for opportunistic government behavior.

Traditional parliamentary systems: Jamaica and the United Kingdom

Jamaica and the United Kingdom have parliamentary systems of government, a strong judiciary, and electoral rules that tend to support two strong parties.[21] As a consequence, the majority party invariably has an absolute majority in parliament and controls both the government and the legislature. Both countries have had extreme policy shifts as parties alternated in power.

Their judicial institutions are also similar. Britain has led the world in the development of a judiciary with an exceptional reputation for probity. Jamaica's judiciary is also well regarded and has ruled against the government on numerous occasions. But in a political system based on a sovereign two-party parliament, the courts have no formal restraining authority, and parliament is free to act as it pleases, so long as it follows generally accepted procedures (on which more later) or, as in Jamaica's case, stays within the bounds of a written constitution.[22] Jamaica and the United Kingdom provide observations along the branch of the decision tree answering "yes" to the question on "unified government" (Figure 1.1).

To a large extent, this feature of parliamentary politics has stunted the growth of administrative law doctrine in both countries, although both have a long tradition of contract law and of upholding contracts against the government.[23] In both countries, then, administrative decisions are essentially made in the dark.[24] Agencies do not have to justify their decisions (although the British Office of Telecommunications Regulation

Table 1.1. *Institutional features of Argentina, Chile, Jamaica, the Philippines, and the United Kingdom*

Country	Legislative and executive institutions	Judicial institutions	Social conflict	Social norms	Other features
Argentina	Separation of powers with fragmented party structure.	Weak and politically manipulable.	Basic urban-rural conflict.	Rent seeking. Lack of respect for constitutional order.	Corrupt bureaucracy, but highly qualified professional class.
Chile	Separation of powers with fragmented party structure. Orderly alteration of power except during Pinochet regime.	Strong and professional, defended private property during socialist period.	Regional balance.	Respect for judiciary.	Highly respected bureaucracy and qualified professional class.
Jamaica	Parliamentary system with two strong parties.	Strong and professional, upheld utility contracts against government prior to 1966 and defended private property during the first Manley administration.	Small middle class holds political balance. No major regional differences. Violent urban poor.	Respect for judiciary and electoral outcomes.	Small professional class. Politicized bureaucracy.
Philippines	Separation of powers with weak parties and strong presidency. Under U.S. supervision until 1960 during Marcos regime.	Weak and corrupt.	Regional competition among members of the elite.	Rent seeking. No outright expropriation of elite ownership.	Weak and corrupt bureaucracy.
United Kingdom	Sovereign parliament with strong two-party system.	Very strong and professional, upholds contracts against the government. Weak administrative law.	Large middle class holds political balance.	Strong respect for bureaucratic process and judiciary.	Strong bureaucracy.

does) or hold public hearings.[25] Judicial review of regulatory decisions is not customary in either country. In the United Kingdom regulatory review is not a strong weapon for regulated firms or intervenors, since regulators can make decisions that effectively preclude judicial review.[26]

Thus, the formal institutions of government in the United Kingdom and Jamaica allow for substantial government discretion. That discretion can translate into important policy shifts, with the judiciary playing a minor role in restraining administrative discretion. But in both countries, informal rules of legislative decision making restrain the government's ability to shift policy without consulting with interest groups and building consensus. The need for consensus building arises as much from the imperative of legitimizing government decision making as from the need to maintain a solid front in the governing party to avoid losing the support of the legislature. Mechanisms for developing consensus and internalizing interest group consultations include ad hoc commissions and white and green papers,[27] collective ministerial responsibility (Cox 1993),[28] and dispute settlement through party organizations prior to parliamentary action. Within-party consensus-building measures are useful for single party governments for imparting stability and conferring legitimacy on party leadership – an important safeguard against incursions by other political factions and a means of maintaining backbencher support.

In the United Kingdom, furthermore, the Westminster model of government defines the prerogatives and responsibilities of politicians and bureaucrats for policy implementation.[29] Even where their power is not explicitly constrained, it is hemmed in by mutually recognized boundaries of authority. While Britain's bureaucracy is professional and largely apolitical, however, the reputation of Jamaica's bureaucracy was dealt a severe blow by its politicization during Prime Minister Manley's first administration.[30]

Thus both the United Kingdom and Jamaica have electoral systems that provide for great legislative flexibility and judiciaries that only weakly restrain administrative actions. As a consequence, neither can base its governance structure on legislation. They need further constraints. As we will see, both found them in contract law.

The archetypal presidential system: Chile

With the exception of the fifteen-year military rule of General Augusto Pinochet (1973–89), Chile has had more than 100 years of civilian rule under a constitution embodying separation of powers, orderly transfer of authority, and regular multiparty election.[31] This long period of stability, broken only by the military takeover in 1973, developed in Chileans a strong respect for institutions.[32] Multiple parties, none strong enough to legislate except by coalition, created an environment of independence from a central party apparatus, allowing the legislature to develop a strong sense of local representation.[33] A series of constitutional reforms between 1958 and 1973 shifted the balance of authority in favor of the presidency and elevated national (rather than regional) politics and parties to center stage. These reforms granted more executive powers at the same time that they developed stronger checks and balances.[34] An increased potential for conflict between the legislative and the executive branches became evident during the administration of President Salvador Allende. Though not entirely resistant to extreme pressure, Chile's long-standing legislative and executive institutions and its system of checks and balances had the potential to provide credible safeguards against arbitrary changes in the regulatory regime. Chile provides observations along the branch of the decision tree answering "no" to the question on "unified government" (Figure 1.1).

Chile's strong and independent judiciary provides an effective check on government power, on both constitutional and statutory issues. For example, Salvador Allende's 1970–3 government repeatedly clashed with the courts over expropriation and compensation, but the courts refused to back down. Chile has been well served by its large pool of highly qualified professionals, which gives all parties access to a broad selection of well-qualified potential political appointees.

The diffusion of political power allows Chile to select its regulatory governance structures from a large menu of options. Because specific legislation is more difficult to change in Chile than, say, in the United Kingdom, legislation may play a more important role in the regulatory governance structure in Chile than in the United Kingdom. And Chile's strong judiciary provides options for implementing regulatory governance based purely on procedures or contract law (McCubbins, Noll, and Weingast 1987).

Rent-seeking presidential systems: Argentina and the Philippines

Argentina and the Philippines have modeled their formal political institutions after those of the United States, creating a complex system of checks and balances.[35] Both countries experienced extended periods of constitutional rule, when the power of the executive was restrained, but both also have had periods of extraconstitutional rule, when authority was concentrated in the president.[36] And in both countries an endemic lack of respect for constitutional order has given rise to a corrupt bureaucracy and judiciary and reliance on the military to resolve conflicts among interest groups.[37] Argentina and the Philippines provide observations along the branch of the decision tree answering "no" to the question of an "independent judiciary" (Figure 1.1).

Both governments have followed beggar-thy-neighbor policies toward political opponents. But in the Philippines, even during the Marcos regime, elites have abided by a tacit nonexpropriation norm that safeguarded the assets of political opponents from outright expropriation since control of government rotates among elite groups. Only business owners who are not aligned with any elite tend to be subject to administrative expropriation. With such weak institutional structures and broad scope for executive dominance, Argentina and the Philippines seem to require regulatory governance that goes beyond reliance on legislation, procedures, or contract law.[38] Alternative options are discussed later.

REGULATORY SYSTEMS AND EFFICIENCY

Successful regulatory policy encourages both private investment and efficient operation. It rests on the development of a regulatory governance structure that constrains arbitrary administrative action and thereby encourages private investment, and on regulatory incentives that promote efficiency as well as investment. Institutional endowments and the requirements of regulatory governance influence which regulatory incentive structures are workable in individual country settings.

To examine this relationship, it helps to look first at the efficiency properties of some regulatory incentive structures adopted by the case study countries, ignoring for the moment the limitations imposed by institutional endowment and the requirements of regulatory governance. The next section reintroduces these constraints, helping to clarify why countries made the choices they did, and explores whether they could have chosen more efficient alternatives. Taking into account the full range of constraints on the design of regulatory systems reveals that some countries will have to settle for second- or third-best solutions when it comes to regulatory rules if their regulatory system as a whole is to be workable.

Competition

Competition can be a powerful spur to innovation and technical efficiency. When a country's major telecommunications company fails to develop an adequate communications network, the normative case is strong for opening up the sector to competition. There is a heated debate about which telecommunications services are subject to diminishing marginal costs and therefore have elements of monopoly power that make competition unlikely. And with the rapid changes in technology in the field of telecommunications, tomorrow's answer may be different from today's. Still, there seems to be some agreement that there is ample scope for competition in telecommunications in value added and long-distance services and in complementary networks (fiber-optics, cellular networks). But opportunities for competition in segments where monopoly power is not inevitable can be realized only if ready interconnection among providers and services is guaranteed. In settings where dominant providers have the potential to wield monopoly power over access to the network, the rules governing interconnection may need to be explicitly spelled out and aggressively enforced.

There is substantial variation in the extent to which the regulatory regimes in the countries studied facilitated competition. Jamaica's policies were clearly the most restrictive. A single firm received an exclusive license to provide all telecommunications services for twenty-five years. In the Philippines getting approvals to provide telecommunications services is a highly discretionary and politicized process. Argentina granted exclusive regional licenses to two firms to provide all local and long-distance voice telephone services (but not value-added services) for ten years. Some service areas were opened for competition from the start. Chile and the United Kingdom have regulatory regimes with the fewest restrictions on entry. Regulators have been liberal in approving requests for entry across the range of telecommunications services, and interconnection has proceeded smoothly. Chile also has liberal licensing policies and interconnection rules and enforcement mechanisms that ensure that firms granted licenses will be able to operate. The Chilean system incorporates a transparent, impartial process for determining which activities are noncompetitive and so are subject to price regulation and which are competitive and can remain unregulated.

Overall, only Chile and the United Kingdom come close to having regulatory systems that facilitate competition. Yet it is premature to conclude that the policies the other countries adopted toward competition were wrong. In some countries the institutional and regulatory governance foundations will be inadequate to support a regulatory system flexible enough to take advantage of the full range of opportunities for competition that technological change might open up.

Price regulation

Mechanisms of price regulation also affect efficiency. Jamaica, Chile, and the United Kingdom adopted different approaches to price regulation. (Argentina's system is too new to evaluate, and the Philippines' system is too vague.) Only Jamaica pursued a straightforward rate-of-return system. The shortcomings of this regulatory approach are legion, but only

15

three are especially relevant here. First, a regulatory system that promises a utility a specified rate of return is inconsistent with free entry, since competing entrants will drive the rate of return below the specified rate. Indeed, Jamaica granted a single firm monopoly power over the entire range of telecommunications services. Second, under rate-of-return regulation firms are in principle free to set their own prices, subject to the overall return constraint, so prices for different services could reflect the differential costs of providing the services. In practice, however, Jamaica has also imposed constraints on the pricing of local calls, preventing the telecommunications company from maximizing allocative efficiency. Third, rate-of-return regulation requires the regulator to monitor the utility's revenues, costs, and capital stock to ensure that the utility remains within the imposed rate-of-return ceiling, an administratively sophisticated and burdensome task.

Chile has also adopted rate-of-return regulation for noncompetitive telecommunications activities, but of a radically different sort. The rate of return is calculated using a capital-asset pricing model that approximates the risk-adjusted earnings of a putatively competitive firm. Chile's regulators feed the information into another model to produce a detailed, efficient maximum price schedule consistent with the target rate of return. These are the maximum prices allowed in the regulated segments of the telecommunications market. Note, though, that Chile permits entry even into these regulated segments.

Properly implemented, benchmark regulation such as Chile's has some powerful properties for encouraging efficiency. Its prices are allocatively efficient. Utilities are not locked into a specific rate of return, so they have substantial incentives to pursue static gains in technical efficiency and to control costs. And as long as the price schedule of the notionally efficient firm is recalibrated relatively frequently (Chile recalibrates every five years), utilities are encouraged to keep up with international best practices.

The price-cap system adopted by the United Kingdom – called the RPI−X (retail price index minus an adjustable X factor) – shares many of the efficiency-promoting virtues of benchmark regulation. In principle, the regulator's task is simply to impose an overall price ceiling on a bundle of services and to see that the utility does not exceed it. In practice, the British regulator has also imposed some restrictions on price increases of individual services. Since RPI−X targets an umbrella of prices and not the rate of return, the utility has an incentive to pursue both static and dynamic gains in technical efficiency. And, unlike in the traditional rate-of-return approach, free entry is not inconsistent with RPI−X regulation. As a consequence, regulated firms are under market pressures to improve technical efficiency in the segments of the industry that are potentially contestable. Should competitive pressures not be robust enough, the regulator can encourage innovation and upgrading by increasing the stringency of the X in the RPI$-X$ formula.

INSTITUTIONAL ENDOWMENTS AND REGULATORY COMMITMENT

The goals of investment and efficiency can be at cross-purposes. Regulation of private utilities in the five countries examined here reveals that the best way to resolve that and other tensions varies from one country to the next. As the analytical framework developed earlier in this chapter suggests, what makes the difference is the country's institutional background. The evidence from the five case study countries suggests that institutional endowments have influenced whether a country was able to put in place a workable governance design for its regulatory system and, if so, the form that the design took.

Traditional parliamentary systems: Jamaica and the United Kingdom

In the history of telecommunications ownership, regulation, and performance in Jamaica and the United Kingdom, several aspects stand out (Table 1.2). Both countries have had sustained periods of high levels of private investment in telecommunications: in Jamaica before 1962 and after 1987 and in the United Kingdom following corporatization (1982) and privatization (1984). Regulatory incentives took different forms in the two countries during the periods of high investment, but regulatory governance systems were similar. Jamaica relied on rate-of-return regulation in both periods, although with important differences, with specific profitability targets and strong limitations on regulatory discretion. The United Kingdom introduced a novel system of price-cap regulation, with no formal profitability targets. Finally, although both countries had periods in which private ownership was associated with strong investment, Jamaica experienced a long decade (from the early 1960s to the mid-1970s) during which private investment lagged.

Both the commonalities in regulatory governance structures in the two countries and the differences in substantive restraints can be traced to similarities and differences in their institutional endowments. During all three high-investment periods regulatory systems were aligned with institutional endowments in a way that created workable mechanisms for restraining arbitrary action. Jamaica's dismal experience with inadequate investment in 1966–75 was a consequence of misalignment between its institutions and its regulatory governance structure.

17

Table 1.2. *Regulatory history and commitment mechanisms: Jamaica and the United Kingdom*

Country, period	Ownership	Regulatory history	Private performance	Restraining mechanisms		
				Substantive restraints	Restraints on system changes	Enforcement of restraints
Jamaica, Pre-1966	Privately owned with separate domestic (Jamaica Telephone Company) and international (Cable and Wireless) companies. Major shareholder was the U.K.'s Telephone and General Trust.	Rate of return of 7 to 9 percent on assets stipulated in the license. Ad hoc rate boards responsible for rate reviews. Decisions challengeable in court.	Sustained network expansion up to 1962. Steady, moderate rate of return.	Monopoly rights and long-term rate of return written in license.	License cannot be altered without consent of company.	Strong judiciary.
Jamaica, 1966–75	In 1962 government announced intention of change regulation system at license renewal time. Jamaica Telephone Company sold to Continental Telephone Company in 1966. In 1971 government takes majority stake in new international	License issued in 1966 specifies Jamaica Telephone Company be regulated by the Public Utilities Commission. License specifies that rate of return be fair and reasonable, though Telephone Act specifies 8 percent return. The Utilities	Initial network expansion then slowdown. Low profitability.	Fair rate of return.	None, given generality of license.	Strong judiciary.

	Events	Regulatory mechanism	Outcomes	License content	License change	Institutional endowment
	operations company and in 1975 takes over Jamaica Telephone Company.	Commission interprets legislative mandate to be binding and institutes rate increases based on investment performance. Sustained regulatory conflict.				Strong judiciary.
Jamaica, 1987–present	Creation of Telecommunications of Jamaica, a joint venture between the government of Jamaica and Cable and Wireless. Privatization starts in 1988.	License stipulates rate of return (17.5 to 20 percent) on shareholders' revalued assets. Speedy arbitration. Government cannot challenge investments. Government to monitor quality and may require improvements.	Major investment in domestic network. Reduction in real prices and sustained profitability.	Monopoly rights and long-term rate of return written into license.	License cannot be altered without consent of company.	
United Kingdom, 1984–present	Privatization in 1984.	License specifies price cap and introduces a complex mechanism to resolve regulatory conflicts.	Take-off investment in 1982, with large gains in national welfare.	Main regulatory issues, including RPI-X written into license.	License can only be changed with consent of company or through a process requiring the approval of three separate bodies. Informal restraints on abuse of power by sovereign.	Strong judiciary and informal norms of governmental decision making.

Brian Levy and Pablo T. Spiller

Institutional foundations of high investment. Jamaica has had two periods of high investment. The first ended in 1962, when the government switched from license-based rate-of-return regulation to a regulatory framework based on a U.S.-style public utility commission with broad participation by interest groups. The second period started with the creation and privatization of Telecommunications of Jamaica in 1987. In the United Kingdom the high investment period began with British Telecom's corporatization and subsequent privatization in 1984.

The regulatory governance structures in Jamaica and the United Kingdom were quite similar during the periods of high investment. In both countries licenses served as contracts between the regulated companies and their governments; attempts by the government to deviate from the specific provisions of the license could be – and were – challenged in court. For the judiciary to serve as a credible arbiter, though, licenses have to be specific enough that judicial outcomes are predictable. In the three high-investment episodes, licenses specified price-setting procedures very clearly. The specific, long-term licenses allowed the companies to feel secure about the expected profitability of their investments, without fear that the government could easily modify the terms of the contract.[39] And because the licenses were enforceable in the courts, companies were assured of substantial regulatory stability.[40] These episodes provide observations along the branch of the decision tree answering "yes" to the question on "legally binding contractual arrangements" (Figure 1.1).

In Jamaica the licenses guaranteed the company a specific rate of return (7 to 9 percent on real operating assets in the pre-1966 period, and 17.5 to 20 percent on revalued shareholders' net worth since 1987). The 1987 license also limits the regulator's ability to disqualify investments or to delay price increases through administrative inaction and provides for speedy arbitration to resolve pricing conflicts. British Telecom's 1984 license (and its amendments) is equally specific about price setting, giving the company full price-setting powers, subject only to later verification by the regulator that the company has adhered to the specified price-cap structure. In all three cases the main features of the regulatory regime could be altered only by modifying the license. In Jamaica the company had to agree to any license modification. In the United Kingdom license modification had to follow a clearly specified process. Any amendment proposed by the regulator to which British Telecom was opposed could be put in place only with the agreement of the Monopolies and Mergers Commission and the Secretary of Trade and Industry (the Board of Trade). Any attempt to circumvent the process could be challenged in court.

In both countries the emphasis on contract rather than administrative law to provide regulatory credibility is consistent with the nature of their political institutions. A law governing regulation, no matter how precise and specific, would offer little assurance of regulatory stability, whereas the courts in both countries have a strong tradition of upholding contracts among private parties. Indeed, Jamaican courts were called on to resolve a contract dispute between the government and the licensee before 1962 (though no disputes have arisen under the 1988 license), and British courts dealt with interpretive issues affecting an electric power license prior to World War II. Though British courts have yet to hear a case involving regulation of a privatized utility, just the threat of legal action seems to be enough to restrain the regulators.[41]

Differences in regulatory governance. British Telecom's license gives regulators a measure of flexibility that Telecommunications of Jamaica's license does not. British Telecom's license can be amended against the company's will. Telecommunications of Jamaica's license cannot. But amending British Telecom's license against its will is no simple matter. An effort by the Director General of Telecommunications to do so requires the agreement of the Monopolies and Mergers Commission and the Secretary of Trade and Industry. These three authorities can be expected to have different regulatory views. The traditional independence of the Monopolies and Mergers Commission and the inability of the Secretary of Trade and Industry to dictate decisions to the Director General of Telecommunications imply that the multiplicity of veto points makes amending the license against British Telecom's will difficult, though not impossible.[42]

Jamaica's licenses have never had that measure of flexibility for the regulator.[43] The requirement that the company agree to any amendment gives the regulated company substantial bargaining power. As a consequence, the regulatory environment might not change even in response to dramatic technological or political changes.[44] Jamaica's institutional endowment explains the need for such institutional rigidities in regulatory governance, despite their shortcomings from a purely normative perspective. Unlike the United Kingdom, Jamaica has never had a system of administrative checks and balances or independent expert commissions. The Jamaican Public Utilities Commission created in 1966 was the first, and only, experiment with independent commissions. The result was calamitous. The politicization of the bureaucracy during the first administration of Prime Minister Manley in the early 1970s eliminated the option of securing commitment through a multilevel delegation of regulatory responsibility.[45] Our framework suggests, then, that installing a regulatory governance system in Jamaica with as much flexibility as that in the United Kingdom would very likely undermine the credibility of Jamaica's regulatory process and result in poor performance in the sector.

21

Differences in regulatory incentives. Jamaica and the United Kingdom also differ in their regulatory incentive structures. Jamaica pursued straightforward rate-of-return regulation, whereas the United Kingdom introduced price-cap regulation.[46] By the late 1980s, when Jamaica introduced its current regulatory system, the normative inefficiencies of rate-of-return regulation had been discussed at length in the economic literature, and price caps were widely considered superior.[47] So, was Jamaica's reliance on rate-of-return regulation a mistake, a case of regulatory capture, or a consequence of the constraints imposed by the country's institutional background?

Neither Jamaica nor the United Kingdom introduced its regulatory system lightly. Both countries gave careful attention to the system's design, in the United Kingdom through the commissioning of white papers (Newman 1986, 8-11) and in Jamaica through numerous cabinet discussions.[48] While mistakes and regulatory capture are difficult to rule out conclusively,[49] it seems clear that Jamaica's institutional background would have been a poor fit for a flexible price-cap regime.[50] Jamaica lacks the multiple layers of independent authority necessary to build in credible restraints in the manner of the British system.[51] In the United Kingdom a regulator bent on revising the price-cap rules is circumscribed by a specific process founded on the integrity and political independence of the multiple layers of authority that have to approve license amendments and by informal norms of behavior that ensure that the process cannot easily be manipulated. This process, shaped over time by a specific institutional environment, could not easily be transplanted to Jamaica. Since price caps are designed to be regularly revised, they would be unlikely to inspire investor confidence without the kind of institutional restraint that is built into the British system. The regulated company would thus limit its exposure, unless the initial price-cap regime provided substantial up-front rents.[52]

Regulatory misalignment: Jamaica 1966–75. In 1962 the Jamaican government decided to switch from a license-based regulatory structure to a public utilities commission-style of regulatory structure. At the time of license renewal in 1966 the government issued new licenses under the Jamaica Public Utilities Act of 1966, which called for "fair and reasonable" rates of return. It also established a permanent and independent regulatory commission, the Jamaican Public Utilities Commission, to oversee domestic telephone and electricity services. The commission had substantial administrative discretion and promoted participation in the regulatory process by a wide range of interest groups. This episode provides observations along the branch of the decision tree answering "no" to the question on "legally binding contractual arrangements" (Figure 1.1).

From the beginning relations between the utilities commission and the Jamaica Telephone Company were acrimonious. Price increases lagged far behind inflation as the commission introduced a policy of conditioning price increases on quality improvements and investment levels. Jamaica Telephone had stopped all investment in 1962 following the government's announcement of its decision to change the regulatory regime. Except for a short period of growth following Continental Telephone Company's takeover of domestic telephone operations, the network was not expanded until the 1980s.

Behind the acrimony and deteriorating performance was an absence of substantive restraints in the regulatory system. The utilities commission was based on the U.S. model, with its considerable freedoms of operation. The Jamaica Public Utilities Commission held hearings, invited participation from interest groups, and made determinations without strong restraints on its decision making. The enabling legislation required only that the commission set "fair and reasonable" rates. Although the new utilities law granted the courts the right to review the commission's decisions, the "unreasonableness" criterion required to overturn a decision was a very stringent standard to meet.[53] Except for direct government intervention, the power of the utilities commission was, for all practical purposes, unchecked.[54] During this period the judiciary was incapable of providing the regulatory credibility it had conferred on the system before 1966.

The archetypal presidential system: Chile

As in Jamaica, regulatory history in Chile splits into high and low investment periods (Table 1.3). Two very different forms of regulation were in place during the high-investment periods – rate of return in 1958–71 and benchmark regulation from 1987 on. Both of them, according to the hypothesis developed in this book, were well aligned with Chile's institutional endowments in ways that restrained arbitrary regulatory action. The low investment periods stretched from the end of World War II to the late 1950s and from the period of government intervention in 1971 and nationalization in 1974 through to the regulatory reforms of the mid-1980s.

Weakness in regulatory governance. Compañía de Teléfonos de Chile (CTC), operating since 1880, entered into a contract with the government in 1930 (later written into Law 4/91/30) that remained in effect

Table 1.3. *Regulatory history and commitment mechanisms: Chile*

Period	Ownership	Regulatory history	Performance	Restraining mechanisms	
				Restraints on changing system	Enforcements of constraints
1930–58	Controlled by International Telephone and Telegraph.	Regulatory law open-ended, no independent regulator. Government could intervene in company operations. Disputes resolved by Supreme Court.	Initial rapid expansion, then slowing.	Vagueness provided for administrative discretion in interpreting law.	Strong judiciary.
1958–73	Partial takeover of Chilean Telephone Company by government in 1967, government intervention in 1971, and total takeover in 1974. ENTeL created to provide long-distance services in 1964.	Regulatory subagreements in 1958 and 1967 eliminated vagueness concerning rate of return adjusted to 10 percent instead of up to 10 percent and imposed new investment obligations.	Network expansion accelerates prior to intervention and nationalization.	Separation of powers and divided legislature. Constitutional changes in 1958 and 1967 increased powers on national parties.	Strong judiciary.

1987–present	Privatization in 1988.	Detailed benchmark regulation for non-competitive segments. Price regulation based on performance of theoretically efficient firm, recalibrated every five years with interim indexation. Law stipulates process to compute rate of return. Explicit arbitration procedures for recalibration. Regulatory decisions appealable to Supreme Court.	Unprecedented rates of network expansion and traffic growth following privatization.	Separation of powers and divided legislature.	Explicit conflict resolution process with strong judiciary as final arbiter.

until the government intervened in the company's operations in 1971. The contract provided CTC with a fifty-year concession, indexed its prices to peso-gold, stipulated a return on assets of up to 10 percent, protected the company against termination of the concession,[55] and defined the investment program for the next few years. The contract allowed the government to take over the company's operations under vaguely defined terms. Though the law initially seemed to stimulate investment, conflict with the government over prices and costs soon dampened investment. The two sides entered into subagreements in 1958 and 1967 to resolve these conflicts. The 1958 agreement ensured CTC a 10 percent rate of return (rather than a return of "up to" 10 percent), and the company agreed to launch an eight-year development program. The 1967 subagreement gave more precision to the definition of costs, and CTC agreed to increase the number of lines by 6 to 7 percent a year.

Although many factors contributed to the low investment levels before the 1958 agreement,[56] the vagueness of Chile's telecommunications law, which provided few safeguards against opportunistic behavior by the government, must have been important. The law stipulated a maximum, though not necessarily binding, rate of return of 10 percent. The vagueness of the law meant that the regulator had wide latitude; it also meant that there were no important limitations on changing the regulatory system itself, since the government could moderate the law through regulatory decrees (and did so in 1958 and 1967).[57] The subagreements of 1958 and 1967 improved regulatory governance, leading to improved performance. This period, then, provides observations along the branch answering "no" to the question of "specific process written in law or contract" (Figure 1.1).

The low-investment period before 1958 resembles Jamaica's experience during the public utilities commission period. In both instances regulatory governance structures were not aligned with the country's institutional endowments, did not restrain the regulator's discretion, and failed to limit the potential for unilateral modification of the regulatory system. And in both cases investment and network expansion suffered.

Regulatory realignment.   Although the regulatory schemes of 1958–71 and 1987 to the present are quite different, both attempted to limit regulatory discretion through specific legislation (Table 1.3). The subagreements of 1958 and 1967 eliminated the vagueness of the law by ensuring a 10 percent rate of return (while imposing new investment obligations). The post-1987 regulatory regime, established after a period of regulatory experimentation in preparation for privatization, details precisely how rate-of-return regulation is to work in the noncompetitive segments of the industry, which are themselves clearly defined.

The regulatory problem: A framework

Price regulation for noncompetitive services is designed to provide a rate of return for an efficient firm following industry best practices. The law is very specific, detailing how to compute the cost of capital of the putatively efficient firm[58] and then how to compute the maximum prices (based on a long-run marginal cost model for each service at the point of departure) for the regulated segments. Entry is permitted even into the regulated segments of the industry.[59] The benchmark rate of return is recalibrated every five years (with indexation in between) by the regulator (Subsecretary for Telecommunications) in consultation with the private companies. The law also specifies an explicit arbitration process to resolve disagreements, with the courts as final arbiter.[60]

Because the law is so specific, providing almost no room for differences in interpretation, regulatory changes require new legislation. And new legislation would be difficult to pass because of such institutional obstacles as a divided bicameral legislature and a president from a minority party – obstacles that were absent under the unified military regime that passed the original legislation. But the regulatory system of 1987 does provide one new source of flexibility. Because only noncompetitive segments of the industry are regulated, the boundaries that define where price competition is applicable are not fixed in the legislation, but may be changed by decisions of the antitrust commission (the Resolutive Commission).

On the whole, during both high-investment periods governance structures were designed to limit regulatory discretion. In addition to specific legislation, which is difficult to change, regulatory credibility was fortified by a judiciary with a record of hearing and impartially resolving regulatory disputes. Any deviation from regulatory instructions or any government attempt to change the system can easily be challenged in the courts. Since the privatization of Teléfonos de Chile, the courts have heard a series of disputes on the regulation of telecommunications, particularly on the determination of competitive boundaries.

The limits on regulatory discretion were quite different during the two periods, however, being much more stringent under the current regulatory regime. The 1987 law specifies not only the procedures for establishing prices, but also how information is to be processed, virtually eliminating any regulatory discretion over pricing in the short run. These episodes provide observations along the branch answering "yes" to the question of "specific process written in law or contract" (Figure 1.1).

Such legislative specificity would not have established the same kind of credible commitment under the parliamentary systems of Jamaica or the United Kingdom, where laws can be amended much more easily than in a presidential system like Chile's. While specificity of the sort designed in Chile could be stipulated in a license instead of in legislation, the complexity of the arrangement demands that those who enforce the license –

company executives, bureaucrats, and the courts – be able to navigate its complexity. While the British bureaucracy has traditionally attracted highly qualified professionals, Jamaica's bureaucracy probably lacks the necessary depth and experience. Introducing Chilean-style regulatory incentives in Jamaica could have triggered continuous litigation that would have forced the courts to make highly technical interpretations – an inherently unstable state of affairs unlikely to inspire investor confidence. Chile (and the United Kingdom) provides observations along the branch answering "yes" to the question "strong bureaucracy." (Jamaica provides observations along the branch answering "no" to that question.)

The evidence presented for Chile is thus consistent with our main hypothesis that the performance of utilities is strongly related to how well regulatory governance structures are aligned with the country's institutional endowments. While it is true that the regulatory incentive structures of the post-1987 period are particularly strong, they would not be credible in the absence of appropriate regulatory governance.

Rent-seeking presidential systems: Argentina and the Philippines

Neither Argentina nor the Philippines has succeeded in putting in place a workable regulatory governance structure. As shown in Chapter 5, the development of telecommunications in the Philippines has followed a "political investment cycle." In Argentina investment levels have been reasonable since privatization, but very high rates of return played a role (Table 1.4). We argue that the gaps in the institutional endowment of the two countries account for their chronic failure to establish workable regulatory governance structures. As a consequence, investment decisions have not looked very far into the future, with harmful implications for long-term performance in telecommunications.

Regulatory governance problems.   Argentina split up its state-owned telecommunications company, ENTeL, in 1990 and later sold each part to a private consortium (one headed by Telefónica of Spain, the other by France Cable and Radio and by Stet of Italy). The rules under which the private companies were to operate have been changed repeatedly. Pricing is a vivid example. One set of pricing rules was announced when private investors were invited to bid for ENTeL, but the rules were changed during negotiations with the bidders. The rules were changed twice more in 1991, when the initial agreements came into conflict with broader macroeconomic policies, and then were renegotiated yet again in late 1992 (see Chapter 6).

The way the initial price level for the pulse, the basic pricing unit in

28

telecommunications, was set exposes the fluid state of the regulatory system at the time of privatization and the lack of substantive restraints on regulatory discretion.[61] The pulse price was negotiated afterafter the companies had submitted their bids and won the contracts but before they had signed their license agreements in 1991.[62] The two winning consortiums negotiated hard to get a favorable initial price level before taking over the two operating companies, suggesting that they had little confidence that the proposed regulatory scheme would actually be implemented. And, in the event, the scheme that was finally implemented (a price freeze, followed by indexation to the U.S. consumer price index) bore no resemblance to the scheme specified in the licenses granted at privatization, which had incorporated substantive restraints (a two-year period of rate of return-based pricing, followed by a period with $RPI - X$ price-cap regulation, with X set to zero). There is no evidence that the affected companies tried to force implementation of the original licenses through appeals to the courts – not surprising considering the politicization and corruption of the judiciary.

In the Philippines as well the regulatory system has not imposed any substantive restraints on regulatory discretion. Formally, the telecommunications sector has been under the control of a regulatory commission since colonial times. Before 1972 the Public Service Commission was responsible for all utilities; subsequently, responsibilities passed to a specialized telecommunications regulatory agency. But at no time have the boundaries of authority of the regulatory agency or the substance of its regulatory mandate ever been clearly delineated. Nor have there been any systematic efforts at telecommunications regulatory reform.

While the fragmented legislatures of Argentina and the Philippines, by making it difficult to change regulatory laws, could provide some support for a stable regulatory regime, that is not enough. Weak judiciaries, disregard for the rule of law, and an absence of informal norms of behavior that restrain discretionary action undermine any effort to enact legislative restraints on changing the regulatory system.[63] Furthermore, problems with judicial corruption in both countries seem to constitute a basic institutional flaw that would undermine the establishment of a credible regulatory system since the courts cannot be trusted to restrain the regulators or to block efforts to change the regulatory system in midstream.

Investing in the face of adversity. It is reasonable to ask how investment takes place at all in countries with such weak regulatory governance structures. The answer resides in the extraction of short-term rents. Measuring profitability rates in the Philippines is an impossible task because there is so much corruption in procurement. But "short-termism" can be seen in the rhythm of telecommunications investment in the Philippines,

Table 1.4. *Regulatory history and commitment mechanisms: Argentina and the Philippines*

Country	Ownership	Regulatory history	Performance	Restraining mechanisms		
				Substantive restraints	Restraints on system changes	Enforcement of restraints
Argentina	Main telephone companies nationalized in 1946 to form a national company, ENTeL. Divided in two regional companies and privatized in 1990.	License-based regulatory framework specified initial two years based on rate of return, followed by five years with price cap of $X = 0$. Exclusive license to be extended to ten years only if minimum investment targets are met. Price freeze instituted four	Highly profitable to initial investors. Investment levels match or exceed license renewal requirements. High prices and quality problems remain. Too soon to determine full impact on welfare.	Explicit price adjustment formula.	License amendments require company's agreement.	Very little. Government seems able to deviate from license specifications without triggering judicial review. Politicized and weak judiciary.

months after privatization. Companies negotiated indexation based on U.S. consumer price index. Regulatory agency created under the Ministry of Economy with appeals only to the Minister. Regulatory framework under review.

				None	None	None
Philippines	Private since inception, with ownership shifting from GTC to Filipino parties in 1967.	Longstanding regulation by commission with vague mandate, lack of political independence, and modest power.	Alternatives between stagnation and periods of moderate investment following political cycle. High unmet demand. Probability unknown.	None		

which is tuned to the ebb and flow of political actors "friendly" to the telecommunications company rather than to the business cycle. Esfahani (Chapter 5) shows a repeated three-stage investment pattern. Investment in telecommunications takes off immediately following the inauguration of a government aligned with the group controlling the telecommunications utility. Investment tails off in the later years of the regime and stagnates in periods when relations with the group in power are more distant. As a consequence, sector performance has been poor, especially in local services. Between 1950 and 1991 the number of telephones in service expanded at the modest rate of 4 percent a year. There were bursts of moderate growth in fixed assets and periods of stagnation. As of 1991 recorded unmet demand for telephones amounted to almost 65 percent of the number of phones in service.

In Argentina short-termism is apparent in the extremely high profitability of the licensees. For example, for the eleven months ending 30 September 1991, the rate of return to Telecom's operator was 26.9 percent, while that of Telefónica's was 203 percent. The returns to both consortiums were also quite remarkable, at 58 percent and 72 percent. While investments were no higher than anticipated in 1991, in 1992 both companies increased their number of lines by twice the number required by their licenses in order to maintain the exclusivity of their ten-year licenses.[64]

SOME OPEN QUESTIONS

Private utilities were aggressive investors whenever the three restraining mechanisms of substantive restraints, restraints on changing the system, and enforcement of restraints were in place (Tables 1.2 through 1.4). That was the case in Chile in 1958–70 and after 1987, in Jamaica before 1962 and after 1987, and in the United Kingdom after 1984. Of the remaining four cases examined where the three mechanisms were not in place, only Argentina has experienced any significant private investment by telecommunications utilities (not much time has passed since privatization, so assessment may be premature). And that investment may have been prompted by the unusually high rates of return.

There were substantial variations in the specific forms that the three mechanisms took in the five countries. These variations appear to derive from the nature of each country's institutions. Chile incorporated substantive restraints into its regulatory incentives structures by specifying precisely how the regulated prices are to be determined. Jamaica and the United Kingdom limited administrative discretion by granting the regulated company freedom to set prices subject to some overall price constraints – rate of return in Jamaica, price cap in the United Kingdom – and limiting the ability of the regulator to interfere with those decisions.

The regulatory problem: A framework

The three countries with regulatory systems that have successfully constrained the discretionary power of regulators also had restraints on changing the regulatory system. These restraints differed in the three countries, reflecting differences in their institutional endowments: the United Kingdom and Jamaica used licenses, while Chile used specific regulatory legislation. These countries also have independent and well-regarded judiciaries, with a record of hearing regulatory disputes and resolving them impartially.

In seven of the nine regulatory episodes discussed here, countries had institutions capable of restraining arbitrary administrative action, but only in five of the seven episodes did governments put in place regulatory systems that restrained arbitrary administrative action and encouraged private investment. The other two episodes – Jamaica between 1962 and 1975 and Chile before the subagreements of 1958 and 1967 – appear to be cases of missed opportunities. In both episodes there was a basic flaw in the design of regulatory governance – a failure to build substantive regulatory restraints into the system itself. Chile's 1930 law imposed a ceiling (but no floor, until amended in 1958) on rate of return and gave the government the right to intervene in the company's operations under vaguely defined circumstances. Jamaica's regulatory system between 1966 and 1975 was modeled on the U.S. system of public utilities commissions and promoted participation in an open-ended regulatory process by a wide range of interest groups, but without the process and judicial safeguards that have traditionally protected utilities in the United States. Consequently, in both episodes private utilities eventually failed to invest, and the resulting conflicts with government culminated in nationalization.

The two remaining cases, the Philippines and Argentina, are more of a mixed bag. Domestic institutions in the Philippines have historically provided an inadequate foundation for a regulatory system capable of restraining administrative discretion. Private ownership seems to be based on rents extracted through the political process. Argentina's political institutions, for all their historical weaknesses, might be able to provide some basis for making credible commitments if the judiciary achieves a modest degree of independence and enforcement capability. If democracy puts down strong roots in Argentina, political power is likely to be more fragmented than it is now, both between the executive and the legislature and within the legislature. That would make it difficult to overturn regulatory reforms that limit administrative discretion through licenses or legislation with specific provisions and might provide an adequate comfort level for investors.

What alternatives are available to countries that lack the crucial formal and informal institutions explored here? Our analysis suggests that convincing utilities to invest will require the development of alternative safeguards. One example of a safeguarding mechanism is the broad distribution of share ownership among the population at the time of privatization, an arrangement that confers a stake in the performance of the privatized company. Building a broad base of shareholders was important in the privatization of telecommunications in the United Kingdom and played a modest role in Chile, Argentina, and Jamaica. For this approach to work, countries need a reasonably well developed stock market and security regulations. It might also require development of private institutional investors (pension funds, insurance companies) that provide a low-cost conduit for widespread and diversified stock ownership. The United Kingdom, Chile, and to some extent Jamaica have developed these types of institutions, thus facilitating the further development of investment safeguards.[65]

Another option is to privatize enterprises sequentially or to privatize a single utility in stages. How diligently the government abides by the agreements made in the earlier stages determines the success of later stages, so the costs to government of reneging on its early agreements can be high. Argentina's privatization of telecommunications was a first, dramatic step in a sweeping program to privatize public enterprises. The new private owners could feel reasonably confident that the government would not later engage in attempts at expropriation since that would jeopardize the rest of the privatization program. But this approach provides only a temporary shot of confidence. Unless the institutions required for a credible regulatory system develop as the privatization process progresses, investors will become increasingly reluctant to invest, fearing that the government's self-restraint will end when the privatization program does.

For cases where domestic institutions do not provide an adequate foundation for any workable regulatory system, a last option might be to substitute an international mechanism for the missing national foundations. Jamaica and the Philippines in the 1950s come closest of all the cases studied to using such a mechanism. Jamaica's judicial system continues to recognize the Privy Council in London as the final judicial arbiter, an arrangement that confers considerable credibility on the legal system. For the first fifteen years following Philippine independence in 1946, the continuity of its institutions, the strong leverage of the United States, and specific agreements that protected U.S. investors provided a predictable and safe environment that facilitated investment by Filipinos and Americans alike.

International investment guarantee programs are a promising innovation for fortifying weak domestic institutions. A multinational institution such as the World Bank can provide private investors (and lenders) with guarantees against noncommercial risk, including the risk of administrative expropriation. The guarantees are provided at the request of the host country, so that in the event that a private investor calls in the guarantee, the host country is liable for repaying the cost of the guarantee. (Note that a program along these lines is quite different from programs of insurance against noncommercial risk, which shift the costs of administrative expropriation to the insurer and so do little to strengthen the resolve of the host country to abide by its commitments.) Failure to repay would provoke a costly rupture of the country's relationship with an important international institution. The country's good standing in the international community and its continuing commitment to regulatory restraint are held hostage to each other – ensuring some commitment not to resort to administrative expropriation.

What is crucially important to the success of private utilities is the goodness of the fit of the regulatory system with a country's institutions. If a country puts in place a regulatory system that is incompatible with its institutions, efforts to privatize utilities to improve their performance might end instead in disappointment, recrimination, and a resurgence of demands for renationalization.

2

Telecommunications regulation in Jamaica

PABLO T. SPILLER AND CEZLEY I. SAMPSON

Jamaica tried several approaches to telecommunications regulations and experimented with both public and private ownership before settling in the late 1980s on private ownership and a new regulatory arrangement that seems to promote reasonably good performance in the sector and to be compatible with the country's institutions. Yet there is widespread public controversy about the current regulatory framework: a tight monopoly over all telecommunications services (including equipment supply), very little administrative discretion, and continuous price adjustments to satisfy what many consider too high a rate-of-return requirement. Should Jamaica change its regulatory system to one with greater institutional flexibility and fewer of the normative inefficiencies of rate-of-return regulation? Or, as the framework presented in Chapter 1 suggests, do Jamaica's institutional endowments explain the need for a system of rigid regulatory governance?

A traditional parliamentary government, strong judiciary, and strong two-party system, in which power is regularly transferred between the two parties, constrain the type of regulatory governance structure that can work well in Jamaica. A regulatory mechanism embedded in legisla-

We would like to thank the following individuals for devoting time to illuminate us about Jamaica's telecommunications, regulations, and political system: Roy Alexander, Ministry of Public Utilities and Transport; Charles Bethume, Permanent Secretary, Ministry of Public Utilities and Transport; Jim Cartner, Senior Vice-President, Telecommunications of Jamaica; Alvario Casserly, former Secretary, Jamaica Public Utilities Commission; Carl Chantrielle, President, Telecommunications of Jamaica; Charmaine Constance, Permanent Secretary, Ministry of Industry, Commerce and Production; James W. Craig, Senior Vice-President, Telecommunications of Jamaica; Richard Downer, Price Waterhouse, Jamaica; Neville Johnson, Vice-President for Personnel, Telecommunications of Jamaica; Trevor O. Minott, President and Chief Executive Officer, Jamintel; Phillip Paulwell, Trade Administrator, Trade Board Limited; and Gregg Shirley, Price Waterhouse, Jamaica; Dr. Damien King of the Department of Economics, Professor Edwin Jones of the Department of Government, and Mr. Audley Harris of the Department of Management Studies, UWI.

tion of the U.S. style is too flexible and uncertain to provide the required safeguards for investment and growth in a system in which the rules of the game can change along with the government administration – or even within the same administration. If the courts rule that a particular administrative decision violates the regulatory statute, the government can overturn the ruling by passing new legislation. Judicial restraint of administrative decisions through statutory (rather than constitutional) interpretation, then, may not be very effective.

What seems to work better in Jamaica is a regulatory mechanism built into the firm's operating license in the form of a specific long-term contract between government and firm. Under those conditions Jamaica's strong, independent judiciary and its long history of protecting property rights seem to provide adequate safeguards to encourage investment. Parliament cannot unilaterally change a regulatory regime based on legal contracts as it can one based on legislation. Jamaica's courts and jurists are professional and insulated from politics. They can credibly be expected to uphold contracts even when the government is a party to the agreement, though they might not have much influence in restraining administrative decisions through statutory interpretation. The courts have consistently viewed violations of a clear license stipulation as a breach of contract. Jamaica's highest court is the British based Privy Council and this further removes the courts from the politics of the day.[1]

Both government and firm have understood the importance of the choice of regulatory instrument to industry performance. The sector developed relatively well during periods when licenses constrained the government's ability to set rates on the basis of political considerations (before 1962 and after 1987). In contrast, the tensions and conflicts that attended the regulatory episode based on the formalistic but substantively unconstrained regulatory structure defined in the 1966 Public Utilities Commission Act led eventually to nationalization of the company in 1975.

Political realities affected the regulatory incentives structure as well. Strong political pressures have long dictated that the price of local phone services be kept low through cross-subsidies from long-distance and international services. The government chose to establish an incentives structure that would keep profits in those activities high enough to finance investments in the sector. It did so by granting a long-term monopoly. Though this regulatory structure looks inefficient since it limits the ability to implement more efficient pricing schemes and it could certainly have been designed better – by opening up some segments to competition, for example – its features respond to the reality of social pressures in Jamaica and to the basic commitment problem of Jamaica's institutions.

Pablo T. Spiller and Cezley I. Sampson

POLITICAL INSTITUTIONS AND
TELECOMMUNICATIONS

Local telecommunications in Jamaica, as in most developing countries, differ from public services such as water or mass transport in that their main customers are middle- and upper-class households and businesses,[2] the swing voters in many elections. That makes local telecommunications services and pricing an important political issue in Jamaica.

The composition of demand for long-distance communications is different. Foreign trade businesses and tourism are more important users than local households, making the pricing of international calls slightly less sensitive politically. And until recently the pricing of international telecommunications was not a major concern for most businesses because Jamaica's foreign trade policies discriminated against dynamic export-oriented sectors.[3] Thus, keeping local phone prices low and expanding the network to provide access to the growing middle class would be key issues for both political parties, which would tend to keep telecommunications policy stable despite changes in administration or ideology.

Meeting middle-class demands to expand the network and keep prices low requires an institutional structure that provides strong enough incentives to induce investment in highly specific, nontransferable assets. A regulatory governance structure based in legislation is unlikely to provide enough of a curb on administrative discretion to satisfy investors since the party in power could unilaterally change the law. The judiciary has only limited ability to uphold the original legislative intent if the current administration decides to change the law. As a consequence, regulations based solely on legislation tend to be unstable, and alternative institutions have been needed to provide the stability required for credible regulatory arrangements.

Telecommunications politics in Jamaica have traditionally been played out in the shadow of the various license negotiations and debates over legislation that have shaped the company-government relationship (Box 2.1). Major turning points in telecommunications regulation have followed the timing of key license renewals. That Jamaican governments have had considerable latitude in interpreting regulation based on law is evident in the emphasis that both sides have traditionally given to the text of the licenses.

Political parties and constituencies

The Jamaican Labor Party and the People's National Party have dominated the political scene since the early 1940s, alternating in power. Patronage and fund raising arrangements give the parties a strong hold on their

Box 2.1.	*Key Episodes in Jamaica's telecommunications sector*
Period	Regulatory Institution/Ownership/Event

- Pre-1962
  - *Telecommunications policy under colonial rule*
  - All Island License (domestic operations license) granted in 1945 to the Jamaican Telephone Company, with the Telephone & General Trust (T&GT), a British concern, as the majority shareholder
  - License requires:
    -Specific minimum return
    -Use of ad hoc rate boards
    -Court enforcement of license
  - Private ownership of domestic and international companies
  - Modest but continued growth in service

- Independence 1962–7
  - *Issuing of new licenses to Jamaica Telephone Company and the creation of the Jamaica Public Utility Commission: 1962–6*
  - Requirement of Jamaicanization of ownership
  - New License in 1966:
    -Specifies maximum rate of return
    -Regulation by a new independent, and permanent, commission (the Jamaican Public Utilities Commission)
    -Participation by interest groups
    -Jamaicanization by 1971
  - *Takeover of Jamaica Telephone Company by Continental Telephone Co., 1967*
  - Continental Telephone Company agrees to:
    -Terms of 1966 license
    -Specific expansion and financing plan
    -Extant price levels
  - Stagnation of service

- 1968–75
  - *The Jamaica Public Utility Commission and the quasi-expropriation of Jamaica Telephone Company's assets*
    -Absence of judicial review
  - Creation of Jamintel (1971); a joint venture between Cable and Wireless (a British government owned company) and the government of Jamaica to take over Cable and Wireless (West Indies) international communications facilities (and international communications operating license) in Jamaica

- 1975–6
  - *The takeover of Jamaica Telephone Company (1975)*
  - Disbandment of Jamaica Public Utility Commission

39

Box 2.1. (*cont.*)	
Period	Regulatory Institution/Ownership/Event
	• Regulation by the Ministry of Public Utilities and Transport • Introduction of international direct dialing • *Boom in the profitability of international communications and the beginning of the policy of subsidization of the domestic network* • Increase in profitability of both the domestic and international companies
• 1987–90	• *Creation of telecommunications of Jamaica and the divestiture of the government of Jamaica's holdings* • Telecommunications of Jamaica (a joint venture of the government of Jamaica and Cable and Wireless) takes over all of Jamaica Telephone Company and Jamintel assets and licenses • New domestic and international telecommunications licenses granted to Telecommunications of Jamaica • Guarantees real returns on equity in a narrow band equal to current levels • Restricts government discretion in approving rate increases • Introduces binding arbitration • Allows judicial review • Regulation by ministry, with no participation of interest groups • Boom in investment

members. Except for the period between the mid-1970s and mid-1980s the two parties have shared similar policies, though their rhetoric has differed. The poor are their core constituencies, and the middle and upper classes the swing voters. The hard-core party loyalists – overrepresented by the very poor, black segment of the society – make up approximately 40 to 50 percent of the electorate, fairly evenly divided between the two parties. The leadership of both parties is normally recruited from the educated Jamaican middle class. Because of the parties' hold on their legislators, the government in power has controlled the parliamentary agenda. Unless the issue is constitutional, requiring parliamentary super-majorities, the party in power can carry its policies through administrative or parliamentary decisions.

Since 1962 Jamaica has experienced three distinct periods of economic and political activity: a period of rapid growth, fueled by import substitution, booming bauxite exports, and tourism, that ended in 1972; a period of stagnation, social conflict, and socialism through democratic means from 1972 to 1980; and a period of restructuring along the lines of the pre-1972, private sector-oriented policies from 1980 till today. These three periods reflect the electoral politics of Jamaica, which since 1944 have been dominated by fierce competition between its two main parties. The two parties have alternated in power within an electoral cycle of about eight years (except during a brief period in the mid-1980s). Power is hotly contested between the two parties, and each has realistic expectations of returning to power in less than a decade following an electoral defeat.

Until 1972 the differences between the two parties were more of style and personalities than of substance. The Labor Party championed the private sector as promoter of growth, and thus has been seen as the party of conservative reform. The National Party also supported the private sector, but envisioned a more important role for government, and aligned itself ideologically with the Democratic Socialist tradition of Great Britain. As a consequence, until 1972 electoral changes did not bring about important political or economic policy changes.

Both parties have engaged in patronage at the local level as a substitute for social welfare policies. Housing, jobs, and contracts in local projects, and contracts and overseas jobs are all part of the patronage package organized by the local party bosses, safeguarded by party youth gangs, and implemented by the local member of Parliament. Political power alternates about every eight years, and with it the power to distribute the spoils (though the minority party also sets to pass out some of the spoils). As a consequence of these arrangements, the very poor see the continuation of their party in power as crucial to their welfare.

To win an election, the party needs more than its hard-core loyalists. It also needs what in Jamaica are called the "floating voters," the predominantly urban middle and upper classes. These voters are influenced more by the economic performance of the country than by patronage or political rhetoric (Stone 1981, 1986). Parties also need the financial support of trade union and upper-class contributors. Until 1972 the upper classes supported and participated in both parties' governments.

Their financial support has not provided these richest segments of society with control over party policies, however, many of which they have strongly opposed without prevailing. What this financial and political support seems to have provided the upper classes is an equivalent sort of patronage to that received by the poor, in the form of special access to contracts, import rights, and licenses (Edie 1991). Until the mid- to late 1980s import controls and licenses provided a steady source of profitable opportunities in import substitution and distribution activities. The richer

41

segments of society also benefited from the continuous expansion of government[4] through their encroachment in the bureaucracy and in the government-related small business sector.[5] Until the mid-1970s the upper classes made up the core of a stable, conservative, senior bureaucracy, with a strong seniority system and professionalism. The growth in the professional bureaucracy and in the small business sector was accompanied by the growth of the professional class in general, which expanded from 2 percent of the employed labor force in 1943 to 11 percent by 1980, making it a stronger and more vocal political force (Stone 1986). Accompanying this process was a shift in senior government jobs from the upper class to the middle class of educated and upwardly mobile black groups.

Along with the political consensus of this period was a similarity in party politics. Control of the national party resided with the national leadership, and members of Parliament seem to have had little direct contact with their local constituencies. District voting outcomes rarely differed substantially from national outcomes, suggesting that voters did not believe their representatives had much of a direct impact on their welfare. Because the governing party usually had a strong majority in Parliament, individual members were unable to extract rents from the leadership. Jamaican Parliament is based after the Westminster model and as such is more a forum for discussion rather than policymaking. Policy decisions are the prerogative of the Prime Minister and Cabinet of Ministers.

The consensus between the two parties began to crumble during the late 1960s as economic growth slowed and urban unemployment grew. As social unrest mounted, the populist policies of both parties gradually changed. The ruling Labor Party government, under the influence of Finance Minister Edward Seaga, introduced measures designed to increase Jamaican ownership of major sectors of the economy, including the finance and telecommunications sectors, to achieve domestic ownership rates of 51 percent. To achieve that ownership restructuring foreign holding companies were required to sell part of their stock in domestic companies through the local stock market.

The old consensus broke down completely following the 1972 ascension of the National Party. Though the party viewed itself as a democratic socialist party, Prime Minister Michael Manley aggressively pursued several controversial socialist policies in addition to aligning Jamaica with Cuba and the developing world. This policy was vigorously opposed by the Labor Party and the wealthier classes. The domestic core of the new policy was land reform, nationalization of large industries, job creation, and new welfare programs. The courts threw up a roadblock to the land reform and nationalization efforts, ruling that the government could not summarily expropriate land or businesses, but had to pay for them. The government's efforts to amend the constitution to eliminate these projections of property rights were abandoned in the face of heavy opposition from the Labor Party and the lack of public support.

The Labor Party regained power in 1980. The new government started a process of liberalization, supported and encouraged by the International Monetary Fund and the World Bank, that involved reprivatizing nationalized companies and liberalizing foreign trade. The opposition party, sensing popular disenchantment with its policies, once again took up its traditional positions. In 1988, when the National Party regained power, it followed and even deepened the policies initiated by the Labor Party, including privatization of the telecommunications industry.

The judiciary and regulatory governance

Though Jamaica's political structure gives the party in power substantial discretion, arbitrary behavior is held in check by the independent judiciary. During the 1970s the judiciary's strong defense of property rights kept the National Party government from expropriating land and industrial enterprises without compensating the owners – a prohibitive expense. The judiciary had less success in restraining government regulation of private utilities, however. For example, although the license granted to Jamaica Omnibus Service Company specified that decisions of the Public Passenger Transport Board could be appealed to the Supreme Court, no appeal was ever lodged despite the contentious relations between the two sides (Swaby 1974b). Regulation of the electricity company, Jamaican Public Service Ltd., by the Jamaica Public Utilities Commission seems to have been so antagonistic that, following a long rate hearing in 1970, the price of the company's stock fell to an all-time low of one-tenth of its (revalued) book value. The Labor government seized the opportunity and acquired majority control of the utility through direct purchases in the stock market.

This case exposes the limitations on judicial restraint of government administrative decisions. Any judicial interpretations of legislation that differ from those of the government can be reversed through new legislation. The government's influence over utility regulation was intensified by the way Jamaica's regulatory commissions and boards were organized during that period. Their members were political appointees, who served for three years and rotated with the party in power (Mills 1981). The system was intended to make the commissioners politically accountable, but it also meant that regulatory agencies were not isolated from local politics or from the political tendencies of the party in power. The populism of both parties translated into very activist regulatory agencies, which the judiciary could not effectively restrain.

The regulatory framework for utilities after 1966 was based on the

43

enabling law (the Telephone Act and the Radio and Telegraph Control Act in the case of telecommunications), a license, and the 1966 act establishing the Jamaica Public Utilities Commission. Of these elements, only the license could be considered a contract between the government and the firm, giving the company grounds to appeal any breach of contract to the judiciary. In addition, the Telephone Law stipulated that the licensee should be allowed a net return of 8 percent on its rate base. So, in principle the telephone company could appeal administrative decisions that deviated from the stipulated rate of return. Jamaica Telephone, however, seldom achieved that rate of return. Yet it appealed to the courts only once following an amendment to its license that stipulated minimum rate of return.

The courts were, however, capable of restraining outright impropriety in dealing with the issues. For example, Jamaica Telephone Company's 1945 license stipulated that the company was to receive a return of 8 percent over the rate base and that any deficit earnings could be accumulated and figured into the next rate review by a rate board. Both the company and ratepayer had the right to appeal the rate board's decisions to the Supreme Court. The Supreme Court ruled in favor of Jamaica Telephone, which had protested a rate board's 1956 disallowance of the company's claim for increased rates to compensate for past shortfalls in the rate of return. That was the last time, however, that the Jamaican Supreme Court restrained the administration in its relations with public utilities. Appeals in 1974 by the Jamaica Tax and Ratepayer Association (to have a rate increase rescinded) and by Jamaica Telephone were both rejected.

INDUSTRIAL ENDOWMENTS AND REGULATORY COMMITMENT, 1880–1985

Until the mid-1980s Jamaica's regulatory framework and policy evolved differently for the domestic and international segments of the industry, so the two segments are analyzed separately. (Major events are highlighted in italics in Box 2.1.)

Domestic telecommunications

Regulatory reforms of the mid-1960s radically altered the regulatory environment and performance of the telecommunications sector. Understanding the implications of these changes requires an understanding of regulatory systems under colonial rule, which were based on the specific provisions of the licenses under which each firm operated.

Telecommunications policy under colonial rule, 1880–1961. Several companies operated telephone systems in Jamaica until the mid-1940s.

Jamaica Telephone Company was incorporated in 1892 and took over the small operations of the West Indies Telegraph and Telephone Company. Well-known Jamaican business families were among the initial shareholders. Jamaica Telephone was granted a nonexclusive license to operate throughout the island; other companies also received nonexclusive rights to operate small-scale telephone systems.

In 1925 Jamaica Telephone obtained a forty-year exclusive license to provide telephone services in Kingston and St. Andrew. The Jamaican Post Office operated the All Island Telephone System over the rest of the island. Jamaica Telephone's license stipulated that the government had the right to take over the company at the time of license renewal at a price to be agreed on by the company. If the parties could not agree, the takeover price was to reflect the revalued assets of the company. The license included two other important provisions. The company (or any twelve ratepayers) could file for rate reviews by a three-member ad hoc rate board (named by the governor) whose decisions could be appealed to the Supreme Court. And Jamaica Telephone was allowed an 8 percent return on its rate base. Current-year earning deficiencies (returns below 7 percent) or excesses (returns above 9 percent) would be entered into an excess and deficiency account for future rate adjustments.

In 1945, one year after the introduction of universal adult suffrage, Jamaica Telephone acquired the All Island Telephone System from the Post Office and received an exclusive forty-year license to operate telephone services over the entire island. As under the 1925 license, rate boards were created for each rate review, so they had no permanent staff or institutional memory. Consultants, paid by the company but selected by the rate board, were hired to review Jamaica Telephone's accounts following an application for a rate increase.[6] Requests for rate increases were to be dealt with expeditiously. Rate boards suffered from a structural informational asymmetry relative to the company, which may have benefited the company. Increases were granted in 1950, 1952, 1956, 1957, 1958, and 1960. The company prepared its own development plan and was essentially left alone between rate reviews.

The number of subscribers grew steadily during the 1950s, and the number of telephones (main lines plus extensions) increased from 13,437 in 1950 to 41,152 in 1962. The ratio of telephones to main lines remained fairly stable at two per main line (Figure 2.1). Accounting rates of return (on the rate base) during the last part of the 1950s were around 5 to 7 percent. While there were some strong disagreements between Jamaica Telephone and various rate boards during the 1950s, the domestic license agreements of 1925 and 1945 performed adequately in supporting private development at a time of low real interest rates, low inflation, and free capital flows. Had the economic environment been less stable, how-

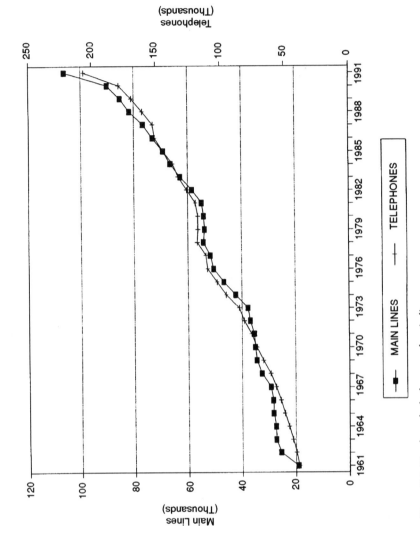

Figure 2.1. Number of telephones and main lines.

ever, these rates of return would not have been adequate. The strict specifications of the license provided incentives for the domestic company to invest and develop the sector.

With the end of the colonial era, though, came the end of Jamaica Telephone's licenses, which were due to expire in 1965. Colonial regulatory institutions were based on contract law rather than on public utility legislation. The renegotiations with Jamaica Telephone during the early 1960s and the introduction of new utility legislation are crucial to an understanding of the development of the sector during the 1970s.

Creation of the Jamaica Public Utilities Commission, 1962–6. The regulatory stability of the colonial period ended with independence and the granting of new licenses to the domestic and international operating companies. The license renewal process clearly demonstrates the hazards of using licenses as safeguards. As long as licenses have finite terms, firms and government will maneuver as the end of the license term approaches to improve their bargaining positions in the renewal negotiations and to safeguard their assets. If renewal is uncertain and the valuation of the assets is not sufficiently advantageous, the firm may hesitate to invest in any more specific assets. The government, meanwhile, may attempt to extract a commitment for a better investment program by delaying the renewal. Uncertainty about license renewal thus has predictable performance implications.

Political influences can also affect the renewal process as did political changes following independence, the growth of the two national political parties, and the disappearance of the independent politician – all forces centralizing power in the Prime Minister's office. License negotiations for Cable and Wireless went smoothly, and under the Radio and Telegraph Control Act the firm was granted an external telecommunications license in 1961 just before the declaration of independence. Jamaica Telephone did not fare as well. The company (under the control of Telephone and General Trust Company, a British concern) refused government requests to expand its services unless it was granted an exclusive all-island license with a specific pricing policy. The company's refusal to invest and expand is evident in the stagnation in the number of main lines during 1962–7 as the number of telephones increased steadily (Figure 2.1). Unmet demand soared. (There were 66,500 telephones in service in 1969, but customer demand was estimated at 184,000 by a 1974 internal World Bank report.) Stagnation was also visible in the company's long-term debt, which remained relatively constant at about J$3 million from 1960 to 1966. Loans to the company from its British parent firm fell from J$1.2 million in 1963 to $0.8 million in 1966.

The company's refusal to invest after 1961 reflects the uncertainties surrounding license renewal following independence. After the first independent elections the company requested a substantial rate increase to compensate for previous revenue deficiencies, as allowed under the 1945 license and the Supreme Court decision of 1956. The government requested a postponement of the rate review as renewal negotiations began. Jamaica Telephone agreed to postpone the rate hearing only if the government would appoint a rate board, allow wage increases to be recovered, and recognize the company's right to recover earning deficiencies, as specified under the 1945 license. Renewal negotiations started in October 1963 and lasted three years. A rate board was established in June 1963, but it allowed no substantial rate increases. It was not until 1971 that an increase was allowed, and by then both the players and the rules of the game had changed. The Public Utilities Commission had been established in 1966, and the British shareholder of Jamaica Telephone had sold its shares to Continental Telephone Company.

During the three years of renewal negotiations relations between the government and Jamaica Telephone's principal shareholder, Telephone and General Trust, became very contentious. A new license was granted in 1965 but was amended in 1966 to accommodate the formal creation of the Public Utilities Commission. The 1966 license was changed in several other ways as well. The term was shortened to twenty-five years (starting 1 January 1967) but was renewable for another ten. To increase Jamaican ownership of the company, no single shareholder was permitted to hold more than a 20 percent share. Telephone and General Trust, which owned 50.2 percent of the stock, was given six years to dispose of its excess holdings. And in place of a fixed rate of return on the rate base, the 1966 license provided for a "fair" return,[7] with the rate base to be determined by the Public Utilities Commission.

By the end of the negotiations, Telephone and General Trust was seeking to divest its interest in Jamaica Telephone, despite the new license. The drawn-out negotiations for license renewal and the uncertainty about the outcome, coupled with the de facto freeze on prices following independence, had made the company reluctant to invest and to maintain the outside plant. By 1967 the system that had expanded continuously during the 1950s was in need of major investments to meet unsatisfied demand and to attend to badly maintained equipment.

The 1966 license made the Public Utilities Commission the regulator of Jamaica Telephone, giving it broad powers and responsibilities for service supervision, planning, and rates. The decisions of the commission, which was set up as a statutory corporation, were subject to review only by the Supreme Court. The commission was to hold public hearings on requests for rate increases and to publicize its proposed decisions, bringing pressures from interest groups to bear on its determinations. To bridge the gap between legislation and licenses, the commission was to take industry legislation into account as it related to minimum rates of return – such as the 8 percent minimum rate of return on the rate base stipulated by the Telephone Act. The nature of the commission's powers, responsibilities, and procedures made bargaining between the company and the government more difficult since any agreement they reached would need the approval of the Public Utilities Commission.

The renegotiation of Jamaica Telephone's license provides insight into the limitations of licenses as a safeguarding institution. Their finite term implies that the company will face substantial uncertainty about its investments unless the license clearly specifies how the company's assets are to be valued at the time of license expiration. License expiration offers the government an opportunity to alter the terms of the license, so the company faces substantially more uncertainty at expiration than at renewal time.[8] The 1945 license stipulated that should the government decide not to issue a new license to the company, the government had to announce a year ahead that the licensee would have to sell its assets to the government at a fair market value plus 10 percent. The 1945 license made no provision for the case in which the government does not force a sale but the company does not agree to the new license. Failure to specify the liquidation terms for that contingency implies that the courts may be called in to arbitrate the terms. Meanwhile, the company would be operating without a license, in a precarious legal environment, and – with overwhelming foreign ownership in this case – limited political support. Telephone and General Trust seems to have understood this eventuality. It froze its investment plans early in the negotiation process, agreed to the new license though it did not intend to operate under it, and began to look for another company interested in operating the domestic network under the new conditions.

The takeover, 1966–7. Continental Telephone Company, a Canadian-based holding company that was undertaking a rapid acquisition program in Canada, the Caribbean, and the United States, expressed an interest in taking over Telephone and General Trust's shares even in this uncertain environment. The conditions under which Continental agreed to take over the shares are important, because they influenced the relationship between the government and Jamaica Telephone.

Continental agreed to several financial and developmental obligations. It agreed to refinance a 1966 fifteen-year World Bank loan for US$11.5 million as a twenty-five-year loan at rates not to exceed 0.5 percentage points above the New York prime rate, to lend Jamaica Telephone US$5 million on similar terms, to reduce its ownership share to 20 percent by January 1971, and to expedite completion of Jamaica

Telephone's J$13 million development plan within three and a half years. The development plan had specific quantitative goals for new service and network expansion.

The government greeted Continental's involvement in Jamaica Telephone with enthusiasm. The government believed that with a large telephone holding company as a parent, Jamaica Telephone would be relieved of its liquidity problems. Continental's commitment to the investment program and to specified service expansion generated strong expectations of improvements after years of stagnation and high levels of unmet demand. Continental, however, seems to have overvalued Jamaica Telephone's equipment, as evidenced by the price it paid for shares and the evolution of its investment plan.[9] Immediately after taking over, Continental increased its expansion plan from J$13 million to J$25 million and then to J$42.2 million because of the poor quality of the outside plant.

Continental's involvement under the terms of the 1966 license is puzzling. Under those conditions Continental should not have expected Jamaica Telephone to be profitable – indeed, its investments did not pay off very well. One explanation is that the acquisition simply reflected Continental's "growing pains," a case of acquisition mismanagement. It is also possible that Continental expected the Public Utilities Commission of Jamaica to operate like utilities commissions in the United States, failing to take into account the institutional differences between the two countries (Jamaica's lack of legislative checks and balances, the weaker role of the judiciary in restraining administrative discretion). Finally, Continental might have expected to renegotiate the terms of its participation once it was in, which would indicate a failure to understand the workings of the regulatory and political structure in which it was supposed to participate.

The quasi-expropriation, 1968–75. The period that follows the regulatory changes of 1966 is crucial to an understanding of the role of institutions in conveying commitment to a regulatory regime. In this case Jamaican politics after independence, in the face of concentrated (foreign) ownership, and a regulatory framework that permitted substantial administrative discretion and interest group participation were unable to restrain discretionary administrative behavior that led to quasi-expropriation of the company's assets.

In 1968 Jamaica Telephone embarked on a new development program, at the same time changing its forecasts of investment and revenue needs and requesting a rate increase (Figures 2.1 and 2.2). The Public Utilities Commission rejected the application outright, indicating that it needed to revise the whole tariff structure, rather than approve piecemeal increases. The commission also questioned whether Jamaica Telephone was meet-

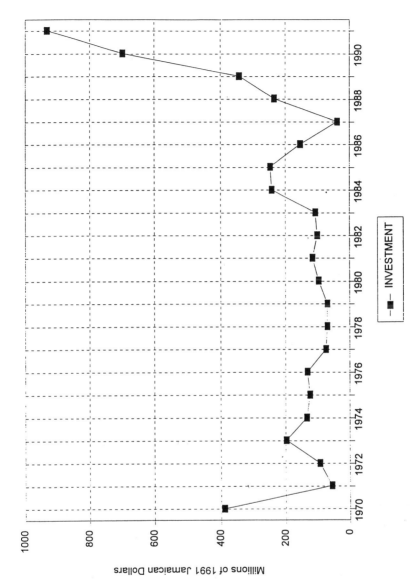

Figure 2.2. Jamaica Telephone Company's real gross investment, 1970–91.

ing its investment agreements. The number of main lines was increasing much more slowly than the number of telephones (Figure 2.1). The company's fixed assets increased until 1970, leveled out until 1972, and then grew slowly again until Jamaica Telephone's nationalization in 1975 (Figure 2.3). The Public Utilities Commission claimed that Jamaica Telephone was reneging on its development promises and that no rate increases would be granted. Jamaica Telephone claimed that its investments were going toward replacing obsolete and badly maintained facilities, rather than toward increasing *nominal capacity* (*The Gleaner*, 9 June 1971). The company halted its investment program entirely in July 1971, at the same time formally applying for a rate increase of 17 percent. The commission granted a 15 percent increase effective December 1971. In April 1972 Jamaica Telephone applied for a new increase of 54 percent. In August 1972 the commission granted an average increase of 35 percent effective September 1972. During this period the price of Jamaica Telephone's shares plummeted. By March 1972 the price was J$0.28, well below a calculated book value estimate of J$1.3 for December 1971 and the J$1.13 a share paid by Continental.

In its August 1972 report the commission stated that price increases would now be contingent on quality of service. It furthermore stated its interpretation that the reference in the license to the Telephone's Act stipulation of a "permitted" rate of return is "not an absolute entitlement." This decision seems to have triggered strong lobbying of the government by Continental and Jamaica Telephone to change the way Jamaica Telephone was regulated. In March 1973 the government imposed a temporary stamp duty tax of 12.5 percent on international and domestic calls, and the proceeds of this tax were to be transferred to Jamaica Telephone as a direct subsidy, despite the opposition of the Public Utilities Commission.[10] In return, Jamaica Telephone issued shares that it transferred to the government, giving the government 10 percent of Jamaica Telephone's outstanding stock.[11] Following the agreement with the government, Jamaica Telephone began a new development program in June 1973. Its license was amended to provide for a minimum return equivalent to "the high point in the immediately preceding year of the gross redemption yield of the last external long-term loan bonds of the government issued in the United Kingdom." In April 1974 Jamaica Telephone requested a rate increase of 81 percent. In July 1974 the commission granted an average increase of 53 percent. This was the last rate increase before Jamaica Telephone's takeover by the government in 1975.

The introduction of a public utilities commission-style of regulatory system, open to solicitation by all interested parties, substantially changed the way the domestic telecommunications sector was regulated by making the process at once more formal and more antagonistic. Rate boards of the

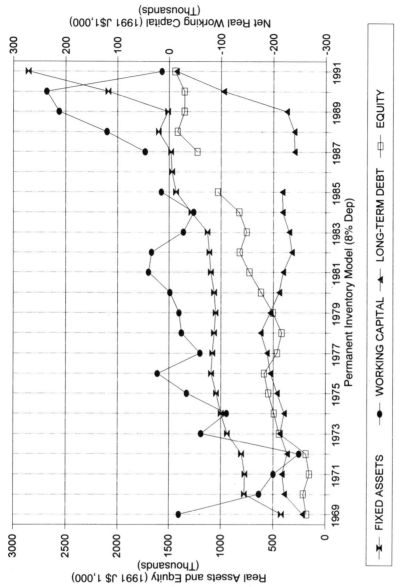

Figure 2.3. Jamaica Telephone Company's fixed and working capital (long-term debt and equity).

past had been ad hoc bodies designed to rule expeditiously on rate changes and then disband. The Public Utilities Commission was an independent commission, with a permanent staff charged with regulating all aspects of the Jamaica Telephone Company and the light and power company, Jamaica Public Service. The regulatory challenges facing the commission were not simple. It had powers similar to those of public utility commissions in the United States, but much less experience and a smaller staff. In the case of the Jamaica Telephone Company, it was charged with regulating a firm whose accounting procedures, information services, and procurement practices had been designed to facilitate control by the holding company rather than by the regulators. And until the takeover by the government, Jamaica Telephone's board of directors was composed of the elite in Jamaica's business and professional communities.

This is the context in which the Public Utilities Commission was to set rates and standards of service. The regulatory environment had changed radically, and Jamaica Telephone now faced a traditional rate-of-return system, but one with no juridically protected implicit or explicit minimum rate of return. Indeed, despite substantial inflation – prices doubled between 1969 and 1971 – no rate increases were granted during 1960–71. Though Continental had stated during negotiations for the purchase of Jamaica Telephone that it believed the pricing structure to be adequate, the company soon claimed that rate increases were needed to cover higher than expected levels of investments (*The Gleaner,* 9 June 1971). The company's claims were received with skepticism by the Public Utilities Commission. A series of acrimonious discussions over related issues followed – on the definition of the rate base (whether the investments that were undertaken were proper),[12] on accounting procedures (how depreciation should be computed), on the company's cost of capital, on what were reasonable costs, and according to a consultant to the rate boards of the 1950s, on procurement practices (Swaby 1981).[13] The license was amended in early 1974 to settle the way depreciation was to be measured and to further specify the minimum allowed rate of return.

At the same time that the regulatory environment was becoming more hostile, new parties were joining the fray. The Jamaican Tax and Ratepayer Association presented evidence at the 1972 rate hearings against Jamaica Telephone's request and again at the 1974 hearings, this time joined by the Jamaican Hotel and Tourist Association. Following the commission's decision, the Tax and Ratepayer Association filed an appeal to the Supreme Court (as did Jamaica Telephone).

Another change was a diminished role for the courts. Though the Supreme Court had reversed a 1956 rate board decision that had blocked the company from recouping a shortfall on its past profits, it denied Jamaica Telephone's appeal in 1974. This was the only case in which the company tried to act against the Public Utilities Commission through legal channels. What had changed? Two aspects of the new regulatory environment may have affected the court's approach to rate decisions. The 1966 license was less forthcoming about minimum rates of return than previous licenses. Also, the Public Utilities Commission was a fully staffed, semijudicial organization whose decisions were given more deference than those of the ad hoc rate boards of the past. Unless the commission clearly violated procedures or an explicit license stipulation, the courts would not find it proper to intervene.

In summary, then, Jamaica Telephone's poor performance and lack of incentives during the first half of the 1970s can be understood in the light of two basic factors: the conditions under which Continental consented to buy out the British majority shareholder and the passage and implementation of the Public Utilities Commission Act. Under conditions of the sale Jamaica Telephone was to undertake a substantial development program, much of it to be underwritten by Continental Telephone. But because of the way the new regulatory process worked, Jamaica Telephone found it difficult to expose any more funds than it already had, seeking instead to finance the expansion through rate increases – which the commission kept in check. Thus, by the mid-1970s Jamaica Telephone's financial situation was precarious. The market seemed to consider the company's assets as already quasi-expropriated. When Jamaica Telephone issued a new public stock offering in 1969 and 1973 to fulfill its obligations to reduce its holdings in favor of Jamaican owners, Jamaicans shrewdly chose not to buy the shares. Since Continental Telephone had to underwrite both issues, by the end of the process it was holding 68 percent of the outstanding shares rather than the 50 percent it had initially acquired.

Takeover, 1975–6. In 1975 Continental sold its stake in Jamaica Telephone to the government, an event that illuminates the role of regulatory institutions in supporting private investment. Nationalization of Jamaica Telephone was the result less of the ideological shift by the Manley government of the mid-1970s than of a series of mismatches between the design of the regulatory regime and the country's institutions. The political changes that accompanied independence seem to have politicized the telecommunications sector and complicated the license renewal process. Telephone and General Trust Company had stopped investing five years before the expiration of its license, a sign of the company's uncertainty about the terms under which renewal would be granted. The new regulatory system introduced by the Public Utilities Commission Act of 1966 seems to have further increased the level of uncertainty in the regulatory process to the substantial disadvantage of the firm. The lack of a coherent conflict-resolution mechanism tilted the balance heavily in favor of the Public Utilities Commission, dooming Jamaica Telephone to continuous financial difficulties. Those difficulties reached a precarious point as Continental's expectations about its ability to renegotiate its operating and financial conditions with the government proved overly optimistic.

By 1975 Continental Telephone's experience in Jamaica was not a happy one. Jamaica Telephone's real profits during 1970–5 were stagnant, barely sufficient to cover real depreciation of its assets – 1970 was the only profitable year (Figures 2.4 and 2.5). The value of Jamaica Telephone's equity rose during the period, mostly because of the stock issue to Continental in 1973 (Figure 2.3), which involved no inflow of funds but rather a cancellation of a short-term bond to Continental, and the revaluation of the Jamaican dollar, which reduced the real value of the company's foreign debt. Nevertheless, Jamaica Telephone's operating return on fixed assets did not exceed the real cost of its long-term debt (Figure 2.6). The company was not sufficiently profitable to attract private investors, Jamaican or foreign. As early as 1971 Continental was asking for direct government investment in Jamaica Telephone. The first step was taken when the government took a 10 percent stake in 1973.

The government's support of Jamaica Telephone did not go far enough. The stamp tax was slated to expire in June 1974, and with it the subsidy to Jamaica Telephone. Meanwhile, the adverse attitude of the Public Utilities Commission toward Jamaica Telephone did not change. Throughout 1971–9 the real price of domestic calls increased in steps with the nominal price increases granted by the commission (and, after 1976, by the Ministry of Public Utilities) to compensate for past domestic inflation. While there seems to have been little difference in the evolution of prices following the announcement by the National Party government of its shift towards government ownership of key enterprises, Continental Telephone took advantage of the change in attitude to negotiate a sale of its equity holdings to the government. In September 1975 Continental agreed to sell its holdings in Jamaica Telephone to the government. The following year regulatory responsibilities were transferred from the Public Utilities Commission to the Ministry of Public Utilities and Transport, though the Public Utilities Commission Act remained on the books.

Jamaica Telephone's financial situation did not improve following the takeover. After essentially breaking even each year since 1973, Jamaica Telephone showed an economic loss in 1977 (see Figure 2.4). Pricing policy did not change with the government takeover, but the steady network expansion since late 1973 seems to have come to an end in the period 1976–8 (see Figure 2.1). Investment also fell during 1977–9 compared with 1974–6 (see Figure 2.2). As a consequence, Jamaica Telephone's real fixed assets, measured in economic terms, fell slightly from

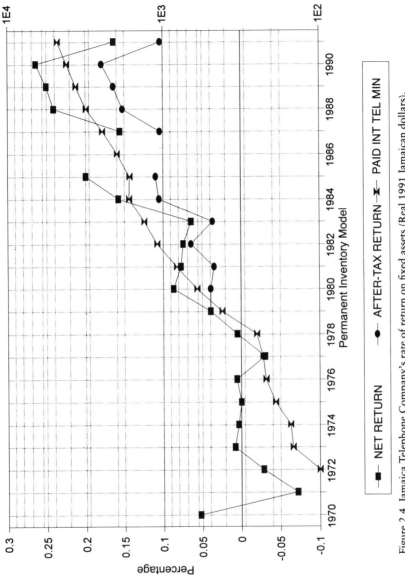

Figure 2.4. Jamaica Telephone Company's rate of return on fixed assets (Real 1991 Jamaican dollars).

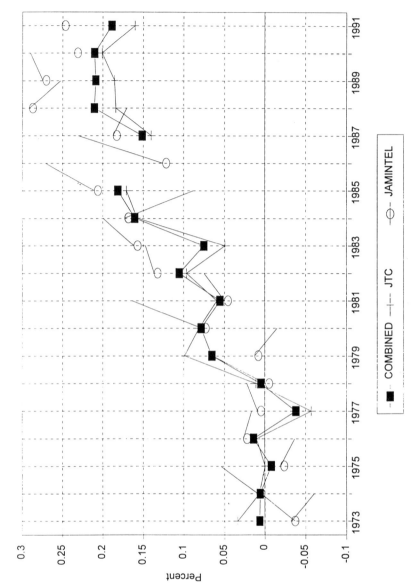

Figure 2.5. After-tax return on equity Jamaica Telephone Company and Jamintel.

58

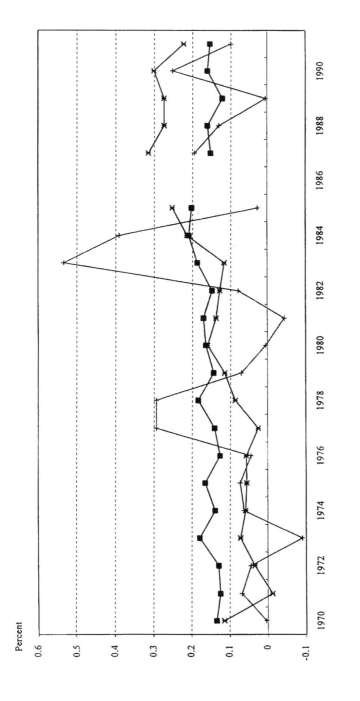

Percent

Figure 2.6. Jamaica Telephone Company's cost of long-term debt and pretax operating return on fixed assets, 1970–91.

── NOMINAL COST ── REAL COST ──✱── OPERATING RETURN

Pablo T. Spiller and Cezley I. Sampson

1976 to 1979 (see Figure 2.3). Consumer surplus, which had increased during 1973–5, remained constant or fell during 1976–80 (Figure 2.7). Thus the takeover produced no positive short-run effect – neither consumers nor Jamaica Telephone gained. Even the government failed to enhance its revenue intake from the domestic telecommunications sector until 1980, when Jamaica Telephone made its first income tax payment in a decade.

International communications

Developments in the international segment of the market show that granting an exclusive license does not, by itself, facilitate private investment. What is crucial is the substance of the license and its implications for the latitude of discretionary behavior allowed the government. Although the government had complete discretion about whether and when to cancel Cable and Wireless's license, it was constrained from taking this course of action because of its relationship with the British Government. Cable and Wireless at the time was owned by the British Government.

The colonial period, 1870–1967. The first international communications line in Jamaica was opened in 1870 by the West India and Panama Telegraph Company, which eventually became Cable and Wireless. International communications were not very important until the late 1970s, with revenues less than half those from domestic services (Figure 2.8). During colonial times Cable and Wireless seems to have operated without a license, under a fixed-price system (Baglehole 1970; Barty-King 1979). There is no record of requests for price increases during the late colonial period; indeed, prices for international calls remained constant until the late 1970s.

The differences between the domestic and the international licenses reflect both politics and ownership. Cable and Wireless was an imperial (colonial) operation, so Jamaica's relation with Cable and Wireless was on a government-to-government basis. Jamaica Telephone was a privately held company. International communications were of little public concern at the time, unlike domestic services, whose users were upper and middle-class urban residents. Thus it is not surprising that ratepayers had the right to call for a rate board review for Jamaica Telephone while Cable and Wireless's customers did not.

The creation of Jamintel, 1961–71. Just three years after Cable and Wireless's license was amended in 1968 and extended for twenty years, Jamintel was established as a joint venture between the government (51 percent share) and Cable and Wireless to take over international

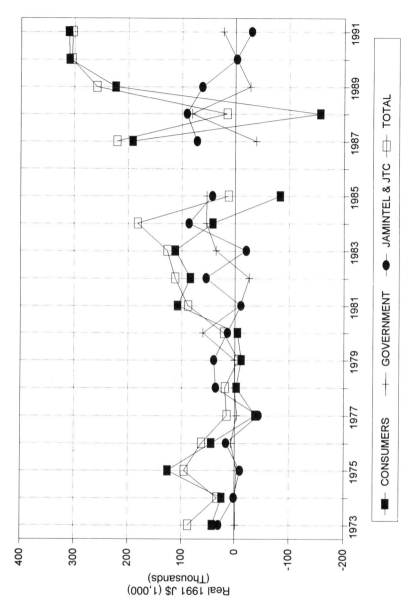

Figure 2.7. Change in total net surplus, 1973–91.

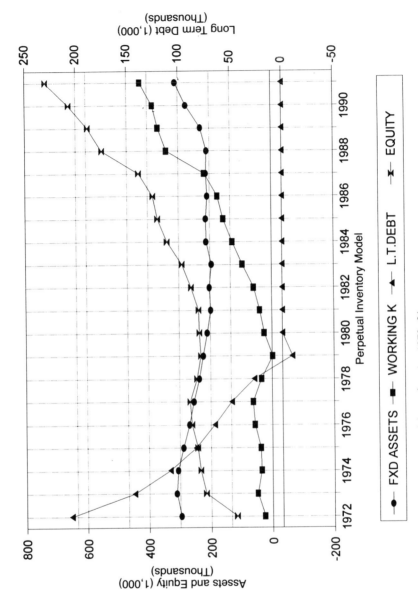

Figure 2.8. Jamintel's fixed assets, debt, and equity, 1972–91.

telecommunications activities. As in the domestic telecommunications sector the granting of an exclusive license did not in itself establish the confidence in the stability and predictability of the regulatory environment needed to encourage any substantial levels of investment. Jamintel, unlike Jamaica Telephone, was not regulated by the Public Utilities Commission, but like Jamaica Telephone, operated on terms that left it with only modest profits, and investment was limited (Figures 2.8 and 2.9).

In the early 1960s Cable and Wireless saw a need for several new investments, in particular for the introduction of an earth station and development of satellite communications. The company requested a long-term extension of its 1961 license (Barty-King 1979). In 1968 the government extended the license for twenty years while amending it in several ways. The government added the right to terminate the license at will. In the case of termination or the failure to renew the license, Cable and Wireless would be required to sell all its assets to the government at an agreed price or at a price set by an arbitrator. The license also stipulated that the company was to earn a "fair" rate of return rather than a specified rate. Less than a year later the government and Cable and Wireless began negotiations for the formation of a joint venture to take over the company's operations in Jamaica. The shareholders agreement gave a 51 percent stake in the venture to the government and 49 percent to Cable and Wireless. (The main features of the agreement are described in Box 2.2.)

There is little evidence to explain what led the government to take over a majority share of Cable and Wireless's interests in Jamaica and to create Jamintel. At the time the 1968 license was granted, the Labor Party's nationalistic discourse promoting Jamaicanization of large foreign-owned companies was at its peak. That the party wanted to have the option of taking over not just a majority share but the whole enterprise is quite clear from the stipulations of the shareholders agreement. Why shares were taken over by the government instead of being offered to the public is unclear, though the failure of Jamaica Telephone's 1969 public issue may have influenced the government's decision.

The joint venture did not turn out to be especially profitable for Cable and Wireless. The shareholders agreement suggests that the company's fixed assets were valued at approximately US$16 million (J$14 million), some US$4 million below the estimate of Jamintel's 1972 fixed assets produced by our permanent inventory model (Figure 2.8). Thus Cable and Wireless may have given away as much as a quarter of its fixed assets.[14] The terms of the agreement were quite onerous for Cable and Wireless as inflation rose during the 1970s with no compensating increase in the nominal prices for international calls. In addition, the formula for sharing international revenues was changed to favor Jamaica

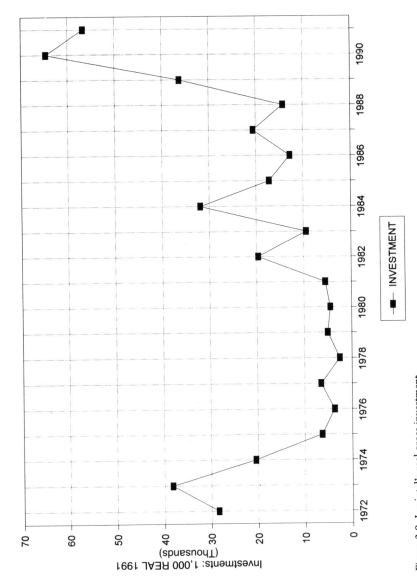

Figure 2.9. Jamintel's real gross investment.

Box 2.2. *Shareholders agreement regulating the creation and operations of Jamintel, 1971*

- Jamintel is to take over Cable and Wireless's international communications license, which was to expire in 1988. Thus, the agreement was valid only until 1988.
- Cable and Wireless would contribute buildings, land, and equipment worth approximately US$4 million.
- Cable and Wireless would lend US$8 million to Jamintel (repayable in seven years, with three years grace, at 8 percent interest) to buy Cable and Wireless's remaining assets and provide working capital.
- The government's contribution of US$4 million (or J$3.4 million) would be provided through a loan from Cable and Wireless. This loan was to be repaid through the use of up to three-fifths of the government's receipts from Jamintel's dividends, without charge of interest.
- Annual dividends were not to exceed 15 percent of equity.
- Jamintel was to be directed by Jamaican personnel.
- The government had the option of further acquiring the assets of Jamintel, a book value, according to a specified formula:
    -Up to 60 percent by 1981
    -Up to 75 percent by 1986
    -Up to 100 percent by 1988

Telephone. In present value terms Cable and Wireless's investment in Jamintel broke even only because the value of Jamintel stock rose following the explosion in international communications in 1978–9.[15] Jamintel's low profitability and the poor quality of the local network retarded investment, to the point that the value of its fixed assets fell throughout the period (Figure 2.8).

The most opportunistic action by the government in its dealing with Cable and Wireless was probably the change in the formula for sharing international revenues. Until 1979 Jamintel (and Cable and Wireless before that) retained 70 percent of international revenues and Jamaica Telephone received 30 percent. By 1979, the government had become the majority shareholder in both companies and was therefore in a position to negotiate changes in the revenue sharing agreement that served to increase Jamaica Telephone's share first to 40 percent, then to 60 percent in 1984, and to 68 percent in 1987.[16]

The boom in the profitability of international communications, 1979–85. The introduction of international direct dialing in 1977–8 created a boom in international long-distance calling that did not subside until

1984–5, following price increases in 1984. While the growth in international telecommunications was also related to the size of the domestic network, the increase in total revenue per line that had also begun in the late 1970s came mostly from the international side (see Figure 2.10). Increases in international rates – 50 percent in 1979–80 and again in 1984 – reflected the Labor Party's determination to reverse the socialistic policies of the National Party. The boom in international communications plus the price increases dramatically increased the profitability of international telecommunications – and of both Jamintel and Jamaica Telephone (Figures 2.11 and 2.12). Jamintel's after-tax return on fixed assets broke the 10 percent barrier in 1982 (Figure 2.13); Jamaica Telephone's did so in 1984 (see Figure 2.4).

While all parties benefited from the increase in profitability, the main beneficiaries were the users of the domestic network. Domestic prices had been falling in real terms since 1980. The boom in international telecommunications provided a windfall to both the local and the international service companies, allowing them to improve their performance even as real prices fell. Also, the government's takeover of Jamaica Telephone relieved the pressure for rate increases whenever prices failed to provide an adequate return. The composition of total telecommunications revenues shifted heavily toward international services – from a 20 percent share in 1978 to nearly 80 percent in 1991 – while the international services' share of direct claims on total fixed assets in the sector was only 20 percent in 1985.[17] It was clear an understanding had been reached between the government and the firm on a policy of cross-subsidization of the domestic network by the international sector in 1987.[18]

By 1985 the system was no longer sustainable. The after-tax return on fixed assets was 10 percent for Jamaica Telephone (see Figure 2.4) and an unusually high 30 percent for Jamintel (see Figure 2.13). As use of the network grew, revealed demand for main lines rose so that by 1986 as many main lines were in held order as in operation. Maintaining the cross-subsidy of the domestic network required either further increases in Jamaica Telephone's share of international revenues or consolidation of the two companies. The government chose consolidation, a move likely to increase pressure to reduce the profitability of the companies – which by 1985 was above 15 percent (see Figure 2.5) – as had happened with the electric company, Jamaican Public Services. The high level of profitability in the telecommunications sector was one of the attractive features which allowed the government to transfer the companies to the private sector without increasing real prices, which made privatization politically feasible. But to make privatization actually happen would require a change in the regulatory system so that it clearly prevented the government from expropriating the sector's assets. Once that regulatory change

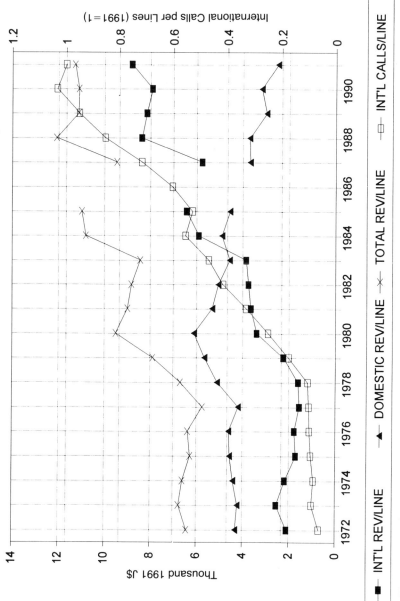

Figure 2.10. Real revenue per line JTC and Jamintel, 1972–91.

INT'L REV/LINE   DOMESTIC REV/LINE   TOTAL REV/LINE   INT'L CALLS/LINE

67

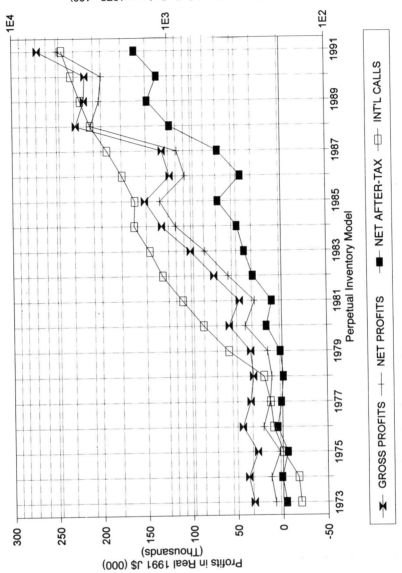

Figure 2.11. Jamintel's total profits, 1973–91.

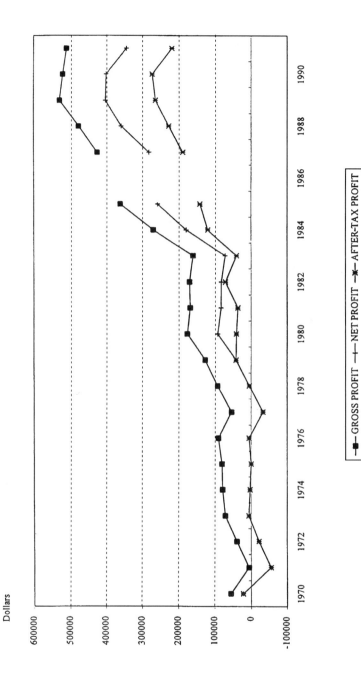

1991 Jamaican
Dollars

Figure 2.12. Jamaica Telephone Company's gross and net profits, 1970–91.

69

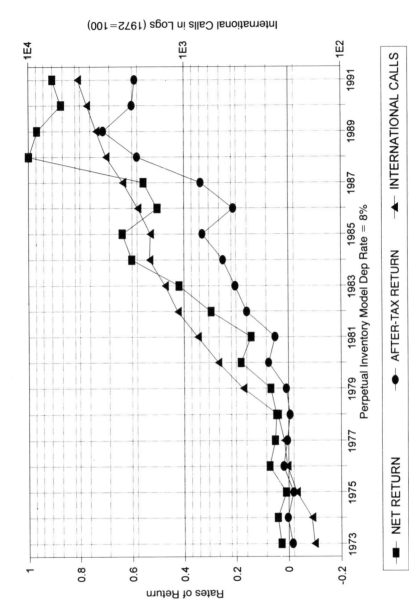

Figure 2.13. Jamintel's net and after-tax return on fixed assets, 1973–91 (1991 Jamaican dollars).

70

was achieved, the government would no longer be able to manipulate pricing in the sector to redistribute wealth for political purposes.

FINDING THE RIGHT REGULATORY MATCH, 1987–90

Structural changes introduced in 1987–90 radically altered the way the Jamaican telecommunications sector was regulated and organized and led to unprecedented vitality in the sector. Performance in the sector responded strongly to the resolution of regulatory design problem through a regulatory contract that was viewed as credible on the part of investors and binding and that was designed to reduce short-run political opposition. What is less clear is whether without the regulatory changes, the increased investment and expansion to the system would have taken place given the political, contracting, and structural constraints involved.

Creation of Telecommunications of Jamaica, 1985–7

Negotiations begun in 1985 on the merger of domestic and international telecommunications companies culminated in 1987 with an agreement between the government and Cable and Wireless to establish Telecommunications of Jamaica as a joint venture. Under the shareholders agreement the two partners would contribute their shares in the two operating companies (Jamintel and Jamaica Telephone) to the new enterprise (independent shareholders in Jamaica Telephone also received shares in the new company). The two companies were to become wholly owned by Telecommunications of Jamaica. A new regulatory mechanism was devised and formally incorporated in amended licenses, stipulating how the government was to set prices (Box 2.3). Divestiture of some of the government's shares in the new company was also agreed on.

The new licenses granted in 1988 marked a regulatory turning point. The licenses commit the government to maintain the profitability levels of the companies at their levels before the new agreement (see Figure 2.5), thus ensuring operating returns sufficient to cover the cost of capital (see Figure 2.6). While Telecommunications of Jamaica would not be able to increase the average real price, which was close to the upper level of the permissible profit range at the time the company was formed, in principle it would be free to rearrange its price structure, giving it an incentive to increase the prices of the inelastic domestic segments. To forestall any move in that direction, a gentleman's agreement seems to have been reached to freeze domestic prices for at least five years. That agreement has been kept; domestic prices have not been increased since 1984; and the company's 1991 annual report noted that increased revenues would allow normal prices to remain unchanged.[19]

71

Box 2.3.   *Components of the 1988 telecommunications licenses*

- Jamaica Telephone, it would appear, has been granted a monopoly over all domestic (local and toll) telephone services, while Jamintel is granted a monopoly over all international telecommunications. Legal arguments are that the monopoly does not extend to domestic wireless and value added services such as digital transmission of computer data.
- Both licenses are for twenty-five years, with a renewal period of twenty-five years.
- Both companies are regulated on a rate-of-return basis, with net after-tax (and special dividends) profits to be no less than 17.5 percent nor more than 20 percent of (accounting) shareholders' equity, where assets are revalued annually.
- Rate setting is as follows:
  - If the company wants to adjust its tariffs, it proposes a new tariff to the Minister of Public Utilities and Transport;
  - If the ministry accepts, the tariff goes into effect;
  - If the ministry does not accept and Ministry's counteroffer is not accepted by the company, a relatively simple arbitration procedure begins, with the arbitrator having to set rates within the stipulated band.

The new arrangements have had three political consequences. First, new incentives for investment have spurred more rapid expansion of the local network, which has kept the middle class fairly content. Second, by focusing increases in nominal revenues on the international segment, the arrangement has avoided alienating the core supporters of both parties.[20] And third, government tax revenues from telecommunications have increased, with average tax collection for the sector doubling in real terms from $J97 million in 1981–5 to J$190 million in 1987–91 (in 1991 prices).

Regulation.   The 1988 licenses created a very simple mechanism for price adjustments and dispute resolution. The government has a short period of time to answer requests for rate increases. If the two parties cannot agree, the issue goes to an arbitrator, who is required to set rates according to the rates of return specified in the license. Public hearings are not required, and license violations may be appealed to the Supreme Court. The regulatory emphasis on contracts rather than legislation reflects to some extent the characteristics of Jamaica's political institutions. Such a contracting approach might not provide the confidence needed to promote rapid private sector participation in a different setting, say, one without a strong judiciary or a history of commitment to property rights.

The licenses stipulate a rate of return based on the shareholders' equity rather than on the rate base. As a consequence, if the rate of return allowed by the license is higher than Cable and Wireless's opportunity cost of funds, the company will have an incentive to increase its participation in Telecommunications of Jamaica, and Telecommunications of Jamaica will have an incentive to finance its investments through retained earnings rather than long-term debt.[21]

Telecommunications of Jamaica has a broad monopoly over telecommunications on the island, including the domestic sale of terminal equipment.[22] This monopoly clearly reflects the impact of politics. To win political support for the privatization, there had to be some assurance that domestic rates would be kept low. The solution was cross-subsidization, even if at the cost of a more dynamic and competitive sector. Allowing competition in the international communications sector would undercut the ability to cross-subsidize. Maintaining cross-subsidization meant that revenues would have to be generated from as many sources as possible. Since demand in the international communications sector is relatively elastic, having other protected sources of revenue (such as surcharges for fax machines) allows the company to reduce the real price of international communications and still achieve its rate of return. The cost of the cross-subsidy, then, is the cost of maintaining a strong monopoly at a time of rapid product development and technological convergence.[23]

Divestiture. Arguments for privatization as a safeguarding mechanism rely on broad-based domestic ownership and multiple providers to increase political support for maintaining private ownership and for restraining government actions to expropriate the sector's assets. The creation of Telecommunications of Jamaica did not result in the kind of widespread domestic ownership that might serve such a role. Originally, the government intended to retain an important share in the new company; foreign exchange and budgetary constraints, however, forced the government to sell its ownership share to Cable and Wireless who took advantage of the offer, eventually owning 79 percent of the stock (Table 2.1).[24] Some moderate safeguards were built into the privatization. Thirteen percent of the government's stock was sold in a way that facilitated acquisition by domestic workers and households. For example, 2 percent of the outstanding stock (21.1 million shares) was reserved for employees, and 51,000 residential customers of Jamaica Telephone were granted priority for up to 1,750 shares each.

One way to tell whether investors had confidence in the 1987 license arrangements is to compare the market valuation of the company's stock and an estimated value based on the assumption that the license holds for its entire life. If the two are similar, that provides an indication that investors considered the 1987 regulatory regime to be credible. Until April 1991

Table 2.1. *Distribution of ownership in telecommunications of Jamaica
(percent)*

Date	Government of Jamaica	Cable and Wireless	Public	Price (U.S.$)
19 May 1987	82.711	9.402	7.88	0.1811
23 July 1987	72.111	20.002	7.88	0.1811
2 October 1987	53.111	39.001	7.88	0.1818
28 September 1988	40.00	39.002	20.99[a]	0.1564
13 July 1989	20.00	59.002	20.99	0.2174
16 November 1990	0+	79.002	20.99	0.2205

[a]Telecommunications of Jamaica employees hold 2 percent.

company shares were being traded at less than US$0.20. Assuming that the licenses hold for the agreed period and that every year the company achieves the lower bound allowed by the license (17.5 percent), the discount rate can be computed that would generate a price equal to approximately US$0.20. Comparing that discount rate with the real rate of interest in Jamaica gives a measure of investor confidence in the performance of the contract arrangement. If dividend disbursements of 4 percent of the company's real equity are assumed, a discount rate of 20 percent implies a stock price of US$0.187 in March 1988.[25] The average prime lending rate in 1988 was 23 percent. The rate of devaluation for the year was zero, implying a real rate of interest (in U.S. dollars) of 23 percent minus the U.S. inflation rate of about 4 percent. Thus a real discount rate of 19 percent for the private sector was reasonable for Jamaica in 1988, which would imply a value of US$0.212 for the company's shares as of March 1988, a bit higher than the price at the public sale, but the same as the price paid by Cable and Wireless in its two latest acquisitions.[26]

Performance and welfare. The terms of the 1988 licenses have implied large changes in the way the sector operates. The real price of international calls stopped falling once negotiations for the creation of Telecommunications of Jamaica had begun in 1985. Profitability has been systematically high (see Figures 2.4, 2.5, 2.13) but well within the prescribed range, which has allowed the companies to increase their level of investment (see Figures 2.2 and 2.9). The number of main lines (see Figure 2.1) and the value of the network's fixed assets have risen rapidly (see Figures 2.3 and 2.8), allowing Telecommunications of Jamaica to finance a large part of its investments through long-term debt.

With expansion of the network have come substantial welfare gains, for consumers, government,[27] and firms (see Figure 2.7). Changes in consumer surplus derive from changes in prices[28] and expansion of the network.[29] Increases in consumer surplus doubled to J$100 million (in 1991 prices) in 1988–90 and reached $350 million in 1991 (Figures 2.14 and 2.15). Most of the gains came from improvement in international services. On the other hand, the installation of fiber-optic cables around the island, the conversion to digital technology, and the introduction of cellular telephony in late 1991 (our measures stop in March 1991) must have surely had a further positive impact on consumer surplus.

While the post-1987 period has been good for consumers, the firms, and the government, it is unclear whether the same welfare gains could have been achieved without the creation and privatization of Telecommunications of Jamaica. Investment in the domestic network increased dramatically in 1990 and 1991. Would similar gains have been possible without the reforms? The history of Jamaica Telephone includes several development programs that went nowhere, as financing and pricing problems delayed or preempted implementation. The regulatory changes after 1987 provided a relatively stable regulatory environment that could have facilitated the implementation of a large expansion program even without the ownership changes.

In the international network investment had been slow throughout the 1970s and 1980s (see Figure 2.9). Working capital increased during the 1980s, and by the end of the decade it exceeded fixed assets (see Figure 2.8). That suggests that neither Cable and Wireless nor the government found it profitable to extend their exposure in the company. Experience since 1988 has been quite different, with rapid development of the international network. The implication is that the combination of privatization and regulatory reform provided Cable and Wireless with the incentives and confidence to invest in its Jamaican operation, which it did not have before 1987.

Assessment of the regulatory reforms of 1987

Notwithstanding the clear benefits, the regulatory changes of 1987 also had several shortcomings, most notably in the areas of competition, pricing, and ownership. The regulatory and structural changes rule out competition even in the more dynamic segments of the sector and maintain a generally inefficient pricing and cross-subsidization scheme. Privatization through direct sales rather than public offerings resulted in foreign ownership concentration and limited domestic ownership. In addition to some fairly important effects on income distribution, these shortcomings may also affect the evolution of the sector in coming years in undesirable ways.

It is easy to lay out a more efficient set of regulatory changes. Telecommunications of Jamaica could have been given a monopoly over the local network, or over basic telephony, domestic and international, with the rest of the system opened to competition. The regulatory incentives scheme could have been more flexible, with a price-cap arrangement that allowed for limited administrative discretion. And the sale could have provided for widespread domestic ownership. Theoretically, such a scheme looks much more efficient. Rapid technological changes in the sector could be counted on to provide adequate incentives to innovate and to reduce costs, and the system might have generated stronger political support for maintaining private sector control of the industry. There is extensive national debate on these issues and the question remains as to whether price-cap regulation is workable in Jamaica.

Competition. Consider, first, the monopoly decision. The Jamaican government chose an extreme point on the competition-monopoly continuum. The main argument here involves the political costs of introducing competition in value-added services and long-distance communications, since that would have undercut the possibilities for cross-subsidization. The extent of these political costs, however, depends on how much competition is allowed. Cross-subsidization would probably not have been seriously affected by competition in the provision of value-added services and terminal equipment only.

But a narrower monopoly franchise would have required more attention to institutional design and regulatory incentives. In particular, administrative latitude in defining the competitive and monopoly segments would need to be carefully detailed. For example, assuming a monopoly for the local network alone, would fiber-optic cables be considered part of the local network and therefore protected by the monopoly? What about cable television? Should large users be allowed to bypass the network? Providing regulators with the right kind of flexibility on these and related matters could motivate the firm to adopt efficient pricing and to innovate. But administrative discretion could as well be used to expropriate the company's quasi-rents. Arbitration or some other conflict-resolution process could be established to counterbalance administrative discretion. Alternatively, the license could precisely define the boundary between competitive and monopolistic sectors by defining either the competitive activities – say terminal equipment, value-added and cellular services, cable television, and international communications – or the monopoly activities, with anything not explicitly mentioned left open to competition. The decision to go with a total monopoly to avoid the short-run political costs of higher prices for local services was, to some extent, a sacrifice of gain tomorrow to avoid pain today. But narrowing the range of the legal monopoly would have had fiscal implications, too, since private investors would have paid less for the company. Society would have paid up front in smaller proceeds for the treasury from the privatization, but in an industry where technological change is so rapid, the tradeoff would probably have been worth making.

What about total liberalization of international or long-distance calls? In principle, access to the local network could have been priced to ensure that revenues from international operations would still subsidize the local network, thereby limiting the political cost. Since Telecommunications of Jamaica would retain the monopoly on the local network, access charges would naturally be regulated. To restrain administrative discretion, though, access charges would have to be included in the rate-of-return system, in which case competition would not have driven prices down. The gains from liberalization of the international calls segment would thus have been substantially lower.

Pricing. Several alternative pricing schemes could have been implemented instead of one based on a target zone for the rate of return on equity. The selected pricing scheme provides adequate incentives to invest, but not to reduce costs. But with Jamaica's political structure and politics, a more flexible pricing scheme would have less investor credibility. Consider, for example, a price-cap system, in which prices are automatically adjusted over a base-price fixed ahead of time. In the absence of periodic adjustments, such arrangements are likely to lead to extremely high or extremely low returns. Yet revisions provide opportunities for substantial administrative discretion, and in systems without a specified minimum expected rate of return, there may be incentives for regulators to set prices so low as to expropriate the firm's assets. As the experience reviewed here has shown, administrative discretion appears to act as a disincentive to attracting private investment in the Jamaican institutional setting, making price-cap regulation unsuitable.

Ownership. Consider, finally, the way the government disposed of its stake in Telecommunications of Jamaica. At the time of the public offering the government was clearly interested in achieving widespread stock ownership by domestic residents. The government selected a price (J$0.88) that would ensure the total placement of its stock,[30] and household customers of Jamaica Telephone and employees of Telecommunications of Jamaica received priority. In the event, however, the sale of the government's remaining stock to Cable and Wireless went against widespread ownership. Strong fiscal and foreign exchange pressures in 1988–9 may have convinced the government to sell its shares to a willing and ready buyer.

The fact that Cable and Wireless was so willing and ready to buy demonstrates the strengths of the new licensing arrangements. But if conflict develops between the government and Telecommunications of

Jamaica, its ownership structure will provide no extra political capital to restrain the administration's actions, as widespread public ownership might have. Thus, it is again possible that Telecommunications of Jamaica may foresee political problems as license renewal approaches and cut back on investment, perhaps triggering an early renewal of the license. More widespread stock ownership might have served as a safeguard and made possible a less rigid regulatory scheme. But ensuring widespread ownership would have required restrictions on the sale of shares outside the country.[31]

FINAL COMMENTS

In Jamaica's strong two-party parliamentary system, legislation-based procedural requirements alone may not provide the necessary regulatory stability to promote private investment. The courts have little restraining power over government policy shifts, though informal norms of consensus building do exert a braking force. Very flexible regulatory schemes with strong incentives, such as the price-cap mechanism, of the United Kingdom, may be less attractive to the investor because of the fear of political opportunism given the nature of Jamaica's politics and the ownership structure of the utilities. The solution adopted in Jamaica before 1962 and after 1987 was to build the regulatory structure into utility operating licenses rather than into legislation alone. The license stipulates a price-setting mechanism and automatic arbitration procedures when disagreements arise. What makes the system work in Jamaica is its independent judiciary and history of protection of property rights, which gives private investors confidence that the terms of the license will be respected. This intermediate approach to regulation limits administrative discretion and provides strong incentives for investment. This outcome was politically feasible because the rapid growth in international communications in the late 1970s allowed the sector to achieve high levels of profitability while continuing to cross-subsidize local services.

While the regulatory system succeeded in encouraging private investment, it did so at some cost in efficiency. To ensure that profits from long-distance and other telecommunications services were high enough to keep the price of local calls low, entry into the entire telecommunications sector was virtually barred. Had some parts of the sector been opened to competition, an array of new products and services could have been developed and the competitiveness of Jamaica's export-oriented sectors would have improved. These foregone opportunities attest to the need for the careful design of regulatory institutions that take into account the politics and political structure of the country and the economic and technological issues in the industry.

3

The United Kingdom: A pacesetter in regulatory incentives

PABLO T. SPILLER AND INGO VOGELSANG

The United Kingdom has been a pacesetter in institutional change in the telecommunications sector. Over the 1980s the government privatized British Telecom, introduced a novel regulatory scheme and a new regulatory institution (Oftel, the office of Telecommunications), and opened the sector to competition in the network, customer premises equipment, and value-added network services. Private investors have shown remarkable confidence in the future of the sector despite the uncertainty generated by the lack of modern experience with regulation of private utilities, the intrinsic discretionary powers of the government in administrative decisions, and continuing institutional change.

The British political system provides no constitutional protection against discretionary regulatory behavior. The party in power controls both Parliament and the government, and there is no tradition of active judicial oversight of regulatory bodies. Thus governments and regulators cannot easily and credibly commit not to use administrative discretion to tighten the regulatory screws to expropriate a regulated firm's specific assets. Even if the courts rejected a particular regulatory interference, the government could get its way just by introducing new legislation or procedures. The puzzle, then, is how the Conservative governments of the 1980s were able to privatize the telecommunications, electricity, water, gas, and airport sectors. Why were private investors willing to invest large amounts in sectors that, in principle, were vulnerable to confiscatory regulation in the future?

At least part of the explanation lies in the way the privatization was

The authors would like to thank senior executives at British Telecom, Mercury, Oftel, Offer, and the Mergers and Monopolies Commission; and Michael Beesley, Martin Cave, John Moore, and Cento Veljanovski for providing extremely useful insights on the way regulation takes place in the United Kingdom; and Brian Levy for challenging and stimulating discussions. Needless to say, the opinions expressed in the paper are exclusively those of the authors.

handled and in the evolution and adaptation of British political institutions. Three elements are especially relevant:

- The privatization was designed to achieve widespread ownership.
- Several basic features of the regulatory governance system work to restrain administrative discretion: the use of licenses to stipulate pricing and access regulations, attention to competition, the involvement of several agencies in any efforts to push through license amendments against the will of the license holder, and the influence of informal norms that limit ministerial discretion.
- The details of the regulatory incentives system, such as use of the price-cap method, limit regulatory discretion.

To a large extent, then, privatization and regulation of the telecommunications sector in the United Kingdom succeeded because they were well suited to the country's institutions (independent courts, informal norms of proper government behavior, the existence of agencies like the Monopolies and Mergers Commission and the Office of Fair Trading). The regulatory system is not without weaknesses, however, and many of them are the result of weak commitment mechanisms inherent in the British system of government.

INSTITUTIONAL ENDOWMENT AND THE IMPLICATIONS FOR UTILITY REGULATION

Utilities are fragile industries. A large proportion of their assets are sunk, many of their technologies exhibit economies of scale, and their customers constitute much of the voting population. Thus utility pricing will always attract the interest of local politicians (Goldberg 1976; Williamson 1976). Such political sensitivity implies that the risk of administrative expropriation rises as regulatory discretion increases. In response to public pressure for cheap phone service, regulators could set prices below long-run average costs, thereby expropriating the companies' specific assets.

In the United States government regulatory discretion has been held in check by the strong tradition of judicial defense of "fair" rates of return[1] and judicial oversight of regulatory agencies. Thus the U.S. regulatory system offers a credible promise of official commitment not to act arbitrarily that enables utilities to expand and provide service in a relatively stable, although not necessarily efficient, environment.[2]

Private utilities in the United Kingdom have not fared as well. Their development from the mid-1800s to the mid-1900s was impeded by political and regulatory systems quite different from those in the United States. The U.S. political system is based on the principle of division of powers, at federal and state levels; the British system, like Jamaica's, is based on a sovereign Parliament. The electoral system that evolved in the United Kingdom following the Reform Acts of the mid-nineteenth century has traditionally granted a majority of seats in Parliament, and therefore control of both government and legislature, to a single party. The judiciary does not play a major role in restraining the administration (Baldwin and McCrudden 1987). Shugart and Carey (1992, 12–13) describe such parliamentary systems as on the road to becoming "principally an electoral college for determining which party holds executive power. [Parliament is] neither a legislature, as legislative authority is concentrated in the cabinet, nor very representative, at least on the level at which its members are chosen, since the national policy concerns that are expressed by parties capable of winning national power become paramount."

As a consequence, politics in the United Kingdom has tended to evolve toward party politics, with members of Parliament more interested in preserving or gaining power than in narrow constituency issues.[3] Cox (1987) calls this evolution the "efficient secret," because it makes a legislature based originally on narrow regional interests take a national perspective. Since backbencher dissent would threaten the government's survival, party and parliamentary organization have evolved in ways that diminish the potential for internal dissent. Thus the British Parliament leaves much less room for individual initiative than, for example, the U.S. Congress (Cain, Ferejohn, and Fiorina 1987). Party resources are also allocated in ways that correspond more closely with the party than with individual performance (Cain, Ferejohn, and Fiorina 1987; Cox 1987).

From this process has emerged a two-party system with a relatively homogeneous Parliament and majority party control of executive and legislative branches of government. The fact that coalition governments are not the norm implies that even minor electoral changes at the national level may have important policy consequences – say, if a government holding a slim parliamentary majority loses the election, and the other party gains control of Parliament, also with a small margin. Formal and informal institutions (or norms) have evolved to rein in this potential for policy reversals and to restrain government discretion in the regulatory arena. We focus here on three of the informal norms: the permanent bureaucracy, white papers laying out the implications of major policy changes, and the delegation of substantive powers to regulators.

Even when the party in power changes, the senior staff of government departments remains virtually untouched. Fesler (1983) finds that the ratio of high-political to high-career officials is one in forty in Great Britain and France and one in five in the United States (see also Heclo 1977). This bureaucratic stability tends to limit the potential for rapid changes in policy.[4] The use of white papers to explore and provide notice of impending policy changes is another institutional check on discretionary government behavior. The commissioning of a report serves to announce the government's intention, providing an opportunity for interest groups to lobby and make their positions known. The process prevents hasty changes in policy, made without public and political consultation.[5] Finally, though ministers retain formal powers to undertake major regulatory changes involving license amendments, it seems to be well understood that a positive recommendation by the director general of the regulatory office is required first. Similarly, if a minister does not want to implement a director general's recommendation, a well-specified process has to be followed. Simply ignoring a director general's recommendation would violate an informal norm of delegation.[6] Since director generals' terms in office are usually longer than those of the minister that appoints them, this delegation of substantive authority provides for a measure of policy stability, especially by limiting radical regulatory changes following a minor shift in electoral power.

These informal norms are not enough, in themselves, to guarantee policy stability (Calvert 1992). Indeed, regulatory policies in the United Kingdom have not traditionally been very stable. Rather, these norms of government decision making provide a base for the design of formal regulatory institutions that reflect the realities of institutional commitment mechanisms. Since changing decision making norms simply to obtain a particular policy outcome is politically costly, basing the formal regulatory institutions on these institutions infuses the regulatory system with greater stability.

The judiciary also restrains government discretion, although more through its long tradition of protecting contracts than through review of regulatory decisions, which remains uncommon at the national level. Judicial review of regulatory decisions is becoming more frequent at the local government level, however, as conflict between local and central governments has intensified. It is not a strong restraining device at the national level because regulators[7] are not required to explain their decisions in detail, so unreasonableness and procedural violations, the main grounds for judicial appeal, are difficult to demonstrate (Baldwin and McCrudden 1987, 292–3). Contracts are another matter. Courts have a strong tradition of upholding contracts among private parties, so it is not surprising that utility regulation has been implemented through licenses, which can specify both substantive restraints on regulatory discretion and restraints on changing the regulatory system as well as the regulatory incentives structure. Such specificity makes procedural violations easier to identify and keeps regulators from deviating too broadly.[8]

Until recently most public utilities were in government hands, suggesting that institutions able to curb regulatory discretion had never developed or could not withstand political change. What was needed was a regulatory structure that would restrain administrative discretion by allowing existing institutional safeguards to influence the regulatory processes. U.S.-style regulation based on rate of return, for example, would not be a good fit in the U.K.'s institutional setting, where the rate review process might not be able to guarantee companies a particular return. Were the courts to reject a particular price-setting arrangement for failing to provide a fair return ("fair" meaning adequate to cover the cost of capital), a government unhappy with the determination could pass legislation making the arrangement legal, thereby voiding the judicial decision and blocking further judicial recourse (Salzburg 1991). Implementing U.S.-style regulation would have required developing new norms of institutional behavior.

INSTITUTIONAL ENDOWMENT AND REGULATORY COMMITMENT: THE HISTORICAL EVIDENCE BEFORE PRIVATIZATION

As early as 1880 licenses were issued by the Postmaster General to private and municipal suppliers of telephone services. Because so many companies desired to promote an integrated national network, the government let the Post Office take over the entire telephone system in 1912, granting it a statutory monopoly (except in a few municipalities, including Kingston-upon-Hull). Thus, the period of private ownership in telecommunications was short, and its historical record poor. For other utilities, however, private ownership continued almost until the end of World War II.[9]

Parliament had considerable discretion over regulatory matters, as is evident in the frequent changes in regulatory legislation. Perhaps to counter these discretionary powers, regulations were implemented through detailed licenses that specified maximum prices, rates of return, sale and takeover provisions, and application of eminent domain. The licenses provided effective safeguards against relatively minor changes in regulatory approach but were vulnerable to the effects of major changes in technology since Parliament unilaterally altered the operating rights of utilities when technology changed. Even then, however, Parliament exercised its power in a way that largely preserved the profitability of the affected utilities and protected their owners from "unfair" expropriation or arbitrary shutdown. Firms affected by a change in operating rights received generous transition rights that compensated them for losses arising from compulsory shutdowns or takeovers. Whether these protections were the result of informal constitutional constraints or the political vision of the day is unclear, however.

Until recently British Telecom and its predecessor, the telecommunications division of the British Post Office, could be said to be synonymous with the telecommunications services sector in the United Kingdom.[10] The Post Office controlled the development and maintenance of the telephone network and the supply and maintenance of terminal equipment.

Box 3.1.   *Telecommunications policies 1960–80*

The 1969 Post Office Act
- Gave the minister the power to appoint members of the board to control investment and borrowing.
- Required the Post Office to provide universal service.
- Called for a Post Office Users National Council to monitor the Post Office from the consumers' perspective and to make recommendations to the minister concerning Post Office initiatives.
- Required the Post Office to consult with the council before implementing any major initiative.
- Transformed the Post Office into a public corporation.

The Carter Report of July 1977
- Criticized the exercise of market power by the Post Office.
- Indicated that the 1969 act provided few incentives to lower costs.
- Criticized the accounting system and data availability.
- Highlighted conflict between managers and government.
- Highlighted lack of accountability and a proper framework for decision making and project evaluation.
- Criticized Post Office management as too rigid and managerial salaries as too low.
- Recommended separating postal and telecommunications divisions into two corporations.

The 1978 white paper on the state of the Post Office
- Did not recommend separating telecommunications and postal services.
- Encouraged greater decentralization of decision making.

It operated as a department of state under the direct control of a minister of the crown until 1969, when it was converted into a public corporation. The Post Office had three business centers, each with its own profit and loss accounts and balance sheet. The telecommunications division was separated from the Post Office in 1981, when British Telecom became a public corporation. In 1984, before its privatization, British Telecom was converted into a public limited company.[11]

Before privatization, telecommunications policy relating to such regulatory incentives issues as prices, investment, and technology adoption emerged from interactions among many players – the Post Office (and later British Telecom), the Secretary of State, Parliament's Select Committee on Nationalised Industries, and user groups. Telecommunications policy changed substantially in the postwar period, as did control and organization of the Post Office and, later, British Telecom (Boxes 3.1 and 3.2). The fluidity of government policy suggests that postwar governments had

---

Box 3.2. *Regulatory changes and proposals prior to British Telecom's privatization*

The 1981 Beesley Report
• Recommended unrestricted resale of leased lines (private circuits).
• Recommended allowing British Telecom to set prices freely for private circuits.
• Recommended promotion of network entry.

The British Telecommunications Act of 1981
• Allowed some entry into value-added networks, with further relaxation to come in 1987.
• Terminated British Telecom's monopoly over customer premises equipment, except for the initial phone (to be terminated in 1985).
• Allowed licensed network entry.
• Separated British Telecom from the Post Office.

The 1982 White Paper
• Proposed sale of 51 percent of British Telecom.
• Proposed creation of an office of telecommunications, with a director general.

The duopoly policy of November 1983
• Stipulated that no nationwide competitor to British Telecom and Mercury would be allowed to supply fixed-link voice telephony for seven years.

The 1984 Telecommunications Act
• Created Oftel and the position of Director General of Telecommunications.
• Required licenses for all private telecommunications operators.
• Stipulated the process of license amendments.
• Brought the Monopolies and Mergers Commission into the regulation of licensees.
• Was silent about price setting, except that it was to be determined in the license.

---

wide latitude in regulatory matters. Most of the regulatory changes were effected not through specific legislation but through executive orders promoted through white papers.

Management of the telecommunications operator was another matter. Both the telecommunications division of the Post Office and later British Telecom under public ownership had serious management problems, attributable to a large extent to political interference and lack of managerial incentives (Moore 1986). Over time most of the changes in regulatory structures reflected attempts by the government to reduce (or formalize)

85

the discretionary authority of ministers or managers. The fact that several white papers as well as the Telecommunications Act of 1969 tried to limit the scope of ministerial interference suggests the government's inherent inability to stick to a policy of noninterference in the management of public corporations.

The movement of prices and profitability in the telecommunications sector since the late 1960s shows the extent of government interference. Most of the price setting process was arranged informally between the government and the Post Office, and no written records are available. Price changes were generally granted without much confrontation between management and government until the mid-1970s, when government interference intensified. Before the financial crisis of 1975, prices for local users were subsidized mostly through increases in long-distance prices.[12] The trend in relative prices began to change in 1976, however, as long-distance rates started to go down and local rates to go up. By 1980 local rates had nearly tripled in real terms while long-distance prices had declined by a third, indicating a move toward cost-based pricing (Figure 3.1). At the same time, however, connection and rental charges were moving away from their cost base. After increasing slightly in real terms from 1967 to 1976, these charges fell by nearly 50 percent from 1976 to 1980 (Figure 3.2). As a consequence, there was substantial excess demand for telephone lines in 1980.

Political interference affected not only prices but also the profitability and investment policies of the telecommunications division. In the late 1960s and early 1970s the profitability of the telecommunications division of the Post Office was among the highest in the public sector. The relatively high rates of return were attributable largely to the setting of high financial targets, which encouraged some degree of monopoly pricing for long-distance calling. Then, from 1973 to 1975, performance declined markedly, reaching its lowest point in 1975 (Figure 3.3), when the government responded to the severe macroeconomic instability (inflation, recession, and the oil price shock) by holding down prices. During the second half of the 1970s the telecommunication division's capital base shrank 5 percent, the productivity of its installed capital fell, and its technology was becoming increasingly obsolete.[13]

Following the abolition of price controls in 1976, prices rose again, resulting in a dramatic financial turnaround for the Post Office and other state industries. Profits in the telecommunications division reached 15.9 percent as a proportion of turnover, with telephone charges increasing an average of 66 percent. Productivity per worker started to grow rapidly after 1980 (Figure 3.4).

In 1981 the Conservative government allowed British Telecom to increase its prices to finance investments. Although fixed assets started to

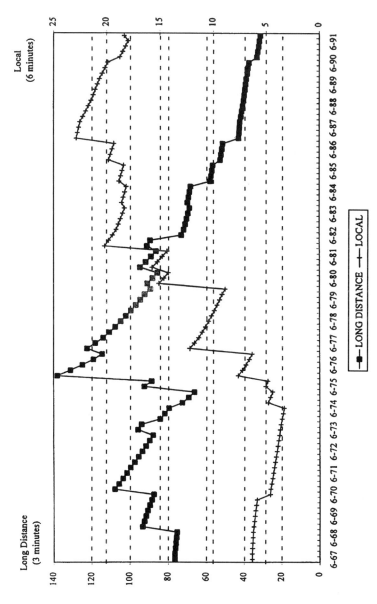

Figure 3.1. Real residential prices of long distance and local calls, 1967–91 (June) (in 1985 British pence).

87

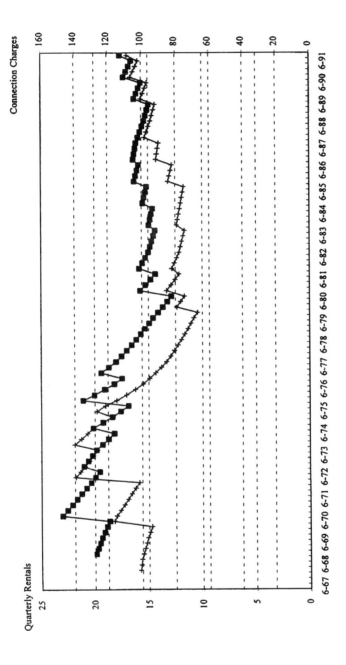

Figure 3.2. Real prices of residential quarterly rental and connection charges, 1967–91 (June) (1985 pounds sterling).

88

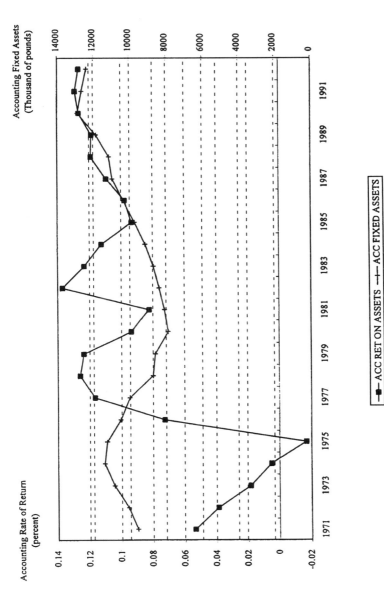

Figure 3.3. Real return on fixed assets, 1971–91, and fixed assets.

89

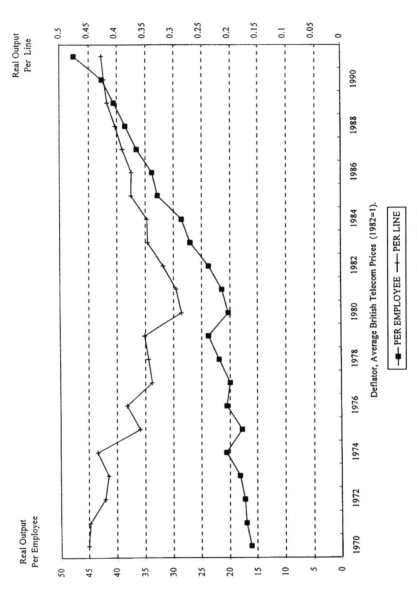

Figure 3.4. Productivity measures: real output per employee and per line, 1970–91.

increase in 1981 (see Figure 3.3), the increases did not get translated into dramatic increases in the number of main lines (Figure 3.5). In May 1982, to a large extent because of British Telecom's failure to invest, the government told the company to reduce prices. British Telecom reduced only its long-distance prices. That was the last attempt by the government to manipulate the company's pricing and investment policies. By this time the government was ready to privatize British Telecom. A July 1982 white paper proposed the sale of 51 percent of the company's shares and the creation of an office of telecommunications to provide regulatory oversight.

THE SEARCH FOR COMMITMENT: PRIVATIZATION, COMPETITION, AND REGULATION

During the 1970s a movement emerged in the Conservative Party to undo the nationalizations of the previous Labour governments. While some supported privatization primarily as a way to improve the fiscal situation, others supported it for political reasons. For example, John Moore, the financial secretary to the treasury, saw "people's capitalism" as a way to change the political composition of the nation (Moore 1986; Newman 1986, 150). This view seems to have influenced the privatization of British Telecom, which was designed to ensure widespread share ownership. The privatization and the introduction of competition, which started with the Telecommunications Act of 1981, were designed in a way that helped to strengthen institutional commitment for private ownership of British Telecom.

Privatization and widespread domestic ownership

The Telecommunications Act of 1981 separated British Telecom from the Post Office. A little more than a year later a bill to privatize British Telecom was presented to Parliament, and the bill received royal assent on 12 April 1984 (Newman 1986). The act formally created a public limited company to which the assets of the public corporation, British Telecom, were transferred. Before that step, however, substantial effort had been devoted to restructuring British Telecom and ensuring that a large part of the company's shares would be sold to individual investors. A massive television and newspaper advertising campaign explained how individuals could buy shares and what it meant to own them. The public offer of 50.2 percent of the shares at 130 pence a share was opened on 20 November 1984, and trading on stock exchanges began on 3 December 1984.

The advertising campaign and various incentive schemes suggest that

Main
Lines

Inland Calls
(percent)

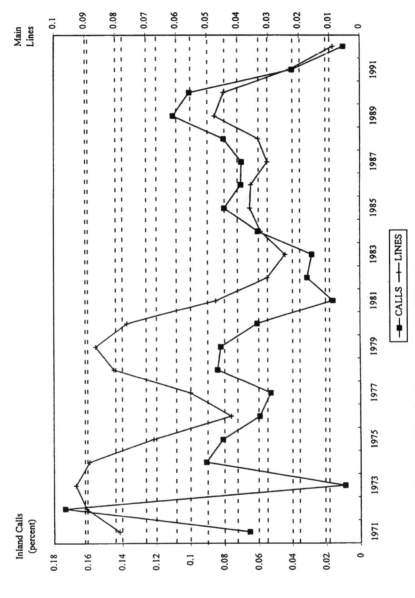

Figure 3.5. Rate of growth of inland calls and main lines, 1971–92.

the government was interested not only in making the privatization a success, but also in achieving widespread ownership in the United Kingdom. In 1981 less than 28 percent of all British stocks were held by British residents, and in 1983 only 3.8 percent of the adult population were stockholders (Newman 1986). Achieving broad public ownership in British Telecom, then, would require substantial incentives and a strong promotional effort.

The government approved three main incentives. The telephone voucher scheme provided individual investors with vouchers worth £18 each. The number of vouchers rose with the size of the investment and the length of time the shares were held. An alternative – and more popular – option offered investors one free share for each ten purchased at the initial offering up to a total investment of £5,000. Another incentive allowed investors to pay only 40 percent of the price at the time of application and to pay the remainder in equal installments in June 1985 and April 1986. A third incentive scheme was designed for British Telecom's 240,000 employees. Each employee received free shares up to a value of about £70. Also, any investment up to £100 at application time was automatically doubled. Employees were also eligible to buy up to £2,000 in shares at a 10 percent discount.

The pricing of shares seems to have been another major incentive. While shares sold at 130 pence, individual investors had to pay only 50 pence up front. The partially paid shares traded immediately at 90 pence and were at 103 pence by the end of December. By the end of the payout period, April 1986, investors were receiving a nominal gain of 110 pence on an (undiscounted) investment of 130 pence (Figure 3.6). The number of shares applied for by the public was five times the number put up for sale. Underpricing was so great that even investors who had to buy in the open market after the initial offer for sale made substantial gains.

Institutional investors bought up almost half the shares (47 percent), followed by the public (39 percent) and overseas investors (14 percent). More than 2 million individuals purchased shares, half of them buying fewer than 400 shares each.[14] By June 1985, though, shares held by individuals fell to a more normal 29 percent. Whether the government intentionally tried to achieve widespread holdings or not, the fact is that most of the shares remained in the hands of residents, turning regulatory policy, as well as renationalization, into a sensitive political issue.[15]

In December 1991 the government reduced its holdings from 47.7 percent to 21.8 percent, cashing in £5.5 billion. This time, instead of selling at a prespecified price, the government divided the shares in two segments. Large investors were required to bid for their shares, with smaller investors then allowed to buy at the price set in the competitive auction, minus a small discount. This sale signaled the government's

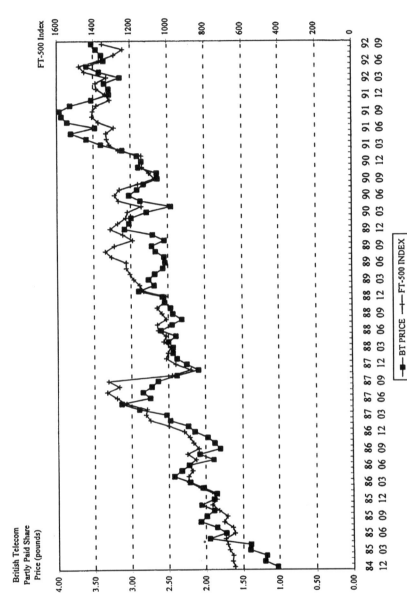

Figure 3.6. British Telecom's share price and the *Financial Times*-500 Index, 1984–92 (December).

commitment to keeping British Telecom in the private sector. At the time the Conservative government was being threatened by a Labour Party victory in the upcoming spring 1992 elections, and relinquishing most of the government's remaining shares was certainly intended to make it more difficult for a Labour government to undo the privatization.

In summer 1993 the government further reduced its holdings almost to zero so that British Telecom is now fully privatized. The privatization process thus suggests that the government tried to create institutional safeguards for private ownership. British Telecom was sold to the public in the largest-ever share issue. But widespread ownership may have come at a short-run cost to the government. Taking the value of the partially paid-up shares at the end of the first day of trading (95 pence) plus the two remaining installments (80 pence) as a measure of what the government could have received in 1986 by selling shares in an open auction (£5.5 million) yields a cost for selling the shares the way it did equal to about half the actual proceeds (£3.6 million). This calculation overstates the cost, however, because if widespread ownership actually provides safeguards against future opportunistic behavior by the government, an open auction that resulted in much more concentrated ownership, would have weakened an important safeguard, reducing the value of British Telecom.

Competition and the rise of Mercury

During its first few years in power the Conservative government considered a series of major changes in the structure of British Telecom (see Box 3.2). Michael Beesley of the London School of Business was commissioned to analyze the potential for competition in customer-premises equipment, value-added network services, and the network. His report (Beesley 1981) recommended major changes in organization and policies, including price flexibility, the right to resale private lines, and competition in the network. British Telecom claimed, though, that these changes would reduce availability of cross-subsidies from international and long-distance calling and force it to increase prices for telephone line rentals, connections, and local calls. Fearing that such a radical change in the price structure would burden residential customers to the benefit of business users, the government did not follow Beesley's recommendations (Bradley 1992, 28), though it did allow some entry into the value-added network market. More important, the Telecommunications Act of 1981 terminated British Telecom's monopoly for customer-premises equipment (except for rental of the first phone, a monopoly that continued until 1985) and allowed for licensed network entry.

Thus, competition was introduced before privatization and without breaking British Telecom up into regional or functional companies, which could have intensified and accelerated competitive forces. Breaking up the company would have required substantial restructuring (or rebalancing) of prices, at a heavy political cost that could have threatened the privatization (Vickers and Yarrow 1986). That British Telecom was privatized intact may reflect both the country's fiscal circumstances and an understanding of the price implications of competition.

Promoting competition had two distinct incentive effects. It reduced the potential profitability of British Telecom, since competition would lower prices in the contested segments of the market. It also reduced the ability of regulators to behave opportunistically toward British Telecom. Setting prices too low would elicit complaints not only from British Telecom but also from its competitors, who would lose customers to the lower-priced British Telecom.

In June 1981 a consortium consisting of British Petroleum, Barclays Merchant Bank, and the recently privatized Cable and Wireless applied for a license for project Mercury, to supply telecommunications network services in competition with British Telecom. British Telecom responded by publicly threatening price increases. It put some of the threatened measures in place when Mercury's license was granted in principle in August 1981. In February 1982 Mercury received a twenty-five year renewable license.[16]

British Telecom's rate rebalancing started well before privatization and seems even to have predated Mercury's license application. Originally, Mercury's license was quite specific, requiring Mercury to build a fiber-optic network connecting thirty specified cities and limiting Mercury's market share in voice telephony to 3 percent of British Telecom's. This restriction was meant as a safeguard for British Telecom's planned expansion and network modernization. Within a year, however, the limitation was dropped and Mercury was to become British Telecom's competitor for all services. Soon it was Mercury's turn to ask for protection from competition so that it could commit funds for its required investments (Beesley and Laidlaw 1989).

In November 1983 the government announced a new duopoly policy, blocking entry to new suppliers of public fixed-link voice telephony for seven years. The new policy, which was announced after the decision to privatize British Telecom, seems to have been motivated by a desire for a more gradual transition to competition that would not affect prices too abruptly. Greater competition was allowed outside of the fixed-link network services. The government licensed two operators of mobile cellular networks (Cellnet, 60 percent owned by British Telecom, and Racal-Vodafone), and awarded eleven pilot cable franchises that could eventually be used for telecommunications services.

Mercury got off to a bumpy start. Its market share remained negligible throughout the 1980s. By the end of the decade, however, Mercury was growing fast, and by 1992 it had achieved a 6 percent share of the telecommunications market. Ninety-six of the top 100 corporations were using Mercury's network.[17] Its cumulative investment in plant and equipment, which stood at £1.5 billion in 1992, was forecasted to double by 1995. Mercury's ambitious investment program has definitely been helped by the financial strength and profitability of its parent company, Cable and Wireless. In recent years, however, Mercury's own profit growth has been so strong that self-financing of its investment has become a realistic possibility. After losing money the first few years, Mercury made its first profits of £17.7 million in 1989. Three years later it had a trading profit of £155 million on a turnover of £915 million. By the time the duopoly policy expired, Mercury had become a viable competitor. It was involved in all three of British Telecom's license modifications, making its own recommendations on license changes to Oftel.

Thus, the way network competition was introduced reinforced the government's commitment to private ownership of utilities, just as the privatization process had. Limiting network competition allowed for a more gradual rebalancing of British Telecom's rates, thus reducing the political cost of privatization, while the emergence of a viable competitor forced the regulator to take its financial interests into account and provided British Telecom with a strategic supporter in its price bargaining. Thus, both privatization and the introduction of competition must have affected performance and investment decisions in the sector.

THE MODERN REGULATORY PROCESS

The United Kingdom has a tradition of loose administrative processes (Baldwin and McCrudden 1987). Public hearings are the exception, agencies do not have to substantiate their decisions (which could open them to judicial review), and standards of judicial review are lax. Thus detailed procedures need to be specified to restrain regulatory discretion (Veljanovski 1991).

Utility regulation has long been implemented through licenses that stipulate what the enterprise can do, the legal basis of the regulation, and the method of price regulation that applies. The underlying legislation, which precedes the granting of the license, also specifies how the licenses are to be amended. In the case of telecommunications licenses, the Telecommunications Act of 1984 specifies how licenses are to be amended. The Telecommunications Act of 1984 specifies how licenses are to be amended when both parties agree and when they do not. Jamaica's utility regulation also relies strongly on licenses, but a license cannot be amended without the agreement of both parties (see Chapter 2).

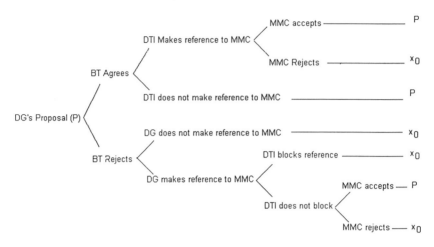

Figure 3.7. The telecommunications regulation game.

Built into the regulatory process is a strong commitment, though not unbreakable, to follow the regulatory bargain struck at the time of privatization. The nature of the country's institutions (particularly the courts and informal norms of government decision making) further reduces the likelihood that major regulatory changes will be imposed without the consent of the regulated company. Among the key safeguards:

- To amend the license against the wishes of the company, the government must follow a complex and a precisely specified process. Failure to do so can be contested in courts.
- Amending the license requires the agreement of several agencies, further reducing the extent of regulatory discretion.
- Major regulatory powers are delegated to the head of the regulatory agency, limiting power at the ministry level.
- Use of a price-cap mechanism limits the price-setting powers of the regulator and, because price-caps are part of the license, limits the regulator's ability to radically change the price-setting mechanism.

The players

There are four key players in the regulatory process: the Director General of the Office of Telecommunications (Oftel), the Secretary of State of the Department of Trade and Industry, the management of British Telecom, and the Monopolies and Mergers Commission. All four are involved in any major regulatory change requiring a license amendment (Figure 3.7).

All utilities in the United Kingdom are regulated by a regulatory agency headed by a director general who responds to a secretary of state. Director generals are appointed by the secretary for a period of up to five years; they cannot be removed except for clear malfeasance or personal incompetence. Ultimately, the director general is accountable to Parliament. Oftel's budget is set by the Treasury and is financed by a levy (approved by Parliament) on licensed telecommunications carriers that covers most of its current expenses (Oftel *Annual Report 1991*).

Because the telecommunications privatization would be scrutinized and would affect investors' expectations about future privatization (particularly of gas, water, and electricity companies), the government had an interest in ensuring the independence of the telecommunications regulator. The first Director General was Sir Bryan Carsberg, formerly Arthur Andersen Professor of Accounting at the London School of Economics. The choice of an academician seems to have been a deliberate effort to emphasize the independence of the office. While the Secretary of State of the Department of Trade and Industry must sign the original license and any modifications, the secretary can sign modifications only on the Director General's recommendation. Thus, the Director General has substantial autonomy even in a parliamentary system. While conflicts between the Director General and the Secretary of State could lead to reductions in the regulatory agency's budget or a failure to reappoint the Director General, firing the Director General is not an easy matter.

While the Director General has substantial discretion, the enabling law enunciates the objectives that the agency must follow. For example, the Telecommunications Act of 1984 (Part 1 ¶3(1), (2)) stipulates the primary and secondary duties of the Director General and the Secretary of State. Primary duties are

(a) to secure that there are provided throughout the United Kingdom . . . telecommunication services as satisfy all reasonable demand . . . ; and
(b) . . . to secure that any person . . . is able to finance the provision of those services.

Secondary duties are

(a) to promote the interests of consumers, purchasers and other users . . . in respect of the prices charged for, and the quality and variety of, telecommunications services . . . ;
(b) to maintain and promote effective competition;
(c) to promote efficiency and economy . . . ;
(d) to promote research . . . and development . . . ;
(e) to encourage major users of telecommunication services whose places of business are outside the U.K. to establish places of business in the U.K.;

(f) to promote the provision of international transit services . . . ;
(g) to enable persons providing telecommunications services in the U.K. to compete effectively . . . ;
(h) to enable persons producing telecommunication apparatus in the U.K. to compete effectively in the supply of such apparatus.

This careful specification of objectives (many of them mutually contradictory) in itself serves as a constraint on the discretionary behavior of the Director General since a failure to meet the objectives could open decisions up to litigation.

Another player with a strong independent tradition is the Monopolies and Mergers Commission, a consultative body created in 1948. Though its determinations on mergers, consumer protection, and regulatory issues are not binding, its concurrence is required to block a merger or to amend a license without the company's approval. Thus, the role of the commission has always been to bless or to veto the policy recommendations of the Director General or Secretary of State. Commission members (there were thirty-five in 1992) are appointed by the Secretary of State for four-year terms. Commissioners cannot be removed or reappointed. Though the Monopolies and Mergers Commission is clearly a partisan agency, there is implicit agreement that its composition should not be wholly partisan. The chairman, together with the Secretary of State of Trade and Industry, convenes a panel to hear each telecommunications license amendment case and to make a decision after a public hearing.

The license amendment process as commitment device

Oftel has to rewrite British Telecom's license every four years because the price-cap formula is valid only that long. That gives British Telecom a strong bargaining position because the amendment process has to be completed before the price cap expires. If the license is allowed to expire, British Telecom could, in principle, set its own prices at will. In general, amending a license requires the agreement of the regulated firm and the Director General. If they do not reach agreement, the Director General may proceed with what is called a "reference" to the Monopolies and Mergers Commission (see Figure 3.7).

Consider the case in which the Director General proposes a license amendment with which the company agrees. The agreement is not enough to change the license, however, because the Secretary of State has to sign the new license. The secretary has fourteen days to block the agreement by making a reference to the Monopolies and Mergers Commission, seeking a judgment on whether the agreement is "against the public interest." This veto power is vested with the Department of Trade and Industry to reduce incentives for collusion between the Director General and British Telecom. If the commission concurs that an agreement would be against the public interest, the Secretary of State may not sign the agreement, and the initial status quo remains in place. If the commission finds the agreement to be in the public interest, the secretary has no further recourse but to sign the license agreement.

Next, consider a proposal by the Director General with which the company does not agree. To change the license without the company's agreement, the Monopolies and Mergers Commission has to determine that the current situation is against the public interest and that the Director General's proposal is in the public interest (Telecommunications Act 1984, Part II, ¶13–15). In other words, the commission may veto the Director General's recommendation, but it cannot impose a particular recommendation on the Director General.[18] If the recommendation gets the commission's approval, the proposed change can be sent to the Secretary of State for formal signature. If the commission does not approve, the status quo remains.

While the Secretary of State has to sign a license agreement that has been sanctioned by the Monopolies and Mergers Commission, the secretary may block the reference to the commission. The secretary may instruct the commission not to consider a particular reference that is considered to be against national security, thus preventing the Director General from getting a proposal enacted against the will of the company (Telecommunication Act 1984, Part II, ¶13 [5]). References can be blocked on these grounds only under extreme circumstances. (A false claim of national security risk, though possible, would taint all of the department's policy decisions if discovered.) To understand the reason for this rule, the nature of references to the Monopolies and Mergers Commission has to be clarified.

A Director General can make narrow or wide references to the commission. Narrow references deal exclusively with issues of contention between the company and the Director General. Wide references deal with all sectoral issues, including organization of the company or competition in the sector. The Secretary of State could consider that a wide reference presents a serious risk, and so may find it proper to block it. Even a narrow reference that implies too large a change in the regulatory system might be considered to be against national security if, for example, the change could bankrupt the company. In any event, moving a reference to the Monopolies and Mergers Commission under the widest terms would naturally require the agreement of the Secretary of State, although relatively minor references would not.

From the company's perspective then a reference to the Monopolies and Mergers Commission may involve substantial risks and costs. References take an average of six months and require the attention of senior management. During that period the integrity of the company may be at stake, raising its cost of capital.[19] References may also be costly for the regulatory agency. Losing a reference, as happened to Oftel in the *Chatlines* case, implies some loss of reputation.[20] Thus, both the regulatory agency and the regulated companies give serious consideration to what the Monopolies and Mergers Commission is likely to do. It is not surprising that the commission has received few references during the last decade.[21]

The Telecommunications Act of 1984 has no provisions allowing the Secretary of State for Trade and Industry to amend a license against the wishes of the Director General. In principle, the secretary could initiate legislation in Parliament to revoke British Telecom's license. But the action could be challenged in court and would deviate so far from accepted norms of behavior that it would call into question the credibility of contract law in the United Kingdom. As a consequence, such an action would be conceivable only under extreme circumstances. As a practical matter, too, the Department of Trade and Industry lacks the specialized bureaucracy that has developed in Oftel.

Another curb on the discretionary powers of the Director General is the availability of information. While Oftel is entitled to all information needed for determining British Telecom's costs and compliance with the price-cap formula, Oftel does not automatically receive that information. Furthermore, Oftel cannot publish the information without British Telecom's consent. Thus, Oftel has very limited power to penalize an operator for breach of license, and there is no provision in the Telecommunications Act of 1984 for damage payments in case of breach. Since revoking the license is unrealistic, the Director General's powers appear to be restricted to cease-and-desist orders and to embarrassing British Telecom publicly for noncompliance.

To understand how the current license amendment system works, and to explore some of its implications for the stability of the system in the face of political change, we developed a model of the regulatory process in the United Kingdom (Spiller and Vogelsang 1992), which we describe briefly here. A regulatory system based on a licensing scheme can help ensure government commitment to private sector activity by restraining regulatory discretion. While the government could change the rules for license amendment through new legislation, that action would deviate from traditional norms of government behavior.[22]

The initial price level or the initial rate of return determines by how much each player in the regulatory game wants to change the regulatory policy and in what direction. Unless prices are at the monopoly level, the

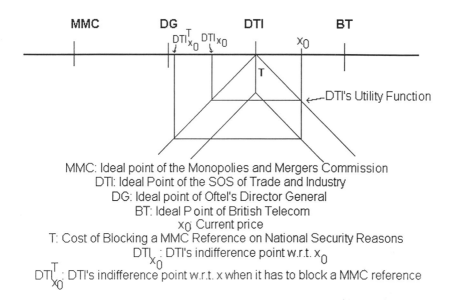

MMC: Ideal point of the Monopolies and Mergers Commission
DTI: Ideal Point of the SOS of Trade and Industry
DG: Ideal point of Oftel's Director General
BT: Ideal Point of British Telecom
x_0 Current price
T: Cost of Blocking a MMC Reference on National Security Reasons
DTI_{x_0}: DTI's indifference point w.r.t. x_0
$DTI_{x_0}^T$: DTI's indifference point w.r.t. x when it has to block a MMC reference

Figure 3.8. A representation of possible preferences.

company wants to increase its average prices and rate of return. For the regulator to get the company to agree to a lower price level or rate of return, the reference to the Monopolies and Mergers Commission must not be blocked by the Department of Trade and Industry on grounds of national security, and then, if the reference is made, the commission must support it. Thus, given the initial status quo, the success of any feasible proposal by the Director General that would make British Telecom worse off also has to be preferred by both the Monopolies and Mergers Commission and the Secretary of State of the Department of Industry and Trade.

Consider a diagrammatic representation of the preferences of all the players in the regulatory arena in a single dimension that represents British Telecom's average price level or its rate of return (Figure 3.8). Each player is assumed to have a preferred policy point and a utility level that falls as the policy outcomes deviate from the preferred policy point. At the time of British Telecom's privatization British Telecom and the Department of Trade and Industry initially agreed to leave the price level, x_0, at a relatively high level somewhere between the ideal points of the two parties. The Monopolies and Mergers Commission under the Conservative governments of the 1980s and 1990s has been free-market oriented, so its most desired rate of return for British Telecom would be close to competitive levels. The Director General of Telecommunications, while also strongly procompetition, had a legal responsibility to watch

103

out for British Telecom's financial well-being (Vickers and Yarrow 1988, 236) and thus might have preferred a higher rate of return than did the Monopolies and Mergers Commission.

Since all three government parties would prefer a lower average price than the initial price level, that level was not at equilibrium. The Director General should be able to find a lower price that the three agencies could support. British Telecom would also go along, given that agreement. How low the price and rate of return would be, though, depends on the exact parameters of the model. First, the Director General of Oftel would not propose a change that would bring prices below its own ideal point, represented by point DG in Figure 3.8. Thus, at most, the Director General's proposal would bring prices down to point DG. Whether such a proposal is feasible depends on how much it would cost the Department of Trade and Industry to block a reference to the Monopolies and Mergers Commission. If it would cost the department a great deal to claim national security considerations for blocking a reference, then Oftel might not feel threatened by the possibility of a block and so might propose its own ideal average price level to British Telecom. But if the potential loss of reputation to the department from blocking a reference is not too high, Oftel would have to take the department's preferences into account.

If it costs nothing for the Director General to block a reference to the Monopolies and Mergers Commission, the Department of Trade and Industry will be indifferent to a choice between the initial status quo x_0 in Figure 3.8 and a point to the left of its ideal point marked DTI_{x_0}. Under those conditions the Director General can propose only policies that lower the price to DTI_{x_0}. If it costs T to block a reference, the department is indifferent to a choice between x_0 and a policy point to the left of its ideal point marked $DTI_{x_0}^T$. Now, if $DTI_{x_0}^T$ is to the right of point DG, the Director General will not be able to implement its desired policy, while if it is to the left, the Department of Trade and Industry cannot block any policy desired by the Director General. Whatever the case, if the initial configuration is as depicted in Figure 3.8, the model suggests that the initial price level would be adjusted downward, toward Oftel's most desired price level. How fast prices drop, though, would depend on the exact preference configuration.

With the current preference configuration the equilibrium average price will be somewhere between the ideal points of Oftel and British Telecom. If, for some reason, the price falls below the level preferred by Oftel, the Director General would propose a license amendment to move prices closer to its ideal point. The Department of Trade and Industry will support the agreement between British Telecom and Oftel. The Monopolies and Mergers Commission, which could have blocked the agreement had the price been between its ideal point and that of Oftel, would not be asked to participate in the amendment process.

Now consider the effects of a change in government to a party less supportive of private ownership. The ideal point of the Department of Trade and Industry would move to the left of that of the Monopolies and Mergers Commission. Since commission members and the Director General were appointed by the previous government, their preferences can be assumed to remain stable through the first years of the new government. If the initial price was higher than the price preferred by the Director General, Oftel could bring prices closer to its own ideal point because the Department of Trade and Industry would always support a reference to the Monopolies and Mergers Commission.

If, however, prices fall below the Director General's ideal point and somewhere between the ideal points of the Monopolies and Mergers Commission and Oftel, Oftel and British Telecom would agree on a license amendment that would bring prices up. The Department of Trade and Industry would then block the amendment by making a reference to the Monopolies and Mergers Commission. The commission would declare the agreement to be against the public interest. So even though the new government had not yet appointed a new Director General or new commission members, the Director General might not be able to bring profitability levels up again if prices have fallen too much because of recession or some other unexpected event, as would be possible in the case when the Department of Trade and Industry's preferences were closer to British Telecom's.

The game is not over, however, because British Telecom's price cap has a sunset provision. If the price cap specified in the license expires before a new license is agreed on, British Telecom may set prices at will. Prices will rise, forcing the Director General to propose a license amendment to bring prices down to its desired level. The action would be supported by both the Department of Trade and Industry and the Monopolies and Mergers Commission.

To bring prices below those desired by the Director General and the Monopolies and Mergers Commission, the government would have to appoint a new Director General and new commission members, which it could not do at will since they are appointed for set terms. Thus, the new government might not be able to pack the commission or change the Director General before new elections take place, at which time the government itself might be out of office. Over a longer period of time, though, if a strong statist-oriented government remains in place, both the Director General and the commission members could be replaced, reducing the government's commitment to profitable private undertakings.

Given the players in the regulatory process and the rules specified for license amendment, the equilibrium price or rate of return might not change much following a large, but short-term change in government. The ability of the current regulatory process to prevent major modifications following a more enduring change in government ideology is very limited, however. By allowing enough flexibility in the license amendment process to adjust regulatory policy to unforeseen technological and economic changes, the current regulatory system runs some risk of being open to the possibility of regulatory opportunism. To restrain that possibility, other safeguards had to be developed.

Whether that flexibility eventually leads to opportunistic behavior by the regulators depends to some extent on the courts, the ownership structure of British Telecom, and public and political perceptions about the role of government in the productive sectors of the economy. Opinion polls show a major turnaround in public opinion about nationalization (Market and Opinion Research International). In mid-1973, 30 percent of those interviewed favored more nationalization and 27 percent favored denationalization (Figure 3.9). By the fall of 1976 those favoring nationalization had fallen to 20 percent while those favoring denationalization had risen to 37 percent (Newman 1986). Also, the large numbers of middle-class citizens and institutions such as pension plans that own shares in British Telecom and other privatized utilities are likely to constitute a strong constituency for "proper" treatment of British Telecom and other privatized utilities.[23]

Price cap as commitment device

All telecommunications operators require a license to operate. The license describes the utility's rights and obligations under the Telecommunications Act of 1984. British Telecom, which holds a twenty-five-year renewable license, is allowed to engage in business activities in cellular telephony, apparatus and equipment supply, and value-added network services as long as it keeps separate accounts showing that it does not cross-subsidize these activities from its telephone network service business. Other activities, such as new mobile technologies or local cable operation face some restriction. The main competitive provisions in British Telecom's license are the requirements to provide universal service, to refrain from cross-subsidization, to purchase equipment through competitive tender, and to interconnect with other operators.

The regulator's discretion is determined by the amount of intervention permitted in the company's price setting and investment decisions. British Telecom's initial license was very specific about who set prices. British Telecom set its own prices subject only to a specified price-cap rule and Oftel's annual supervision. The price-cap rule is very simple. Prices for a

Percent

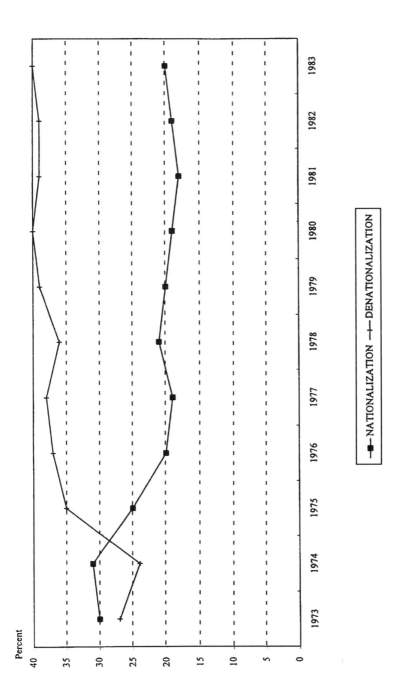

Figure 3.9. U.K.: Share of population in favor of nationalization and denationalization, 1973–83 (Taken during fall, except summer 1973).

Box 3.3. *Development of the RPI−X price-cap system*

The price-cap system was devised by professor Stephen Littlechild, who was commissioned in 1982 to report on two suggestions for regulating British Telecom's prices: a U.S. style rate-of-return and an incentive scheme designed by Professor Alan Walters, economic adviser to Prime Minister Margaret Thatcher. Walters had proposed a profits levy, a tax inversely related to British Telecom's output growth; his plan had no further price regulation. The scheme appeared to have some drawbacks, both in theory and in its practical application (Glaister 1987; Littlechild 1983). Littlechild rejected both schemes, suggesting instead what he called a "local tariff reduction scheme" that would subject only local services to price regulation.

Prices on a defined basket of regulated services would be allowed to grow at the rate of inflation (expressed by the retail price index) minus X percentage points. Within the regulated basket British Telecom could rebalance its prices as long as the RPI−X constraint held for the average, expressed as a chained Laspeyres price index. After five years British Telecom would either be deregulated or the scheme would be revisited by the regulator. Littlechild also proposed a number of steps to open up the sector to more competition. While the government did not follow all his suggestions, Littlechild's regulatory proposal, with some modifications, became part of British Telecom's license, including Littlechild's recommendation of an initial value of 3 percentage points for X. Long-distance calling services were included in the regulated basket, however. Littlechild's suggestion of an RPI−3 for a basket that included local telephone service only would have been much tougher on British Telecom than the scheme that was implemented (Bradley and Price 1988; Vogelsang 1989).

---

basket of regulated services are allowed to increase by RPI−X, the retail price index minus an adjustment factor (Box 3.3). The initial pricing scheme was valid for five years unless amended. The basket of regulated services included local and domestic long-distance rates and covered slightly more than half of British Telecom's total sales. International telephone services, private circuits and apparatus, and connection charges were not part of the regulated basket. Within the RPI−X constraint British Telecom can change its prices with twenty-eight days' notice. Since the RPI−X regulation is part of British Telecom's license, any change of the price regulation requires a change in the license. After the initial five-year period for the RPI−X price-cap, two new four-year license agreements were reached, the latest in 1992.

Including long-distance services in the regulated basket gave British Telecom more flexibility to rebalance its prices because reductions in long-distance rates could be offset by increases in other rates. British Telecom expected competition from Mercury mainly in long-distance services, so including long-distance prices in the basket appreciably increased British Telecom's ability to compete. The greater scope for rebalancing also allowed British Telecom to move toward subsidy-free, allocatively more efficient prices. In 1984, however, British Telecom agreed to hold increases in exchange line rentals to RPI+2, limiting the amount of rebalancing it could engage in.[24]

British Telecom's initial license provided very limited regulatory discretion in price setting, so getting British Telecom to lower its prices would have to depend on competition or a change in the license. There, too, the regulator's freedom of action was tightly circumscribed. Changing the license required negotiating several institutional hurdles, while the 1983 duopoly policy, which restricted fixed-link competition to Mercury and British Telecom until 1991, limited Oftel's ability to foster competition. The license provided slightly more regulatory flexibility on quality supervision, but the 1984 Telecommunications Act did not grant Oftel the power to impose penalties. Thus with the price-cap mechanism substantially constraining the ability to influence British Telecom's prices, the regulator's attention turned to quality control and competition.

REGULATION AND PERFORMANCE SINCE PRIVATIZATION

The regulatory model developed in this chapter suggests that British Telecom's initial price level (and consequently its rate of return) after privatization was relatively high and unlikely to be at its equilibrium level, given the likely objectives of the other players in the regulatory game. Indeed, the various license amendments following privatization can be viewed as efforts to adjust British Telecom's prices to a level that reflected the politics of the day, subject to the procedural constraints imposed by the regulatory system. The process of regulatory change closely followed the pattern that would be predicted by the simple model of regulation described above.

Major regulatory changes

British Telecom's license has been modified four times, always through agreements between Oftel and British Telecom. Two of the modifications were required by the sunset provision in the license for the price-cap regulation, and they came at their regular times (1989 and 1992). A third modification was prompted by the expiration of the duopoly policy in 1991. While the only change required by the expiration of the duopoly

---

Box 3.4. *Major regulatory changes since British Telecom's privatization*

First price-cap renewal, 1988–9
  Regulatory issues
  • Price restructuring since 1985
  • Quality problems, particularly during 1987
  • Large price increases in private circuits
  • British Telecom's high rate of return
  • Interconnection with Mercury
  Regulatory outcome
  • Increase from RPI−3 to RPI−4.5
  • Extension of RPI+2 for exchange line rentals
  • RPI−0 price cap for private circuits
  • Quality guarantees and monitoring
  • Interconnection agreement by regulatory intervention

Duopoly policy review, 1990–1
  Regulatory issues
  • Duopoly policy review
  • British Telecom's continuing high rate of return
  • British Telecom's continuing high market share
  • Government sale of British Telecom shares in November 1991
  Regulatory outcomes
  • Liberalized entry (except for international)
  • New interconnection agreement for Mercury
  • Inclusion of international calls under price caps
  • Increase from RPI−4.5 to RPI−6.25
  • British Telecom allowed to offer volume discounts

Second price-cap renewal, 1992
  Regulatory issues
  • British Telecom's continuing high rate of return
  • Mercury's high rate of return
  • Further rate rebalancing by British Telecom
  • Further government sale of British Telecom shares planned
  Regulatory outcomes
  • Increase from RPI−6.25 to RPI−7.5
  • Restrictions on rebalancing
  • British Telecom accounting separation and current cost accounting

---

policy concerned network entry, Oftel used the occasion to negotiate changes in the price cap as well. The fourth license modification – not discussed here – involved restrictions on the sale of *Chatlines* (similar to 900 lines in the United States). (Box 3.4 summarizes the major regulatory changes since British Telecom's privatization.)

United Kingdom: A regulatory pacesetter

Examination of the three license modifications that involved substantive changes in regulatory policy shows that regulation has grown in scope and stringency since 1984, as reflected by several indicators:

- The adjustment factor X in the price-cap formula has been increased in several steps.
- New revenue items have been brought under price regulation.
- British Telecom's ability to rebalance its rate structure has been severely curtailed.
- Regulation has been extended to the quality of service.
- British Telecom's interconnection charges to its competitors have been subject to a number of regulatory interferences.
- Oftel's personnel and budget have grown steadily.

These changes, though they might appear to be unanticipated modifications in the nature of telecommunications regulation, can be seen as a regulatory adaptation to a new equilibrium more in tune with the political realities of the United Kingdom.

First price-cap renewal, 1988–9. About 50 percent of British Telecom's outputs (in value terms) were initially subject to the RPI−3 price cap following privatization. British Telecom immediately increased prices for the capped services an average of 2 percent in November 1984, which represented an average real price cut of 3.1 percent for the regulated basket, or slightly larger than the regulatory requirement. Because of the composition of the average nominal change, however, the average customer faced a rate increase well above RPI−3. The price for exchange line rentals, off-peak calls, and local and short long-distance calls rose 7 percent while rates for peak and standard national long-distance calls dropped 12 percent. This price restructuring, which should have been expected given the initial extent of cross-subsidization, came as an unwelcome surprise to the British public.

British Telecom's increasing profitability after privatization suggests that the company did not find the RPI−3 regulation to be too onerous. The Director General of Oftel, in a December 1985 report on British Telecom's pricing, raised the issue of the company's rate of return: "I shall consider the need to propose a license amendment if British Telecom's rate of return shows a further significant increase or if rebalancing is carried beyond the point justified on economic grounds" (Oftel 1985, 2). He notes that he would prefer not to consider revising the X factor yet because it was "so recently established and approved by Parliament." This early document already hints at the changes to come.

Telecommunications regulation is not bound by any specific rate-of-return considerations. The Director General of Oftel made clear in his

111

1986 report that under the RPI−X mechanism British Telecom may earn more than its cost of capital, a principle that was upheld in the 1988 and 1992 reviews of the price-cap regime. Nevertheless, over time British Telecom's rates of return, both actual and projected, have come to play an increasing role in the determination of X and in the scope of price caps. And the Director General's 1986 report indicated a willingness to change British Telecom's license at any time should its rate of return become excessive (Oftel 1986).

In 1987 British Telecom experienced quality control problems. While these could have been a manifestation of efforts to avoid the stringency of price-cap regulation by cutting corners, it is more likely that the labor disputes and strikes of 1986−7 lay behind at least some of the problems − especially considering that British Telecom never fully exhausted its legal options for seeking price increases. Whatever the cause, the quality control problems gave rise to enough bad publicity that, perhaps as a goodwill gesture, British Telecom agreed to a price moratorium from 1987 to 1989. In negotiations with Oftel, British Telecom agreed to contractual guarantees on response time for fault repairs and to penalty payments to affected customers in case of delays. In addition, the company resumed detailed reporting on its quality of service. Oftel initiated its own quality observation and reporting.

With the RPI−X provision in British Telecom's license set to expire in 1989, Oftel invited comments in January 1988 on all aspects of the regulatory regime. There was overwhelming support for extension of the regime, with some differences in opinion on issues such as the basis for setting X (Oftel 1988b). At the same time the Director General started discussions with British Telecom on rate of return, productivity performance, and investment and employment plans. Oftel used a quantitative model of British Telecom to simulate the effects of different regulatory changes on profits, capital employed, and other variables under various scenarios (Cave 1991) and proposed an X factor of 4.5 for essentially the same basket of prices for the next four years. British Telecom was allowed to carry forward unused price increase potentials within the four-year period, but not beyond. British Telecom agreed to introduce discounts for low-volume users. (See Oftel 1988a for a discussion of agreed changes.)

The tightening of X from 3 to 4.5 came as no surprise, considering British Telecom's substantial improvement in profitability since privatization (see Figure 3.3) and the Director General's decision against a one-time adjustment of prices at the beginning of the new price-cap period. Yet in real terms British Telecom's price moratorium from 1987 to 1989 came close to being just such a one-time adjustment. Without any adjustment in regulated prices the company realized RPI−4.4 in November 1987 and RPI−5.9 in November 1988 (Meek 1988, cited in Johnson

1989). Thus, the first Director General succeeded in establishing himself as an advocate of consumers and of competition, without hurting British Telecom's profitability.

The duopoly policy review, 1990–1.   During the seven-year period of the duopoly policy (1984–91) British Telecom invested heavily in modernizing and expanding its network and restructured its prices, making it a far more formidable competitor than it had been at the beginning of the period. Thanks to its pricing policy and its large share of residential customers (who call primarily during off-peak hours), British Telecom also had much better load characteristics than Mercury. Problems still remained, however. British Telecom had not yet fully rationalized its price structure and was probably still cross-subsidizing switched customer access and analog private circuits.

The duopoly policy had also spurred investment at Mercury and induced Mercury to go after a larger share of the market. By the time of the duopoly policy review, Mercury had made heavy inroads into British Telecom's market share with large business customers, international telecommunications, and digital private circuits and was starting to gain new small-business and residential customers. It was clear for the first time that Mercury was aiming for more than a niche market. British Telecom had been trying to counter Mercury's success with big business customers by offering quantity discounts but had been prevented from doing so by Oftel.

A government green paper review of the duopoly policy, *Competition and Choice: Telecommunications Policy for the 1990s* (November 1990), recommended a policy of open entry for qualified new competitors and restrictions on competitive moves by British Telecom and, to a lesser extent, by Mercury. A white paper followed in March 1991 and reflected extensive comments from British Telecom, Mercury, and others.

The government decided on a policy of further liberalization of the telecommunications market by encouraging new operators for fixed services, but decided to limit competition in the international market. Here, only British Telecom and Mercury could offer facilities-based services, and only international resale and private satellite links were left open to competition. British Telecom and Mercury were also prevented from transmitting television signals for another ten years and from operating radio-based networks of their own. While there was considerable opening up of the market – as of July 1992, thirty-six license applications were received, ten licenses were issued, and twenty-four cable television systems were allowed to offer telephony services (Cave 1992) – there was still little more than token competition, most of it in niche markets.

The original regulatory framework left interconnection issues to be decided through private negotiations between the parties involved, with official intervention only if these negotiations failed. Oftel set interconnection charges in 1985, and they followed the RPI−3 formula until 1990. Interconnection with other operators, particularly Mercury, soon became a large business for British Telecom (£300 million in 1992). Mercury began feeling the squeeze as British Telecom's interconnection rates increased more than Mercury's retail prices. Also, any British Telecom subscriber wishing to switch to Mercury had to change telephone numbers, so Mercury's new subscribers usually stayed with British Telecom for their incoming calls.

As Cave noted, "because new entrants typically rely on interconnection with the dominant firm, at prices usually determined by the regulator, entry changes the nature of regulation rather than eliminating the need for it" (1991, 8). Thus interconnection was an important issue in British Telecom's license change of September 1991. By that time British Telecom's real output prices had, for four years in a row, been falling at a much faster rate than RPI−3, and Mercury's connection rates were being squeezed. A retroactive reduction was enforced for 1990–1 (making 1991 RPI−9), and a new (unpublished) adjustment formula was installed for the future.

Somewhat surprisingly, changes in British Telecom's price-cap regulation also emerged from the duopoly policy review. Only somewhat surprisingly because these changes can be linked to the competition-increasing intent of the duopoly review. Price-cap-related changes included a more generous RPI+5 for most business rentals, for low-volume users rebates, and the possibility of introducing volume discounts for bulk users provided British Telecom adhered to RPI−0 for the median residential bill. Allowing an RPI+5 for multiline business rentals and volume discounts for bulk users would make British Telecom more competitive in the big-business market, in which Mercury was developing a monopoly. Rebates for low-volume users would establish rates for customers that would not benefit from competitive price restructuring.

The most visible pricing change was the inclusion of international services in British Telecom's price-cap basket, with the X increased from 4.5 to 6.25 and an immediate 10 percent reduction in international rates. Bringing international services under regulation can be viewed as the tradeoff for reserving facilities-based international services to British Telecom and Mercury. Though competition was supposed to be keeping the prices of international calls in check, British Telecom's profit contributions from international calls had increased sharply since 1988, and Mercury had established itself as a viable competitor. Making international services part of the main regulatory basket clearly benefited British Telecom by allowing more flexibility in price rebalancing.

Second price-cap review, 1992.   Responses to two consultative documents commissioned by Oftel on price regulation and on British Telecom's cost of capital generally favored the continuation of price caps based on the RPI−X formula, at least for another four to five years. After the round of responses, including its own, British Telecom expected to be consulted on Oftel's proposal for the new price caps.[25] Instead, the Director General informed British Telecom's management of Oftel's price-cap decision the night before the press conference called to announce the decision on 2 June 1992. The Director General made it clear that should British Telecom oppose the proposed amendments, he would make a reference to the Monopoly and Mergers Commission under very wide terms that, according to British Telecom, could include the possibility of breaking up British Telecom.

British Telecom seems to have been taken by surprise by this move, which came less than two weeks before the incumbent Director General was to leave Oftel (to become Director General of Fair Trading). Two factors appear to have influenced the decision to act without consulting British Telecom: the desire to demonstrate the regulator's independence from the regulated firm[26] and the need to get the amendment through before the price-cap provision of British Telecom's license expired. The Director General wanted to leave enough time for the option of a reference to the Monopolies and Mergers Commission, which can take six or more months.

The Director General's proposal retained the RPI−X concept, while making price regulation substantially more stringent and broader in scope. The X was increased to 7.5 for the general basket of prices, which was expanded to include connection charges, and British Telecom was given no credit for additional volume discounts to large users. Rebalancing within the general basket was further restricted by an RPI−0 constraint on all other services in the basket. For the private-circuit basket, X remained at 0, and only very restricted rebalancing was allowed. The proposal also included new accounting rules for British Telecom based on current costs and separation of accounts by business activities.[27] Though chafing at these and other provisions of the proposal, British Telecom decided not to contest the Director General's recommendation for a license amendment.

British Telecom's acquiescence has to be seen in the context of the Director General's threat to use the Monopolies and Mergers Commission. Several factors make such a threat credible. Information about the company is revealed during the proceedings, senior management has to devote time to the case, and license conditions become uncertain, which can hurt the company's share price. Perhaps most persuasively, the outcome could have been catastrophic for British Telecom had the commission called for its breakup.

Two other cases may have influenced British Telecom's decision to avoid a reference to the commission. In one case the commission had approved British Telecom's request to acquire 51 percent of Mitel, a Canadian manufacturer of private exchange equipment, but with harsh conditions. British Telecom was prohibited from purchasing or dealing with Mitel equipment for at least four years (the restriction was later eased). In the other case, involving British Gas, the commission expressed the view that the company's rate of return in 1988 (19.1 percent using historic cost accounting, or 6.1 percent in current cost accounting) was "very substantial for a company in its position" (cited in Cave 1991, 16). The commission also found evidence of refusal to supply, of price discrimination in the company's industrial prices, and of failure to provide adequate information on charges for common carriage. The commission issued a prohibition against any refusals to supply and insisted that price information be published. It also threatened British Gas with the possibility of structural change in the gas industry if the situation failed to improve within the next five years.

A unified view of regulatory changes since privatization

British policy on telecommunications regulation is fluid. Although the price-cap formula calls for moderately long periods of passive price regulation, those periods have been punctuated by interference in pricing formulas and in the composition of regulated baskets of services and by advance preparation of new $RPI-X$ formulas. Issues of quality control and competitive access have also kept the regulatory process in flux. Nevertheless, some analysts view the current arrangements as much more stable than conditions a decade ago. Beesley and Laidlaw (1992, 24) see a fundamental change in the regulatory process since the early 1980s, when only the Department of Trade and Industry and British Telecom were involved and few other commercial interests had to be taken into account. "This very informality allowed ministers to take radical decisions to change the structure of the sector. Now, a complex regulatory framework of rules and institutions is in place, and a multiplicity of interests has to be balanced. As the duopoly review has shown, the regulatory process can best be characterized as successive rounds of negotiation in which the regulatory authorities have sought to accommodate the express demands of incumbents, potential investors, and consumers. This inevitably constrains radicalism."

While Beesley and Laidlaw view the last few years as creeping realism, Veljanovski (1991, 1992) interprets the regulatory record as creeping overregulation. He cites the complaint of British Telecom's chairman, Iain Valance, at the 1992 annual shareholders meeting: "Regrettably, the trend in regulation in the U.K. – and not just telecommunications – appears to be toward greater intervention in management, without a clearly expressed vision or set of long-term objectives" (1992, 20).

Which assessment is supported by the three episodes of regulatory adjustments described above? During the first episode of price-cap renewal in 1988–9, the Director General of Oftel faced and successfully handled many problems for which he needed British Telecom's cooperation to gain information about the issues. To establish a reputation for integrity and toughness, he had to appear confrontational and maintain some distance. Responsibility for the rate restructuring could be shifted to British Telecom since the regulator could be said to have inherited the RPI−3 price cap. Since British Telecom had kept the price moratorium from 1987 on and was making good profits, the move from RPI−3 to RPI−4.5 was fairly easy on the company, and also made the regulator look good.

The increase in the X factor at the time of the duopoly policy review is more problematic. British Telecom was continuing to show high and increasing profits, and there was little real competition since Mercury was concentrating on large-volume users and British Telecom could not. Director General Carsberg could no longer say that he had inherited the RPI minus 4.5 price cap. Yet there was no explicit need to increase the X factor at the mid-point between formal price-cap reviews. A plausible explanation, though, is that moving the X to 6.25 was not really a tightening of regulation since British Telecom now benefited from a new, larger basket that included more competitive services and from the ability to grant volume discounts. The company's share price rose after the announcement of the results of the duopoly policy review, further suggesting that it remained unharmed by the new regulations. At the same time, the Director General managed to look tough in taking a firm stand on British Telecom's rising profits.

At the time of the second price-cap review in 1992, there was still no real regulatory problem, except for British Telecom's high profitability. The elections were over. Director General Carsberg had secured a promotion as Director General of Fair Trading and made his decisive proposals for the next four years just before leaving Oftel. Interviews with his immediate successor, William Wigglesworth, elicited not a hint of disagreement with the opinions of his predecessor.

Overall, then, the three episodes show a steady tightening of British Telecom's price regulation. The process has become more public; there are no more negotiations behind closed doors. Regulation coverage has expanded from about 55 percent of British Telecom's revenues in 1985 to about 64 percent in 1991.[28] Regulation has become more stringent and has moved closer to a rate-of-return approach. In fact, the move from RPI−3 to RPI−7.5 in several steps is quite remarkable. Viewing the change optimistically, it could be said to have helped British Telecom improve its productivity while maintaining a consistently high rate of return, even in the midst of a recession. British Telecom reduced its work force by 30,000 from 1990 to 1992 and by another 38,000 in fiscal 1993. That clearly leaves some room for regulatory stringency.

Viewing the change from a more pessimistic perspective, however, exposes the possibility of overshooting and the specter of declining profitability, as occurred in the mid-1970s. The three-step rise in the X factor definitely looks like the ratchet effect in action. The X factor became a focal point in the regulatory process. Perhaps the Director General intentionally held back in earlier rounds, to gain more leeway for later rounds. Or perhaps, from a public relations perspective, the regulator had to increase the X factor in each successive round unless British Telecom's profitability started to fall. Success in one round becomes the yardstick for the next round. And since British Telecom had overcome its quality problems and Mercury got its interconnection agreement, there was little for the regulator to do other than to focus on the X factor.

Director General Carsberg had declared at least from 1988 on that he was against a one-time adjustment of prices in the regulated basket to bring British Telecom's rate of return in line with its cost of capital, favoring adjustment of the X factor instead. The move from RPI−3 to RPI−4.5 was clearly motivated by the desire to reduce British Telecom's rate of return. But the rate of return stayed high even after X was increased to 6.25. Thus by 1992 Carsberg seems to have been determined to get British Telecom's rate of return down to its cost of capital by increasing the X factor to 7.5. At the same time, however, British Telecom's ability to serve and invest must not be compromised. It seems likely, then, that even without major political changes, a new price-cap round could develop before the current cap expires in 1997. If British Telecom's profitability fails to fall, the Director General will move to amend the license, once again using the threat of a reference to the Monopolies and Mergers Commission as leverage. If British Telecom's profitability falls below its cost of capital, all parties would support a change in the X factor to bring profitability up.

It is also possible that the 7.5 X factor may turn out to be too high only after a change in government. If a new government comes in that opposes private ownership of utilities and wants to extend the 7.5 factor, it may face the opposition of the Monopolies and Mergers Commission and the Director General, if they have not been replaced. And unless a new pricing provision is agreed on by 1997, British Telecom will be free to set its own prices. So if 7.5 turns out to be too high, the new government may have to agree with British Telecom on a new X factor that the Monopolies and Mergers Commission will support. Thus unless the new government wants to take the radical step of changing the license amendment process itself, the licensing arrangement that British Telecom will face at least for the next few years seems likely to assure its profitability.

LESSONS

Telecommunications regulation in the United Kingdom shows the importance of a country's institutions as guarantors of commitment to a regulatory policy that offers adequate safeguards for investment and incentives for efficiency. The existence of an independent judiciary with a strong tradition of upholding contracts and property rights allows regulatory bargains to be enforced through licensing arrangements. Using a license to specify the price-setting mechanism and the means of amending it brings to the regulatory governance process a clear threat of judicial action should the regulator deviate from the license provisions. Also, informal but clearly understood and broadly accepted limits on ministerial discretion help make the delegation of regulatory authority another source of commitment. Similarly, bringing the Monopolies and Mergers Commission, an established institution, into the process provides yet another check on regulatory discretion. The diffused ownership structure of British Telecom also helped to develop broad-based support for retaining private ownership. The regulatory incentives system (price-cap) provided for gradual price reductions while avoiding too much regulatory interference in price setting. And finally, the promotion of limited competition also supported gradual price reduction while creating further support for private ownership.

The regulatory system has several weaknesses, however, in both regulatory governance and regulatory incentives. A major weakness of regulatory governance is that the government can unilaterally change the license amendment process by passing new legislation. However, because licenses stipulate precisely the legislation on which they are based, a license amendment might be required to bring the license under the new procedural requirements. This eventuality is not an entirely remote possibility. A conflict between the government and the Monopolies and Mergers Commission could trigger an act of Parliament giving responsibility for license amendments to a more tractable agency. Instituting such legislative changes against the company's will would not be costless, however, because they would clearly be seen as attempts to change the rules of the game in an opportunistic way.

To a large extent, then, the answer to the puzzle presented at the beginning of this chapter may reside in the nature of the institutional environment in which regulation takes place in the United Kingdom. Several features of that environment reduce regulatory discretion by creating a division of powers in a political system with strong political cohesiveness. Other elements of the institutional environment may have reassured private investors that they could trust the stability of the rules of the regulatory game, notwithstanding the Labour Party's opposition to the privatization of British Telecom. Two of the most important were having the regulatory system in place before the utilities were privatized and building in limits on unilateral actions by the regulators. British Telecom's broad-based ownership structure and the extent of competition in the sector provided additional safeguards. Furthermore, differences in preference among the Department of Trade and Industry, the Monopolies and Mergers Commission, and Oftel make regulatory policy more stable. Thus, as in the United States, though in a very different manner, process fortifies commitment.

Admittedly, the regulatory structure rests on several weak pillars of commitment and has not yet weathered a change in the ruling party. How the system will respond to major disturbances is uncertain. Nonetheless, history suggests that response will be well balanced. British Telecom is not likely either to reap exorbitant returns or to be strangled by regulation. The success of the combined policy of privatization, competition, and regulation has already dimmed the specter of renationalization after a Labour Party victory. While a Labour government might tilt the regulatory process in another direction, the boundaries stipulated by the licenses and the Telecommunications Act of 1984 would certainly remain for the near future. Given the rapid rate of technological obsolescence, perhaps that is all that is needed to provide commitment in this sector.

These results have important implications for regulatory innovation in many countries undertaking utility privatization. In particular, countries without a strong tradition of judicial restraint of administrative decisions may find that attempts to design a U.S.-style regulatory system will fail because of the time needed to develop the relevant jurisprudence. For some countries the British system could provide an alternative, as long as their courts have a tradition of upholding contracts. Licensing arrangements that require companies to agree to major regulatory changes or that stipulate complex procedures for unilateral changes may restrain regulatory discretion and provide private investors with adequate assurances against opportunistic behavior by the regulator.

4

Chile: Regulatory specificity, credibility of commitment, and distributional demands

AHMED GALAL

Chile's experiments with regulatory regimes and ownership patterns in telecommunications have produced radically different results. Between 1930 and 1970 firms were privately owned and regulated but the sector grew only modestly after the agreed investment obligations were fulfilled. In the 1970s the government took over ownership of the two firms providing local and long-distance services and ran them as regulated monopolies. The sector grew even slower than before. Beginning in 1982 Chile deregulated some segments of the sector, improved regulation of others, and returned the firms to private ownership. The gains have been substantial: The number of new lines doubled in four years, unmet demand has declined, new services are being introduced, and modern technology is replacing old. Why has this latest episode been so much more successful than the others?

Chile's experience shows how the proper match of regulatory regime and political institutions can foster efficient development of the telecommunications sector. Though regulatory incentive structures have been important (pricing, entry), more important have been the distributional demands of various interest groups and the effect of institutional factors on the credibility of government commitment not to behave opportunistically.

Three questions guide the analysis:

- How clearly did the different regulatory regimes spell out pricing rules, entry policy, and conflict-resolution mechanisms?
- Did these different regulatory regimes equally persuade firms to invest in the sector and operate efficiently?
- If not, why? Can the failures of certain regulatory regimes to encourage investment and improve performance be explained, at least in part, by changes in Chile's political institutions and pressures by interest groups?

121

The paper argues that Chile, with its stable political institutions and independent judiciary, has always had the capacity to write credible regulatory contracts and enforce them. The poor record of regulation between 1930 and 1970 is attributed to deficiencies in contracts, particularly with respect to the rate of return on investment (until 1958) and the conditions under which the government could intervene in firm operation.[1] These incomplete contracts were the product of populist policies and a widespread lack of concern for telecommunications. The publicly owned telecommunications companies in the 1970s had no greater success, in part because they were caught in an ideology shift toward greater reliance on markets forces and private ownership, which curbed public investment. The success of the regulatory reforms of the 1980s is attributed to the emergence of an influential entrepreneurial class and the spread of technological changes that made telecommunication services indispensable for private sector development.

Two policy implications emerge from this analysis. First, regulatory reforms cannot succeed if they lack a strong constituency. This point is illustrated by the absence of regulatory reforms in telecommunications until 1958 and the ineffectiveness of the early reforms. Second, the ability to write and enforce credible contracts does not mean that regulatory incentives (pricing formulas, entry rules, and the like) are not also critical. This point is illustrated by the limited development of telecommunications between 1982 and 1987, when no price-setting procedures were specified.

REGULATORY EPISODES

Before the Great Depression the government had little involvement in telecommunications except to grant concessions. The Chilean Telephone Company was the main provider of telecommunications services, with 26,205 telephone lines in 1927. Except between Santiago and Valparaiso, Chile lacked communication links between cities and an integrated network. (For a detailed history of the sector see Melo 1992.)

To integrate telecommunications across the country and expand coverage, Chile negotiated a contract with the Chilean Telephone Company in 1930 that created Compañía de Teléfonos de Chile (CTC); International Telephone and Telegraph (ITT) owned an 80 percent share. In 1964 the government created the Empresa Nacional de Telecomunicaciones (ENTeL-Chile) to provide national and international long-distance services.

Telecommunications regulation since 1930 has gone through three phases. Between 1930 and 1970 the government relied on private ownership and regulation by specific contract for CTC and on public ownership and an implicit contract for ENTeL. Between 1971 and 1981 both companies were publicly owned. In 1982 there was a shift to deregulate some segments of the market, better regulate others, and reintroduce private ownership. During all three episodes the key elements of regulatory concern have been prices, entry rules, concession rights, and conflict resolution.

Early regulation of the sector, 1930–70

Though other utilities in Chile operated under a general utilities law issued in 1925, CTC operated under a specific law (4791/1930) that remained in effect until the government intervened in the company's operations in 1971. This law detailed the terms of CTC's concession prices and conflict-resolution mechanisms. Under a fifty-year concession the company could provide local and long-distance telephone services and supplementary services. At the end of the concession period the government could acquire the company, but it had to purchase the entire company and pay the owners the value of net fixed assets. Otherwise, the concession would automatically be extended for thirty years and, following the same procedure, for similar periods thereafter.

As part of the concession, CTC was to modernize the network, interconnect certain regions according to an established schedule, and invest in specified infrastructure plants and equipment. To help it meet these obligations, CTC was given the right to buy other regional companies at a mutually agreed price or a price estimated by a three-member committee (one member appointed by the government and one by each of the disputing parties). CTC was allowed a rate of return on net fixed assets of up to 10 percent. The company and the national treasury shared any profits above 10 percent. In addition, the company was allowed to establish a reserve fund equal to 2 percent of net fixed assets provided the accumulated value of the reserve did not exceed 20 percent of net fixed assets. Prices were indexed to the value of the peso in gold at the time the concession was granted. The company's board of directors decided on price revisions, subject to government objection within thirty days.

The company was managed by up to fifteen directors, three of them government appointees. The general director of electric services was an ex officio member and the other two were appointed and removed by the president. Disputes between the government and the company over the terms of the concession were to be resolved by the Supreme Court.

The law had a few other stipulations. For example, Chilean nationals were to constitute at least 80 percent of the company's staff. The central government and municipalities were to receive a 50 percent discount. And the law gave the government the right to intervene in the company's operations in cases of war or internal disturbance, though the government was obliged to compensate the company for any damages incurred. In short, the law limited government discretion in terms of outright expropriation of assets and relied on the Supreme Court for resolving conflicts. However, it did give the government the right to intervene in the company's operations under vaguely defined circumstances, and it did not guarantee a specific rate of return.

CTC met its initial investment commitment. But, as time passed, expansion slowed, and ITT was accused of inflating costs. These factors prompted the government to enter into subagreements with CTC in 1958 and 1967. The 1958 agreement ensured CTC a 10 percent return (instead of *up* to 10 percent) on fixed assets. In return, CTC agreed to an eight-year investment program. Under the 1967 agreement, CTC pledged to expand the network by 144,000 lines between 1967 and 1971, and thereafter to increase the number of lines by 6 to 7 percent a year. Costs were redefined,[2] and enforcement was strengthened by requiring the approval of the board of directors, including at least two of the government's representatives, for decisions on such matters as additions to fixed assets and fees for financial and technical assistance provided by ITT.

The government also used the occasion of the 1967 agreement to announce a new national telecommunications policy. The government would assume control of the basic network to develop underdeveloped regions, to guarantee national and international telecommunication service, and to meet the ordinary and extraordinary needs of government. The state holding company, CORFO, would purchase up to 49 percent of CTC's shares. A long-distance market would be carved out for the newly created state company, ENTeL, excluding CTC's microwave segment between Santiago and Valparaiso (Agurto 1991).

The government created ENTeL in December 1964. Just why it did so remains unclear but whatever the reason, the company was established to offer only long-distance services, even though CTC's concession was not exclusive and the government had been intensively involved in economic activity since 1930. ENTeL operated under the general utilities law of 1959 which governed all utilities except CTC. The terms of the law were similar to those under which CTC operated. Prices were to be set to allow a 10 percent return on the sunk cost of useful capital, defined as intangible assets, working capital and the replacement cost on construction, plant, and other fixed assets. Intangibles were defined as expenditure on studies at up to 5 percent of the value of fixed assets. Regulatory authority was assigned to the Superintendency of Electricity, Gas, and Telecommunications, and a Tariff Commission was established to revalue net fixed assets. The commission was composed of the Superintendent of

Electric and Gas Services and representatives of the president, the Ministry of Economy, CORFO, and the National Planning Office.

The law stipulated that tariffs would be revised every five years, with interim adjustments for inflation. If ENTeL's rate of return exceeded 12 percent, the superintendency could set provisional prices that would reduce excess profit by 50 percent. Excess profits were to be deposited in a special account, to be amortized in case of profit shortfalls. If the rate of return fell below 10 percent, the firm could request a change in prices.

Regulation under public ownership, 1971–81

Under authority of a clause of the 1930 law, the Allende administration intervened in CTC's operations in 1971. That law was revoked in early 1973, and CTC operated under the general law of 1959. In 1974, despite the laissez-faire policy of the new military regime on most other economic matters, CORFO acquired CTC from ITT. The Chilean telecommunications sector was now dominated by three public enterprises. CTC provided local services throughout most of the country. ENTeL provided national and international long-distance services. And Correos and Telegrafos provided domestic telex and telegram services, sharing the market for international services with ITT and Transradio.

Though CTC and ENTeL were supposed to operate according to the regulatory rules of the 1959 utilities law, public ownership made a big difference. For example, under the system of concessions laid out in the 1959 law there were no restrictions on the services that could be provided by utilities, public or private, except for domestic telegraph and telex services. But the government assigned local telephony to CTC and long-distance services to ENTeL. Conflicts between the two companies were for the most part resolved by CORFO, their joint owner. Whenever disputes between the two companies escalated, management of the two companies was shuffled around.

The 1959 regulation also guaranteed firms a 10 percent rate of return on net fixed assets. Yet during the 1970s prices were often adjusted by less than the rate of inflation, especially in the early years of the decade. As a result CTC and ENTeL lacked the resources to expand the network, develop new products, or adopt new technologies. In addition, cross-subsidization between local and long-distance services intensified the vertical and horizontal integration of the two government-owned firms.

Finally, the 1959 regulation vested regulatory authority in the Superintendency of Electricity, Gas, and Telecommunications and the Tariff Commission. But CORFO, as the owner of the two companies, played a more active role. Further, the management of both companies was ap-

125

pointed by the president, largely from the military. In 1977 the Tariff Commission and the Superintendency of Electricity, Gas, and Telecommunications were replaced by a new regulatory agency, Subtel. The regulator was outranked by the heads of the two companies, and the companies were essentially left alone.

A new telecommunications policy was announced the next year that was more consistent with the government laissez-faire approach in economic matters. The policy emphasized the importance of the private sector and telecommunications to economic development and the need to eliminate preferential treatment of state enterprises. Among the new principles announced: public services such as telecommunications, radio, and television were to be provided by the private sector; concessions would be granted on the basis of objective criteria; and prices would be freely negotiated between suppliers and clients except where markets were not competitive. Until 1982, however, this new policy remained merely a statement of intentions.

Deregulation and evolving regulation, 1982–present

In 1982 Chile introduced a new legal framework for telecommunications based on market principles. The General Law of Telecommunications places no limits on the number of concessions that can be granted to provide any service, except for technical reasons. Concessions are required to provide local and long-distance public services, cellular telephony, point-to-point private transmission, and private data transmission. Concessions are not required to provide telephone directories, facsimile services, private exchanges, and supplementary services or to sell or lease telephone and facsimile equipment.

Concession holders of public services are required to connect their networks in compliance with the technical norms established by Subtel. The parties are free to negotiate the terms of the interconnections. Product and service prices were to be unregulated, except in monopoly markets where rates were to be set by the Ministries of Economy and Telecommunications on the basis of the direct and necessary cost of service provision.

These changes lacked adequate specificity in several important areas. The law was ambiguous about the right to refuse to grant concessions, so there was a proliferation of requests in the more profitable segments of the market. The law did not address pricing, which continued to be established through informal negotiations between the companies and Subtel and the Ministry of Economy. Cross-subsidies also persisted, so prices remained divorced from costs. Finally, Subtel's role was not well defined, and it lacked the resources to perform the tasks assigned to it.

The new law did not ensure producers a fair rate of return on investment or consumers the right to a phone within a specified period.

Not surprisingly, the regulatory history since 1982 has been largely a series of attempts to remedy these deficiencies. In 1985, Subtel's right to reject concession applications was clarified, and an arbitration process was introduced for interconnections between existing companies and newcomers. Subtel was authorized to supervise the resolution of legal, procedural, and technical disputes between service providers and users.

The issues of universal service and price setting were not addressed until 1987, when the 1982 law was modified to prepare for the privatization of CTC and ENTeL. The new law stipulated that requests for service be met within two years, though a ten-year grace period was allowed to deal with the backlog. To ease the financial burden of this new requirement, companies were allowed to request reimbursable deposits from customers applying for phones. The deposit could be reimbursed in bonds, shares of the company, or any other mutually agreed form.

The law also introduced an arbitration process to settle disagreements between firms and regulators and a new pricing scheme for local and long-distance fixed telephony (Box 4.1). The law identified the agencies responsible for setting prices and defined the criteria, procedures, and timing to be followed. Prices of other services were left to the determination of market forces.

In 1988 CTC and ENTeL submitted their price proposals to the Ministries of Telecommunications and Economy through Subtel. CTC was allowed a 12 percent rate of return, and ENTeL a 14 percent rate of return because of the greater volatility of revenue from long-distance service. The new rates phase out cross-subsidizes between local and long-distance services over five years.

Two problems remain. First, Subtel is still relatively weak. Unlike other Chilean regulatory agencies, Subtel is neither financially nor administratively independent. It falls under the Ministry of Transportation and Telecommunications. The agency also lacks the resources to undertake necessary studies. These circumstances have made it difficult for Subtel to attract or retain the right mix of skilled staff to handle its regulatory functions.

The second problem concerns market segmentation. CTC and ENTeL were able to coexist peacefully for a long time largely because both firms were owned by the government. Competition intensified following their privatization in 1988–9. Both firms are trying to maximize profit, but the long-distance market is more lucrative than the local market. This rivalry is causing costly disputes. Efforts are being made to address these problems by strengthening Subtel and by introducing a multicarrier system in the long-distance market.

Box 4.1 *Price setting procedures for fixed telephony*

- Demand is estimated for each service, zone, and firm.
- The incremental cost of development for each service, is then calculated based on the concept of "efficient firm." The incremental cost of development is nothing but the long-run marginal cost (LRMC). The law defines the efficient firm as one that starts from scratch and uses only the assets necessary to provide that service. It further stipulates that regulated companies have to have a minimum of a five-year investment program, prepared by the company and presented to Subtel following the detailed outline specified in Law 18, 168 (article 301).
- Revenue is then estimated for each service, such that the net present value of providing the service is equal to zero. This revenue is the incremental cost of development.
- To move from the incremental cost of development to the long-run average cost (LRAC), efficient tariffs are increased in a least distorting fashion so that firms make a fair rate of return.
- The fair rate of return is defined as the sum of the rates of return on the risk-free assets and the risk premium of the activity, weighted by the systematic risk of the industry. That is
$$R_i = R_{rf} + \beta_i (R_p - R_{rf}),$$
where R_i is the rate of return on revalued capital of firm i, R_{rf} is the rate of return on risk-free assets, β_i is firm i's systematic risk, and R_p is the rate of return on a diversified investment portfolio.
- Prices are recalculated only every five years, but the law allows firms to adjust prices every two months, using the inflation index of each service and the Divisia index.

REGULATORY STRUCTURES AND SECTORAL PERFORMANCE

How did these regulatory episodes affect the development of the telecommunications sector in Chile? Until 1970 government regulators and regulated companies remained skeptical about each other's intentions. After an initial boost in the 1930s, network growth was sluggish, prompting the government to create ENTeL and to enter into subagreements with CTC in 1958 and 1967 ensuring a 10 percent rate of return and imposing new investment obligations. When the government assumed ownership of the two companies in the early 1970s growth was even more modest than before. The government's fiscal circumstances constrained investment. The regulatory structure was clear, but regulations were rarely applied. Pricing was politicized, and conflicts between the two companies were

Table 4.1. *Telephone expansion in Chile, 1934–91 (average annual growth rates)*

	1934–60	1961–70	1971–81	1982–91
Telephones in service	5.6	6.7	4.2	8.9
Lines in service		7.5	3.9	9.9
	1960	1970	1981	1991
Telephone density	2.7	4.1	5.4	10.8
Pending telephone applications (as percentage of lines in service)	54	25	42	24

Source: CTC.

resolved by the government. The regulatory structure changed again in the 1980s. Private ownership, deregulation, and regulatory reform produced significant benefits for the economy as the network expanded and new services were introduced. Numerous disputes erupted, however, increasing the costs of doing business. These disputes could have been avoided if the government had more clearly specified the boundaries between competitive (nonregulated) services and noncompetitive (regulated) services.

Sectoral performance

Whatever measure of telephone expansion is used – investment, number of telephones, lines in service, density, or automatization and digitalization – the rate of expansion was highest in the 1980s and lowest in the 1970s (Table 4.1 and Figures 4.1–4.3). The number of telephones in service grew at nearly 9 percent a year during 1981–91, but at only 4 percent a year during 1971–81. Network expansion before 1970 was uneven, proceeding at 7.3 percent a year in 1934–48, slowing to 2.6 percent in 1948–57, and picking up again to 6.8 percent in 1957–70, when subagreements between the government and the telecommunications companies ensured the companies a set rate of return. Pending applications for telephone installations (as a percentage of lines in service) were highest in the periods preceding expansion. Pending applications have increased in recent years, even as the network was being doubled, reflecting a surge in demand and higher consumer expectations about telephone services.

The regulatory reforms of the 1980s coincided with the fastest expansion of the network. Public ownership and tight fiscal policies inhibited expansion in the 1970s. In the preceding period CTC's service was slack until its contract was modified in 1958 and 1967 to improve the specificity of regulatory incentives and reduce regulatory discretion.

129

Thousands of lines, telephones

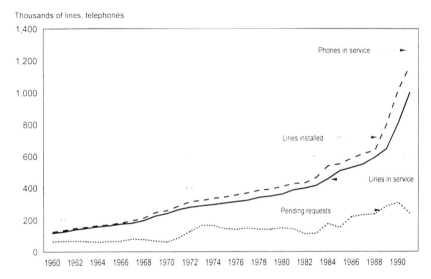

Figure 4.1. Telecommunications expansion (CTC), 1960–91. *Source:* CTC annual reports, 1982–91; Statistical Yearbook of Development in Telecommunications 1960–89, Santiago, Chile; J. R. Melo.

Millions of US dollars

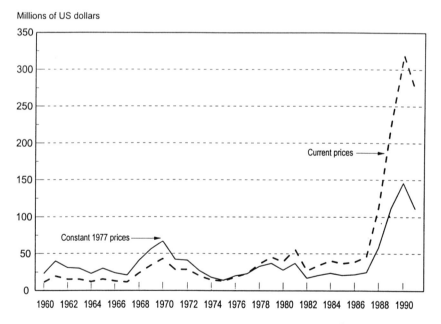

Figure 4.2. Fixed capital formation (CTC), 1960–91. *Source:* CTC annual reports, 1982–91; Statistical Yearbook of Development in Telecommunications, 1960–90, Santiago, Chile.

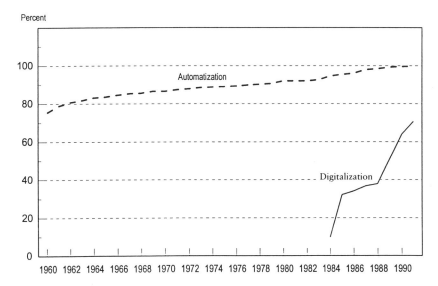

Figure 4.3. Automatization and digitalization of lines (CTC), 1960–91. *Source:* Statistical Yearbook of Development in Telecommunications 1960–89, Santiago, Chile; CTC, various documents.

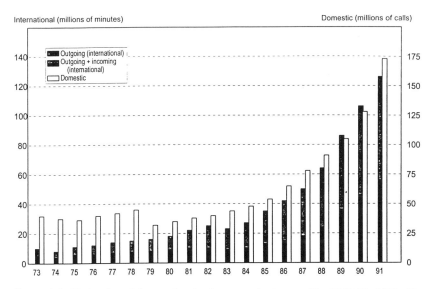

Figure 4.4. National and international telecommunications traffic (ENTeL), 1973–91. *Source:* ENTeL annual reports, various years; J. R. Melo.

131

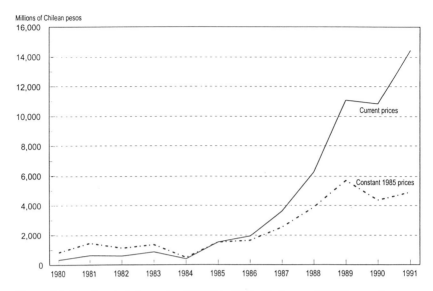

Millions of Chilean pesos

Figure 4.5. Fixed capital formation (ENTeL), 1980–91. *Source:* ENTeL annual reports, various years.

The same pattern emerges for national and international long-distance services (Figures 4.4 and 4.5). Services increased dramatically following ENTeL's privatization and CTC's expansion. ENTeL's privatization eased the resource constraint experienced under public ownership, and CTC's network and service expansion made it possible for more consumers to make long-distance calls.

There was also an explosion of value-added services in the 1980s. Consumers now have access to such services as paging, mobile telephony, and data transmission. CTC-Cellular and CIDCOM provide mobile phone services in the Santiago metropolitan region and Region V, and VTR-Cellular and Telecom-Cellular serve the rest of the country. International communications are provided by Telex-Chile, TEXCOM, VTR, and ITT World Communications. VTR, Chile-Pac, and ECOM provide data transmission. Finally, there has been a huge expansion in the market for equipment, including telephone sets, modems, and private exchanges.

Prices and profitability

Identifying long-term price trends for telecommunications is difficult because of the difficulty in compiling consistent price data. The composition of prices differs between fixed and variable charges, peak and off-peak

1985 Chilean pesos per line

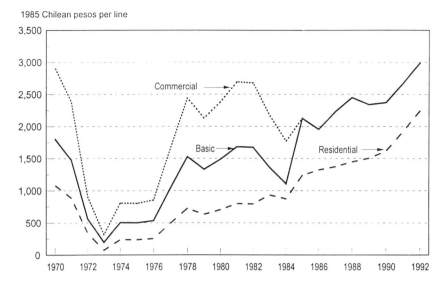

Figure 4.6. Monthly charges for local services, flat rate system, 1970–92. *Note:* December rates for each year, except for August 1992. *Source:* CTC, various documents.

1988 Chilean pesos, net of taxes
Per 3 minute call   Per minute

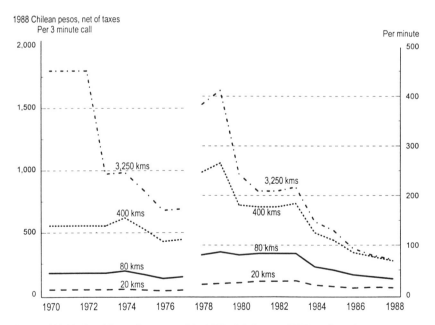

Figure 4.7. National long-distance tariffs, 1970–88. *Source:* CTC, various documents.

133

Ahmed Galal

Table 4.2. *Index of telephone prices 1990–3*
(1989=100)

	1990	1991	1992	1993
Local metered service				
Monthly charge	123	138	154	171
Variable charge	100	100	100	100
Local flat-rate service	114	125	136	147
National long-distance	80	74	65	65
International long-distance	100	100	100	100
Allocation fee	82	25	12	0

Source: CTC.

periods, and flat and metered systems. Nevertheless, certain observations can be made about price trends (Figures 4.6 and 4.7).

The real prices of local services declined in the early 1970s, following Salvador Allende's election. Prices picked up again in 1974 and have been rising ever since with the exception of 1984. Long-distance prices also declined in the early 1970s; this trend has persisted. Both trends reflect continuing efforts to reduce cross-subsidization from national and international long-distance services to local services and from commercial to residential subscribers. In 1981 the flat-rate system was replaced by the metered system, but not until 1989 did the price schedule formally incorporate the complete phasing out of cross-subsidization (Table 4.2).

Except in the early 1970s, prices for local services have kept up with and even exceeded inflation. Prices for long-distance services have declined consistently in real terms, largely to eliminate the cross-subsidy. The question is whether the charges have provided firms with adequate returns on their investment.

Since 1958 firms have been assured a rate of return of 10 percent – increased to 12 percent for CTC and 14 percent for ENTeL in 1989 – on the sunk cost of useful capital. However, trends in profitability on revalued assets reveal significant differences between CTC and ENTeL (Figure 4.8).[3] CTC's reported rates of return exceeded 10 percent only after privatization in 1988. ENTeL, by contrast, consistently had rates of return of more than 10 percent in the 1980s. In recent years the company's rate of return has exceeded 40 percent on revalued assets despite falling prices.

The rate of return on revalued assets should be interpreted carefully, however. These figures underestimate the rate of return actually received by the companies because (the numerator) profits after tax are unduly reduced by deductions for interest payments and because companies may be inflating net fixed assets (the denominator). Nor can these rates be

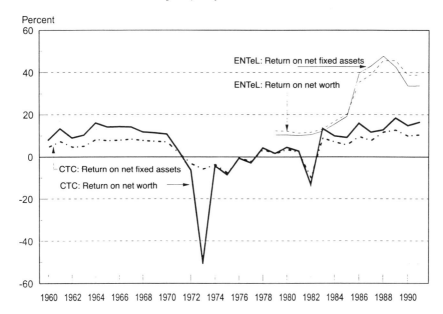

Figure 4.8. Return on net fixed assets and net worth, 1960–91. *Source:* CTC and ENTeL, various documents, author's own calculations.

used to determine whether CTC and ENTeL received the 12 and 14 percent rates of return to which they have been entitled since 1989, because rates are based on revenue from regulated and unregulated services. (It was not possible to correct for these factors.)

CTC's rate of return on net worth was 10 percent or more during the 1960s and 1980s, except in 1982 (Figure 4.8). Under public ownership in the first half of the 1970s, rates of return were negative. Data for the 1980s for ENTeL indicate that the company had rates of return far exceeding reasonable returns on investment in telecommunications. This windfall profit is largely due to revenue from incoming international calls.

Effects on welfare

Several considerations affect any assessment of the welfare impact of regulatory reforms. Consumers are better off the larger is the network, the better is the quality of service, and the lower are prices; producers are better off the higher are prices and the greater are the returns on investment. Competition would be expected to reduce the returns for competitors, and network expansion would be expected to benefit providers of complementary services.

Galal and others (1994) performed this kind of welfare analysis for

Table 4.3. *Welfare effects of privatizing CTC*
(1988 net present value; billions of pesos)

	CTC under private operation	CTC under public operation	Net gains from privatization
Government	97	64	33
Domestic shareholders	19	11	8
Consumers	1104	588	516
Competitors	43	27	16
Domestic welfare	1263	690	574
Foreign shareholders	39	0	39
World welfare	1301	689	612

Source: Galal et al. (1994).

CTC, comparing the social net present value of CTC under private operation with its estimated value had it continued under public ownership.
Their main conclusion is that privatization and regulation in the 1980s
improved the welfare of Chileans and foreigners (Table 4.3). Consumers
were the biggest winners, but shareholders, government, and, interestingly, ENTeL (which benefited from CTC's expansion) also gained.

Although no similar analysis has been conducted for ENTeL, a broad
conclusion based on the indicators noted earlier is that ENTeL's expansion and lower tariffs must have benefited consumers. Yet ENTeL's excessive rate of return indicates that consumers could have done much better.

Anticompetitive behavior and transaction costs

Notwithstanding these positive effects, recent regulatory reform and
privatization have also resulted in a number of costly lawsuits alleging
anticompetitive behavior.[4] Several factors lie behind these claims, including a failure to define the boundaries between competitive and noncompetitive activities, the drive for profit maximization following privatization, the industry's large sunk costs, and the strong incentives for
vertical integration, cross-subsidization, and the skimming off of the
most lucrative market segments. But the issues are not entirely clear-cut,
and there are trade-offs involved: the cost of lawsuits should be weighed
against the benefits of having the flexibility to cope with rapidly changing technology. Whatever the merits, the lawsuits have increased the
costs of conducting business and burdened the judicial system. A few of
the cases are reviewed here to illustrate the nature of these disputes and
their resolution.

Local fixed telephony.   To promote competition and private sector participation, Subtel granted concessions to several small companies in 1981 to provide local fixed telephony services in certain regions of the country, some of them overlapping CTC's concession area. These firms accused CTC of infringing on fair competition.[5] CTC was found guilty of anticompetitive behavior in all instances.[6]

Most of the complaints concerned interconnection. A new firm is generally required to provide transmission and switching equipment to interconnect its customers and to connect its network with that of other companies. Interconnection costs are shared by agreement between the parties involved, subject to rules set by Subtel. The problem, of course, is that the incumbent is not likely to negotiate in good faith because of an inherent conflict of interest. So even after agreement is reached on cost sharing, CTC can find plausible reasons to delay installation.

Long-distance markets.   The same weaknesses affect the market for long-distance services. The government could have anticipated in the early 1980s the lack of compatibility between unfettered competition (multiple concessions) and the absence of a multicarrier system in the long-distance market. Failure to recognize this problem led, following the privatization of CTC and ENTeL, to a costly lawsuit that is still working its way through the judicial system.

The conflict began in June 1989 when CTC applied through its subsidiary CTC-Transmisiones Regionales S.A. for a concession to provide domestic long-distance services through satellite links. In September 1989 CTC applied for a concession to provide domestic long-distance services in the Santiago-Valparaiso and Santiago-Temuco markets through a fiber-optic cable system. ENTeL objected to CTC's applications, arguing that the concessions would constitute a monopoly for CTC.[7] CTC maintained that its participation would enhance competition and introduce advanced technology in the sector.

Subtel referred the matter to the Fair Trade Enforcement Office, requesting a ruling on the following questions: How would competition be affected by vertical integration? Can local and long-distance services be considered different markets? And should local companies be barred from participating in the long-distance market?

In October 1989 the Regional Preventive Commission, the first tier in the dispute resolution process, ruled against CTC, declaring that local service companies could not participate in the long-distance market (and that long-distance companies could not enter the local market). CTC's preexisting long-distance concessions (including the Santiago-Valparaiso and the Santiago-Buin radio links) were exempted from this decision. In November 1989 the Resolutive Commission, the second tier in the dispute-resolution process, ruled in favor of CTC. The ruling stipulated that local companies could enter the long-distance market and long-distance companies the local market on two conditions: if the company entering the new market created a subsidiary for that purpose (to identify transfer costs) and if the local company modified its system (at its expense) to provide interconnection with all long-distance carriers through a multicarrier system.

ENTeL appealed the ruling to the Supreme Court in December 1989. In May 1990 the Supreme Court returned the case to the Resolutive Commission without reviewing ENTeL's appeal, on the grounds that the commission had not adequately investigated the feasibility of implementing a multicarrier system or the effect on competition. The court ordered the commission to conduct an in-depth study. In the meantime the government developed a draft law for a multicarrier system.

REGULATORY CREDIBILITY AND DISTRIBUTIONAL DEMANDS

So far, the discussion has skirted the puzzle of why Chile did not introduce a more efficient regulatory system until recently and of why the private sector found this regulatory system to be credible, unlike previous schemes. Chile's regulatory incentives structure has ensured a 10 percent rate of return on net fixed assets for CTC – since 1958 – and even higher since 1989. On that basis alone performance and growth in the telecommunications sector since 1958 would be expected to have been strong. They were not. Something else is clearly at play. The credibility of a regulatory incentives structure depends not only on the nature of its pricing formulas and entry rules, but also on the stability of a country's political institutions, the independence of its judiciary, and interest-group demands.

Political institutions

The momentous political changes in Chile over the past two decades – from the election of Salvador Allende in 1970, the first freely elected socialist-Marxist leader, to the military overthrow of the government by General Augusto Pinochet three years later, to the election of Patricio Aylwin, a Christian Democrat, in 1989 – give the impression of dizzying political instability. Unstable political institutions undermine confidence in the ability of regulatory structures to protect against government expropriation of asset-specific utilities such as telecommunications. But the political turmoil of the 1970s and 1980s in Chile was an aberration in a more than 100-year history of orderly transfer of civilian rule. That

Table 4.4. *Popular votes in Chilean presidential elections, 1952–89*

Year	Candidate (party or coalition)	Percentage of vote
1952	Carlos Ibanez (Independent)	46.8
	Arture Matte (Right: Conservative, Liberal)	27.8
	Pedro E. Alfonso (Center: Radical)	19.9
	Salvador Allende (Left: Socialist)	5.5
1958	Jorge Alessandri (Right: Conservative, Liberal)	31.6
	Salvador Allende (Left: Socialist, Communist)	28.9
	Eduardo Frie (Center: Christian Democrat)	20.7
	Luis Bossay (Center: Radical)	15.6
	Antonio Zamorano (Independent)	3.3
1964	Eduardo Frei (Center-Right: Christian Democrat, Conservative, Liberal)	56.1
	Salvador Allende (Left: Socialist, Communist)	38.9
	Julio Duran (Center-Right, Radical)	5.0
1970	Salvador Allende (Left: Socialist, Communist, MAPU, Radical Left)	36.6
	Jorge Alessandri (Right: Independent, National)	35.2
	Radomiro Tomic (Center: Christian Democrat)	28.1
1989	Patricio Aylwin (Center-Left: Christian Democrat, Radical, Socialist, PPD)	36.6
	Hernan Buchi (Right, UDI)	35.2
	F. J. Errazuriz (Center: Independent)	28.1

Source: Falcoff (1989) and Mendez (1990).

suggests that Chile could have at any time in the past established and enforced a regulatory governance structure that could have credibly committed the government to refrain from arbitrary administrative actions. Why didn't it? This question is taken up next after a brief review of Chile's political and judicial institutions.

Since Chile's independence from Spain in 1818, the country has, with brief exceptions, maintained a multiparty system and a liberal view of civil and political rights. Its constitutions since 1883[8] have embodied principles of separation of powers, the orderly transfer of government, and regular parliamentary elections. This has resulted in elected presidents of diverse political leanings (Table 4.4).[9] Moreover, of the five presidents elected between 1946 and 1973, only one was elected by an absolute majority – and then only because one candidate withdrew. As a result, presidents faced opposing majorities in Congress.

The resilience of Chile's political institutions is demonstrated by recent events. When Allende won the election in 1970, the opposition (mainly Christian Democrats) feared that the new administration would try to change the country's political institutions. Allende received only

36.6 percent of the votes, just slightly more than his challenger, Jorge Alessandri, who received 35.2 percent. Under the Chilean constitution, Congress selects the president when no candidate receives a majority of the vote – normally the candidate receiving the largest popular vote. Out of concern for the country's political institutions, the Christian Democrats agreed to support Allende only in exchange for a number of constitutional amendments known as the Statute of Democratic Guarantees. These amendments affirmed the right to free association in political parties and equal access to state-controlled media. Newspapers could be expropriated only by an absolute majority vote of both houses of Congress. And only Congress could authorize changes in the size of the armed forces. These safeguards proved formidable obstacles to the Allende administration's efforts to change the country's political institutions.

Allende's successor, General Pinochet, also tried to reshape Chile's political institutions. A new constitution, passed by a plebiscite in 1980, gave Pinochet an eight-year term. But the constitution also stipulated that another plebiscite was to be held before the end of the term to determine whether the military junta would propose another candidate or whether the country would return to civilian rule. A new Congress was also to be elected, the first since 1973. In 1989 Chileans voted against the continuation of military rule and later that year elected a new president (Aylwin) and a new Congress. It can be argued that this shock, rather than destabilizing the country, provided motivation for consensus and reconciliation.

The judicial system

Chile has a tradition of an independent judiciary that has restrained government discretion with respect to property rights and contract law. This judicial independence is well illustrated by events during the agrarian reform of the 1960s and the nationalization of enterprises in the early 1970s. Under the 1925 constitution, the government had to pay for expropriated land immediately in cash. Lacking the resources to meet this provision during the agrarian reform program of the 1960s, the government passed a law that allowed compensation to be paid over a ten-year period. The law established a government agency to oversee the valuation and expropriation of property and a system of land tribunals to settle differences between the agency and landowners.

The nationalization of enterprises that occurred during the Allende administration was allowed by an article in the 1925 constitution that permitted expropriation "when the interests of the national community so require." But the constitution also limited such action, stating that expropriation required "a general or special law which authorizes the expropriation for reasons of public utility or social interest, as defined by the legislation." The Allende administration skirted this provision by using an obscure decree (law 520 of 1932) that allowed the president to intervene in certain industries under vaguely defined conditions – for example, when producers of a "basic necessity" decided to halt production or "unjustifiably" produced an inadequate supply.

The administration used the decree extensively, but Congress refused to give the president the legal mandate to support expropriation and the comptroller-general repeatedly invalidated Allende's actions. In April 1972 the judiciary declared the government seizure of several factories by their workers to be invalid. By late 1972 relations between the administration and the Supreme Court were strained, with the administration insisting on the validity of its actions and the court insisting otherwise. The deadlock was broken the following year when the military junta overthrew the Allende government.

Distributional demands

If the stability of political institutions, the nature of Chilean politics, and the independence of the judiciary meant that the country could at any time have established and enforced a credible regulatory structure for the telecommunications sector, why were regulatory systems so much more successful in the 1980s than before? The question can be explored from two sides.

Why earlier reforms were less successful. Perhaps the most important explanation for the failure of earlier reform is a difference in political constituencies. Until the 1980s demand for telecommunications services came almost entirely from the wealthier classes. During most of that period Chilean politics was concerned with the interest of the low- and middle-income classes. Chile's industrialization strategy was based on import substitution, price controls, and public ownership of important economic activities. The government was not only active in social sectors like health, housing, and education, but also in productive sectors such as electricity, fertilizer, and steel. Telecommunications, however, was basically ignored – not surprising given the low- and middle-class constituencies of the radical party, which controlled legislation during 1938–52.

The government's interventionist approach continued into the 1950s, until the economy was brought to its knees by acute inflation and a foreign debt crisis. In response Chileans elected the Liberal Party candidate Jorge Alessandri president in 1958. To lower inflation and stabilize the economy, Alessandri proposed a program of fiscal restraint, credit restrictions, a unified exchange rate, and import liberalization. He also proposed to free prices and promote competition. But since the Radicals were the largest party in Congress at the time, Alessandri had to submit reform measures that supplemented rather than supplanted previous policies. Telecommunications reforms also fell short. CTC's contract was improved in 1958 by defining the company's rate of return, but the contract failed to remove the threat of government intervention.

The Christian Democrats won the 1964 election, returning in large measure to policies in the Radical mold. Chile experienced a wave of nationalizations and agrarian reform. In a 1967 agreement with CTC the government invoked the clause permitting government intervention (49 percent of its shares were sold to the government-owned CORFO).

Two other factors also contributed to the relative neglect of the telecommunications sector until the late 1970s. Telecommunications had not yet become essential for businesses, and the incipient private sector, composed mostly of small businesses, often shared the values of the landlord oligarchy, because of cultural homogeneity and perceived common economic interests. Thus, there was no vocal constituency for improving performance in the telecommunications sector.

Why recent reforms have been more successful. The military regime that ruled Chile between 1973 and 1989 introduced sweeping structural reforms that continue to shape the economy today. They opened the economy and allowed market forces and the private sector to determine the structure of production. The government substantially liberalized trade and prices and privatized public enterprises, banks, pension funds, and even the delivery of health and education services. Public enterprises that were not privatized were commercialized, and a number of regulatory reforms were introduced. Despite these reforms, telecommunications continued to lag.

Reform of the sector gained momentum in the 1980s because broad support emerged during this period for better telecommunications services. Much of the demand arose from a larger, more entrepreneurial private sector and coincided with an increase in the importance of telecommunications services for business.

Though the ruling coalition under the military regime consisted mainly of the armed forces and the upper classes, a new group of economists (known as the Chicago boys for their neoclassical leaning) was soon having a profound impact on the economy. Their policies of privatization, economic liberalization, and cutbacks in public sector employment helped create an important class of entrepreneurs that included small businesspeople, shopkeepers, and farmers, as well as larger enterprises.[10] The new bourgeoisie is an important influence in the telecommunications sector because it includes three new politically influential groups that depend on telecommunications services to remain competitive: members of the middle class who left public sector employment to become entrepreneurs in commerce, transportation, and services; local entrepreneurs who formed partnerships with international investors in new conglomerates in such dynamic sectors as fishing, fruits, wood, paper, and mining; and market entrepreneurs in agricultural and other exports (Montero 1990).

CONCLUSION

Before 1958 the regulatory structure was too vague to persuade CTC to invest adequately. The government eventually responded by specifying more of the details and creating its own long-distance telephone company. But the government did not press harder for development of the sector because there was not much of a political constituency for expanding telecommunications services. In the 1970s the government took over ownership of the sector, but the new arrangement led to even slower growth. Beginning in the 1980s technological changes and the emergence of a stronger business class provided the impetus for developing the sector. The sector has grown substantially, with privatization providing needed capital and better regulation providing a fair rate of return for the private sector.

The success of the recent regulatory reforms in Chile is thus the product of the emergence of a new entrepreneurial class and a near perfect fit between regulatory design and the country's institutions. The specificity and fairness of the regulatory rules and the difficulty of changing these rules are critical to success. Chile could have more clearly defined market boundaries and strengthened its regulatory bodies, reducing the transaction costs resulting from settling disputes through the courts. But specifying market boundaries more narrowly in an industry with such rapidly changing technology could have reduced efficiency. The cost of such specificity could have been high.

Two lessons emerge from the experience of the telecommunications sector in Chile:

• Stable political institutions and an independent judiciary increase the capacity of governments to establish a credible regulatory system and to enforce it. Attempts to develop telecommunications may not succeed, however, without the added push of interest group pressure to get government to act.

- Private sector investment depends not only on the credibility of government commitment but also on the regulatory incentives provided by pricing and entry rules. Failure to specify such regulations appropriately may inhibit private sector commitment.

5

The political economy of the telecommunications sector in the Philippines

HADI SALEHI ESFAHANI

Policymakers the world over have come to see privatization as an important remedy for the ills afflicting economies long dominated by state-owned enterprises. Private sector involvement is expected to bring increased resources and efficiency to ailing public enterprises. Yet it is still an open question whether private enterprises can perform well in situations where public ones have failed. Indeed, many private enterprises in developing countries have track records no better than those of typical public enterprises in similar situations. What are necessary conditions for the success of the private sector in a developing economy? Certainly, it takes more than a simple transfer of ownership for a firm or industry to prosper.

The experience of the telecommunications sector in the Philippines provides an opportunity to study the underlying causes of success and failure in an infrastructure sector in which most firms have been privately owned since the industry's infancy. The main operators in the sector have had direct access to international capital markets and have managed to raise large amounts of debt capital relative to their equity, yet the sector has not performed very well: telephone density is low (about 1.7 telephone sets and 1.1 main lines per 100 people), waiting lists for basic services are long, and service quality is roundly attacked (Gavino 1992). Even taking the country's level of development into account, it seems that the sector has had no edge over its counterparts in other countries, including those under public ownership or with more restricted access to foreign capital.

These observations compel us to ask what factors impeded growth of the sector. Why wasn't there any effective regulatory reform to create stronger investment incentives? Why did the sector remain in private hands despite its poor performance? The analysis that follows traces the sector's poor performance to the weakness of commitment mechanisms needed to make contracts between various players in the economy credi-

145

ble. The inadequacy of commitment mechanisms, of regulatory governance structures, springs from a system of government in which the legislature and judiciary are relatively weak and dominated by a strong executive. This institutional structure can in turn be related to a "fundamental" characteristic of the Philippine society: dominance by a small elite who engage in competitive politics among themselves, but try to bar the rest of the population from active participation without formally taking away their citizenship.

Certainly this characteristic, shaped by the country's past is not immutable. The changes in the distribution of political power that occur in response to external factors and internal dynamics need to be taken into account before any implications for future policy are drawn from the analysis that follows. Indeed, the economic and political developments in the country over the past four decades seem to be bringing about a wider distribution of power. This change has the potential to mitigate some of the main shortcomings of the telecommunications policy.

To make the task of the study manageable, the discussion focuses on the history of the sector's dominant firm, the Philippine Long Distance Telephone Company, which owns about 90 percent of the working phone lines and has a virtual monopoly over domestic and international long-distance telephone circuits in the country. A government-owned company, TELOF, operates about 2 percent of the country's telephones, and more than sixty small private and local-government-owned operators control the remaining 8 percent. There are also several other firms providing telegraph, telex, paging, cellular telephony, and similar services.[1]

POLITICAL STRUCTURE AND COMMITMENT CAPABILITY

Identifying the origins of the weak commitment capability of the regulatory system in the Philippines is critical to an understanding of the dynamics of telecommunications policy and performance and to the design of institutions that can contribute constructively to rapid development of the sector.

The making of basic Philippine institutions

The Philippines became a U.S. colony in the closing years of the nineteenth century, following four centuries of Spanish rule. An important legacy of Spanish domination was an open economy based on exports of primary products by large farms, a pattern that continued under U.S. rule. Over time a strong patronage system developed headed by an agrarian elite with close ties to U.S. politicians and business leaders. The group's small size,

146

common interests, and pervasive kinship network enabled it to overcome internal political and economic rivalries and promote the group's interests over those of the rest of the population. U.S. policy interests in the region worked to foster the economic and political dominance of this group as well, since the U.S. government was interested in establishing a political system in the Philippines that would remain stable and friendly to the United States. Through a process of negotiated independence, this elite group gradually acquired the knowledge, skills, and institutions necessary to run the government and following independence in 1946, that group took control. The country's institutions reflected the dualism of Philippine society, the objectives of the U.S. government, and the elite's desire to maintain its privileges. Some of its prominent features are noted briefly here.

Competitive politics. To ensure stability and effectiveness, the institutions of government had to have legitimacy in the eyes of the populace and had to minimize damaging infighting among the elite. A U.S.-style constitution in 1935 called for separation of powers and competition for control of the executive and legislative branches through elections. The executive, headed by a directly elected president, was to lead the country. Presidents were limited to two four-year terms. A bicameral legislature, consisting of a 110-member House of Representatives elected from the provinces and a 24-member Senate elected at large, was to provide an arena for political brokerage. The judiciary, led by an 11-member Supreme Court, was to serve as referee.

Qualifications control and plurality rule. To restrict political competition to members of the elite, a nine-member Electoral Tribunal – three members from the Supreme Court and three members each from the two parties with the largest number of votes in the Congress – was established to rule on the qualifications of members of Congress. This arrangement effectively undermined any third party stirrings and kept political outsiders at bay.[2] The influence of those outside the political elite was further weakened by the plurality rule for elections: the candidate with the highest share of the popular vote won the seat. The plurality rule reduced the bargaining power of the nonelite and contributed to the weakening of third parties and the entrenchment of a two-party system.

Dominant executive. Power was concentrated in the hands of the president, and the functions of the legislature and the judiciary were circumscribed. It would be risky to give Congress too strong a hand in setting policies and allocating resources. Its members were in close contact with the voters, which could give political outsiders opportunity to exploit rivalries among the candidates and influence them once elected. The most effective powers vested in Congress were negative powers (restricting budget allocations, limiting civil service salaries, blocking entry of new firms). Similarly, a strong and independent judiciary was viewed unfavorably because it could be used to restrict the actions of the elite. The presidency, on the other hand, as a single, nationally elected office, could hardly be influenced by the nonelite.[3]

The power of the presidency was embodied in a number of constitutional and legal provisions.[4] The president could issue decrees with the force of legislation, had line-item veto power (overrule required a two-thirds majority of both houses), and could suspend elected officials for cause (Wurfel 1988, 76, 77, and 90). In times of national emergency Congress could authorize the president to rule by decree for a limited period. The president could also declare martial law without the consent of the Congress. While Congress could not increase budget items proposed by the president, the president could treat the budget approved by the Congress as partially fungible. Thus members of Congress needing to keep their patronage machines well oiled were at the mercy of the president.

Weak judiciary. The judiciary's weakness was manifest mainly in the control of its resources by Congress and the president.[5] The president, with the approval of Congress, appointed judges at all levels, while Congress set judicial budgets and salaries. Although the Supreme Court gained respect for some measure of independence, political appointees in the lower courts were often entangled in patronage politics (Wurfel 1988, 88–90). This system allowed the elite to control the judicial process while the nonelite suffered the effects of inordinate delays and costs in pursuing justice. The system also gave the president a relatively free hand in issuing executive orders and taking arbitrary action without being challenged.[6] The Supreme Court was further restrained by a number of constitutional provisions, particularly the requirement of a two-thirds majority vote for declaring a law or treaty unconstitutional.

Two-party system with weak, indistinguishable parties. Competition for control of the presidency was intense, since the presidency brought with it the power to channel enormous resources. Elite groups outside the ruling coalition were always looking for ways to replace those inside.[7] Given the electoral rules, their best chance was to coalesce as an opposition party and support those in the coalition with the greatest political talents. All involved realized that if their coalition won, some members would gain more than others, eventually forcing some of them to switch sides. Thus, political alliances were constantly shifting. These incentives gave rise to a two-party system in which parties had no serious role in policymaking and were indistinguishable by platform or program (Tancangco 1988). Belonging to a party was essentially a means of declaring allegiance to the patronage system of a particular leader and benefiting from the distribution of the spoils. Parties alternated in power every four to eight years. The succession of generations and the term limitation on the presidency created the potential for shifting fortunes among elite groups.

Weak constitutional restrictions on rent extraction. The constitution restricted the types of rent extraction allowed by those in office, guaranteeing that at least some of the rents would remain for the elite who were out of power at the time. For example, transfer of ownership of private enterprises to government officials was prohibited.[8] As a result, rent extraction could not be complete, because it required changing regulations and taxes which allowed some of the surplus to be left for those in control of the enterprises. However, the weakness of the judiciary meant that detailed restrictions on rent extraction could not be enforced. Thus, it made little sense to engage in effort-intensive consensus building to establish strong constitutional restrictions that could not be enforced and that, furthermore, could undermine the system of power sharing among the elite. The elite avoided formal restrictions on rent extraction since any explicit redistribution rule they would find acceptable would have to discriminate in their favor against the nonelite, thereby jeopardizing the system's legitimacy among the nonelite. Instead, a complex set of informal constraints – incorporated in institutions such as kinship, religion, and patron-client networks was developed to regulate group relations and to limit opportunistic activities (Wurfel 1988, chap. 2).

Free trade and economic parity rights for U.S. citizens. As conditions for independence and future assistance, the U.S. government imposed a number of long-term restrictions on Philippine government policies that were intended to maintain U.S. influence in the country (Wurfel 1988, 14). The Philippines agreed to accept a U.S. military presence in the country and to maintain a fixed exchange rate and free trade with the United States (free trade was to be phased out gradually after 1954). The Philippine Congress also amended the 1935 constitution to grant U.S. businesses twenty-eight-year parity with Filipinos in exploiting natural resources and operating public utilities.[9] To preserve U.S. interests in the country, the United States offered substantial foreign aid, credit, trade, and investment opportunities for the elite. This level of U.S. involvement helped make Philippine international commitments credible, providing U.S. investors in the Philippines with a sense of relative safety.[10] As a result, the flow of foreign investment and loans to the country was greatly facilitated.

The dynamics of the system

These basic institutional features changed somewhat over time, and with them the commitment capabilities of the Philippine government. For the telecommunications sector these changes induced a repeated pattern of stagnation and growth (discussed later in this chapter; for a summary, see Table 5.1).

As the economic parity and free trade agreements with the United States expired, the Philippines expanded its economic ties to Europe and Japan, diminishing the prominence of relations with the United States. These changes meant fewer guarantees for U.S. direct investors in the Philippines. Indeed, as time passed, U.S. businesses found it increasingly difficult to defend their interests through the legal system.[11] However, this weakening of U.S. influence domestically did not jeopardize foreign lending because loans could be more effectively backed by the threat of various sanctions. As a consequence, many U.S. businesses divested their assets in the Philippines and concentrated on lending, trade, and some joint ventures.

During the 1950s the Philippines introduced import and foreign exchange restrictions in response to the downward trend in the relative price of primary products in international markets, large government deficits driven by the reelection concerns of incumbent presidents, and rising demand for foreign assets under a fixed exchange rate regime that resulted in foreign exchange shortages.[12] These moves ushered in a period of import-substitution-based industrialization and the emergence of a large industrial urban working class and a burgeoning middle class. These developments introduced new elements into Philippine politics that reduced the cohesiveness of the old elites and raised serious challenges to their continued rule (Wurfel 1988, 20–2, 112–13). As education and employment opportunities improved, the nonelite gained greater independence. Patron-client relationships started to break down, and it became increasingly costly to satisfy clients. Voters outside the political machines gained increasing influence on elections and on policymaking. Given the structure of the Philippine government, these dynamics intensified policy uncertainty.

As new players joined the political game, conflicts arose within institutions that had been designed to prevent a shift in the balance of power away from the elite. Demands for a constitutional overhaul began to build. In 1970, largely under political pressure from students, Congress voted to form a constitutional convention.[13] By then even the elite had grown dissatisfied with the rules of the game (Fernando 1974) and hoped that a new constitution would correct the problems of "excessive centralization of power in the presidency and the penetration of partisan politics into every type of government decision" (Wurfel 1988, 108).

Meanwhile, President Marcos was looking for ways to extend his rule beyond the end of his second term in office in 1973. The increasing political turmoil, especially the formation of the constitutional convention, provided him with the opportunity he was waiting for. He lobbied for support at the convention and, using the pretext of political agitation, declared martial law in September 1972. With the strong support of the military and of members of the elite who felt threatened by the rise of the new political forces, Marcos was able to suppress the opposition. His position was further strengthened by the support of the U.S. government and its allies, which saw in the political changes of the early 1970s a threat to their own long-term interests (Wurfel 1988, 191, 330). Congress was prevented from convening, elections were suspended, and opposition political leaders were coopted, imprisoned, or exiled. Labor and peasant organizations were suppressed, and strikes were outlawed.

To help legitimize Marcos's continued rule, he kept the constitutional convention open, despite the move by its members to suspend deliberations. More than a dozen delegates were arrested, and a similar number went underground or fled the country. Marcos then prevailed on the convention to pass a set of transitional provisions for the new constitution that was being drafted confirming the legitimacy of all presidential orders and decrees and giving the president extraordinary powers. The new constitution, ratified in a plebiscite of dubious legitimacy, effectively abolished the old Congress and took away all forums from the opposition.

The judiciary was neutralized as well. Though the Supreme Court proclaimed that the new constitution had not been properly ratified, it dismissed the challenge to the constitutionality of martial law, apparently apprehensive about its own survival. The two swing votes in the court feared that Marcos would claim that he could replace the members of the court following ratification of the new constitution since one of his transitional powers was the right to remove any justice by appointing a successor.[14] The Supreme Court ruling conferred a measure of legitimacy on the martial law regime, and Marcos moved boldly and virtually unchecked, serving as both legislature and executive. He prevented the Supreme Court from ruling on the constitutionality of any law by keeping a number of court seats vacant. All lesser judges had been required to submit signed resignations, which were kept on file, allowing Marcos to free himself of the constraints of the judiciary while maintaining the appearance of constitutionality (Wurfel 1988, 133).

Table 5.1. A chronology of PLDT's performance, 1934–92

Period	Political conditions	Economic conditions	Regulatory conditions	Growth rate			Real return on equity	Causes
				Assets at cost	Number of telephones	Number of lines		
1934–40	Colonial administration	Slow recovery	Favorable to PLDT	–	8.6	–		• U.S. policy credibility • Recovery from great depression
1946–60	Independence, with guarantees for U.S. interests (fixed exchange rate and Parity Amendment)	• Steady growth • Very low inflation • Current account deficient	Favorable to PLDT	22.2	14.2	–	12.0	• Foreign ownership (GTE) and U.S. policy credibility • Stable economic conditions and fixed exchange rate
1960–4	Erosion of guarantees for U.S. interests	• Moderate growth • Moderate inflation	Conflict over rate increase in response to devaluation	6.1	7.4	–	5.1	• Renegotiation of treaties with the United States

Period	Context	Economic conditions	Policy toward PLDT					Outcomes
		• Devaluation in 1962						• U.S. acceptance of currency devaluation • Decline of U.S. role in domestic policy
1964–70	Increased pressure for Phi-lippinization (Parity Amendment nearing expiration)	• Slow growth • Low inflation • Growing current account deficit	Favorable to PLDT	25.6	13.0	21.7	9.4	• Takeover by a Filipino elite group close to President Marcos • Marcos secures position • Large unmet demands
1970–2	Nearing the end of Marcos's second term	• Slow growth • High inflation • Devaluation	• Favorable to PLDT • Immediate rate raise following devaluation	2.0	11.5	4.3	−2.9	• Endgame effect
1972–5	Martial law	• Rapid growth • High inflation	• Favorable to PLDT	2.1	7.1	2.7	0.3	• Demand restriction as a result

Table 5.1. (*cont.*)

Period	Political conditions	Economic conditions	Regulatory conditions	Growth rate			Real return on equity	Causes
				Assets at cost	Number of telephones	Number of lines		
			• Large rate increase • Indexation of PLDT tariffs to the exchange rate • SIP plan					of income concentration and large price increases
1975–8	Martial law	• Rapid growth • Moderate inflation • Income concentration • Large current account deficit	• Favorable to PLDT • Takeover of small operators encouraged	3.7	5.5	3.4	2.4	• International scrutiny • Termination of supply, credit, and other arrangements with GTE [related companies providing long-distance telecom facilities grew]

Period	Political conditions	Economic conditions	Regulatory conditions					Other
1979–83	• Movement toward normalization • Rumor of Marcos's terminal illness • Succession crisis	• Growth slowdown • High inflation • Easy foreign credit • High international interest rates	• Favorable to PLDT • Takeover of small operators mandated	19.4	6.2	7.5	−2.3	• Uncertain political conditions • Expanded capital flight opportunities
1984–6	Political crisis	• 10% decline in GDP • High inflation • Tight foreign credit	• Favorable to PLDT • Large rate increase	2.8	4.4	3.1	−6.6	• Endgame effect • Very uncertain political conditions
1986–90	• Regime shift • Political turmoil	• Recovery, moderate growth • Moderate inflation	• Not favorable to PLDT • Rate reduction • Tax hike • New entry permitted	0.3	5.4	5.4	1.3	• Strength of interests unrelated to PLDT in the administration
1990–2	Normalization	• Growth slowdown • Rising inflation • Increasing current account	• Turning favorable to PLDT; approval of government-guaranteed loans	9.6	5.6	6.0	4.1	• Establishment of ties to the administration • Endgame effect

Martial law completely changed the institutional structure of the Philippines. A small group of the elite, Marcos's cronies, could enjoy the spoils of absolute power for an unspecified period.[15] However, opposition to their rule was growing from elite and nonelite quarters alike. In search of a stable outcome and to supplement the use of force, they attempted to introduce a new system of governance in which the legislature served as an arena for political brokerage. In time, Marcos's illness signaled the possibility of an abrupt end to the existing regime (Wurfel 1988, 234). A succession crisis loomed. Fearing a serious change in their fortunes, Marcos's cronies began to act in such a short-sighted, blatantly venal manner that Marcos's regime collapsed long before his death.

A successful opposition coalition of political parties took control of the government in 1986. The opposition coalition was quite diversified and spanned a very wide range of interests, including those of the now larger and more influential middle class. As a result the new government was initially somewhat unstable, and the ruling coalition went through several realignments. The institutional structure that emerged from this process resembles the system in place before Marcos and martial law, but with fewer restrictions on the participation of nonelite groups and more safeguards against the abuse of executive power.[16]

While politics is now more competitive and open, the old elite has managed to maintain a large part of its control of the system. The Presidential Commission on Good Government, created in the first few weeks of the new Aquino administration to dismantle the Marcos crony system, hit major obstacles after a few months as its findings began to implicate many members of the elite still in positions of power (Clad 1987a,b; Manapat 1991). Many of the investigations were closed, and the commission failed to recover any significant part of the assets transferred abroad by Marcos and his cronies.

Investment and ownership in a predatory state

Under the institutional structure of the Philippines the group in power faced a high probability of ending up on the losing side some time in the future, so its members had to devise mechanisms for protecting their assets when they were out of office. One way was to shift away from sectors with nonsalvageable assets such as public utilities and to place some assets outside the country. Thus, as the probability of turnover in the executive branch increased, real investment tended to fall. Another protection mechanism was to finance investment with debt rather than equity, which helped shift the risk and increased the number of people concerned about expropriation, while involving little loss of control for the original owners. Foreign debt was particularly desirable for this purpose because foreign lenders had strong leverage over the elite, and default by any borrower could hurt those controlling the government at the time.

The relatively strong enforceability of international borrowing contracts had other far-reaching effects as well. The elite group in power could borrow against the future income of the country and then invest the proceeds abroad (Boyce 1992). Essentially, once in power, members of the elite tried to cash in as much of the country's long-term surplus as possible and then to allocate their portfolios, inside and outside the country, according to expected returns. The more the group could cash in, the more of its assets it tried to shift out of the country, fearing retaliation from future ruling groups who would be left with less to extract. However, to be able to borrow and keep assets abroad, Philippine enterprises had to make some investments at home. Thus, real domestic investment rose along with foreign borrowing, but not dollar for dollar.

Direct foreign investment was not as secure as foreign lending because it was more vulnerable to expropriation through regulations and taxation. When the economic parity agreement with the United States neared its end, foreign investment declined. Foreign investors sought to share control of their subsidiaries with the Philippine elite and limited their involvement to simple lending and contracting whenever the transfer of intangible assets was not a major concern.

Though there were no prohibitions against state ownership, economic assets remained largely private. Public ownership of an enterprise meant the total loss of the associated surplus once the ruling group was out of power. Turning an enterprise into the group members' private property, in contrast, could help maintain the group's control over the assets and at least part of the returns. Thus, many foreign-owned enterprises were "Philippinized" but not nationalized, as enterprises in other developing countries had been. Philippine leaders could put pressure on foreign investors to sell their assets to members of the ruling coalition rather than to the government. Also, when the enterprises of rival groups could be expropriated or when failing domestic firms fell into government hands, the ruling coalition arranged for its members to purchase the enterprises and secure them as their private property.

Since the nonelite had no access to executive power, their investments could never be safe. That meant that ownership was highly concentrated in the hands of the elite, with most enterprises owned by families or cliques of friends. Corporate forms of ownership with widespread share subscription were rare. When an elite group was in control of a corporation, its members could siphon off profits to their private accounts and leave other shareholders with little return. As a result the nonelite rarely invested their savings in corporate stocks, and the elite who invested committed very little money to corporations they did not control. Consequently, the Philippine stock market remained undeveloped.

Under martial law, incentives to invest greatly diminished for all but the Marcos cronies, who were able to acquire the enterprises of opposition members and to create investment incentives for themselves (Hawes 1987; Manapat 1991). Thus, lack of commitment did not reduce investment in the early years of martial law. However, investment did not rise significantly either, because the cronies understood that their rule would end someday and that when it did, their losses could be substantial. Foreign borrowing and capital flight became more important than before (Figure 5.1). Investment finally came to a halt after 1983, when the Marcos regime entered a crisis stage, and foreign lending came to a halt following the assassination of the opposition leader, former Senator Benigno Aquino.

POLITICS, REGULATION, AND IMPLICATIONS FOR TELECOMMUNICATIONS

To maintain control of political and economic rents, the Philippine elite have helped shape a political structure that has stunted the development of institutions for market governance and resource mobilization. This institutional failure is clearly reflected in the characteristics of the Philippine regulatory system. Though the initial form of the country's regulatory institutions was borrowed from the United States, key aspects were modified to adapt those institutions to the political structures of the Philippines.

Characteristics of the regulatory structure

Several characteristics of the regulatory structure in the Philippines make efficient regulation virtually impossible.

- *Lack of independence.* Regulatory agencies are quasi-judicial bodies whose decisions can be appealed to the Supreme Court. Agency heads are appointed by the president, subject to approval by Congress, and have no fixed tenure. The president can dismiss regulators unilaterally.
- *Legislative control of the budget.* Congress maintains influence over regulatory agencies by controlling their budgets, including salaries and other expenses.
- *Inadequate resources.* Regulatory agencies often lack the equipment, experienced staff, and other resources needed to perform their tasks.

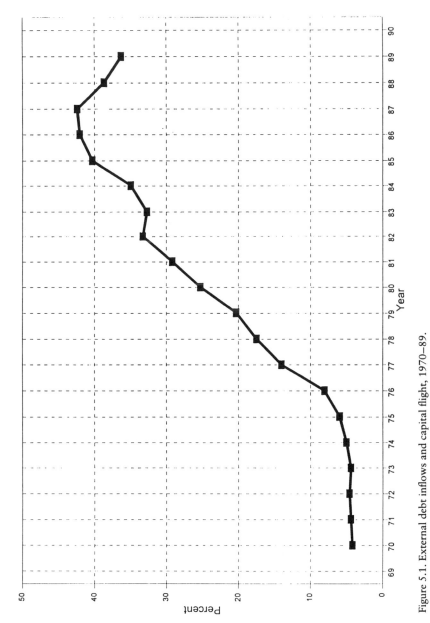

Figure 5.1. External debt inflows and capital flight, 1970–89.

Their budgets are too restrictive to allow them to effectively monitor or evaluate conditions in the sector for which they are responsible.

- *Ambiguity of regulations.* The mandate of regulatory agencies is typically so general that there is wide scope for discretionary behavior. Congress has not tried to achieve sectoral goals by providing detailed instructions about the content of regulatory rules. For example, there is no fixed rule for setting utility prices, though Congress could have stipulated specific procedures or even specific price formulas.
- *Bias toward restricted entry.* Public utility regulators control the entry of new firms by issuing or canceling investment permits, known as Certificates of Public Convenience and Necessity, in response to applications from franchised companies, but they have no control over franchises. Franchises must be obtained from local governments or, if the coverage is nationwide, from Congress. Therefore, regulators' control of entry is circumscribed, and the system is biased toward entry restriction.

Thus lack of resources prevents regulatory agencies from collecting the data and developing the expertise necessary to design and implement appropriate policies, while the discretionary power of the president makes regulations uncertain and limits their credibility. The reasons for such institutional limitations are easy to identify. Specific rules, such as price formulas, that can create investment incentives are difficult to guarantee in a system in which the executive has so much discretionary power. The president can use a variety of means, often difficult to predict, to circumvent a specific rule. If the judiciary were strong enough to establish and defend a particular interpretation of the rule, the government could be forced to abide by it. However, when judicial power is constrained, the judiciary may yield to executive demands. That makes it a futile exercise to try to muster the political support necessary to get a specific rule established in law or in the constitution.

A strong, independent regulatory agency could bring stability to regulatory policy, but such an institution would be a threat to the interests of the elite. Professionals running such an agency could use their control to redistribute the assets of businesses owned by the elite. The interests of those in power are better protected when regulatory agencies have no independence and few resources. Even the elite outside the coalition in power may favor weak regulatory agencies, which keep the president from being too effective in taxing the assets of rivals. Congressional veto power over the entry of new firms also seems to be a means of reining in the president's power to share the profits of businesses owned by members of the opposition. In this sense, congressional control of franchises and of the budgets of regulatory agencies is a means of maintaining some harmony in the balance of power within the elite.

The problem of regulatory institutions in the Philippines is similar to that of the judiciary. When these institutions are strong, they can be used by the nonelite to achieve power and rent sharing. When they are weak, corruption and inefficiency thrive, but the institutions remain under the control of the elite.

Implications for the telecommunications sector

The historical dominance of a small and competitive elite has been an impediment to the emergence of credible regulatory policy in the Philippines. For utilities, the weakness of regulatory commitment mechanisms is an especially severe impediment to investment and efficient operation because nonsalvageable assets constitute such a large share of their costs. There is, however, a sliver of space for some policy credibility in this system if opportunistic changes in policy that bring private investment to a standstill impose large costs on the government. In a country where investment in a sector is grossly inadequate and there is a large pool of new technology that could be imported, private operators can guarantee a minimum return on investments because of their ability to "punish" the government for regulations that would expropriate their specific assets. However, this implicit contract mechanism works effectively only in a stable environment. When changes in the country's political or economic conditions cause the benefits of implicit expropriation to fluctuate, the government may find it worthwhile in some situations to engage in rent extraction even though it jeopardizes investment. Thus, some mechanism guaranteeing strong irreversible commitment is necessary to reduce the risk of such possibilities.

The analysis of the Philippine political economy developed in the previous sections has numerous implications for the country's telecommunications sector:[17]

Implication 1. *Telecommunications enterprises are primarily domestically owned.* Foreign ownership was possible only under colonial rule or in the early years of independence, under the Parity Amendment. When foreign-owned firms are Philippinized, they are sold to members of the ruling coalition rather than being nationalized.

Implication 2. *Telecommunications enterprises are primarily privately owned, with ownership typically concentrated in the hands of the elite.*

Implication 3. *Telecommunications enterprises with more widespread corporate ownership are controlled by a minority elite with friendly ties to the administration.* The enterprises generate large surpluses but

161

Hadi Salehi Esfahani

yield low rates of return to stockholders. The difference is captured by
the elite by overreporting costs and underreporting revenues.

Implication 4. *Public telecommunications firms tend to be privatized
before the end of the administration under which they are established.*

Implication 5. *Private investment in telecommunications firms is likely to
be high under colonial rule, in the early years of independence under
the Parity Amendment, and in the early years of a friendly administration. Investment declines toward the end of friendly administrations
and remains low under unfriendly administrations. Reduced investment is accompanied by capital flight.*

Implication 6. *Telecommunications firms tend to finance their investments through debt, especially foreign debt, rather than equity. They
maintain high debt-equity ratios.*

Implication 7. *Real investment by domestic telecommunications operators rises with their foreign borrowing, but less than dollar for dollar,
with capital flight accounting for the difference.* Their foreign borrowing depends largely on supply rather than demand factors.

Implication 8. *Price, tax, and regulatory conflicts between telecommunications enterprises and the government develop mostly during unfriendly administrations or during periods of increased political competition, when the nonelite become influential.*

Implication 9. *Price adjustments under administrations friendly to the
telecommunications firms are favorable to the industry. Under a friendly
authoritarian administration, prices approach monopoly levels.*[18]

Implication 10. *Because of the bias of the regulatory system against the
entry of new firms, established telecommunications firms are likely to
succeed in fending off competition whether the administration is
friendly or not.* In addition, under unfriendly administrations or intense political competition, excess demand will grow since the government is unable to bring in new firms. Entry may be blocked even in
undeveloped regions of the country because established firms may
want to reserve the markets for later development, when more friendly
administrations take office.

Implication 11. *Private investment in international circuits is not much
influenced by the commitment capabilities of domestic regulatory structures.* The international network is far more difficult to expropriate
through regulatory action than the domestic network. Regulators have
no control over a company's agreements with foreign operators on the
settlement price of international calls. If regulators try to lower international long-distance rates for calls originating in the home country, the
company can claim that it needs to collect more to pay high settlement
costs to foreign operators. It can also limit the number of outgoing
calls, forcing domestic customers to have their calls originate outside

162

the country. Revenues will then be collected by foreign operators and will not depend on the rates set domestically.

HISTORICAL PERSPECTIVE ON COMMITMENT CAPABILITIES

The history of the telecommunications sector in the Philippines provides strong evidence that the commitment capabilities of government have had a significant impact on investment in the sector. The focus is on the experience of Philippine Long Distance Telephone (PLDT) and a number of other closely related enterprises.

Policy credibility during colonial administration

PLDT's experience under colonial rule supports implications 1 and 5. Under colonial rule the administration depended on U.S. institutions and adhered to the strategic interests of the United States in the Philippines. As a result, the danger of opportunistic policy changes was minimal, and the credibility of regulatory governance and incentives structure was high. Thus, effective performance and rapid growth should be expected in this period.

The basis for telecommunications regulation in the colonial period was a vaguely written law requiring regulators to approve investments that affected "public welfare" and to set prices so that utility companies received a "fair" rate of return on investments. A decision by the Supreme Court defined the fair rate as a 12 percent return on revalued assets. All public utilities were regulated by the Public Service Commission and all decisions were made by the commissioner, a centralization of authority that placed the administration in firm control of regulatory decisions.

In November 1928 PLDT was franchised as a U.S.-owned company. Under the terms of its fifty-year franchise PLDT was allowed to operate in several large cities and on all intercity routes. The franchise stipulated a 1 percent tax on the company's gross receipts in lieu of all other taxes. The company soon took over many of the local telephone companies in Manila and other population centers and supplemented their networks with long-distance circuits. During the depression of the 1930s the company's local service stagnated, but PLDT continued to invest in long-distance services. Investment in local service resumed after 1934, and until 1940 the number of telephones grew at an average rate of 8.6 percent a year. The Japanese invasion during World War II destroyed most of PLDT's network. Thus, the company invested vigorously during the period of colonial administration except during the depression and the war.

Hadi Salehi Esfahani

Foreign ownership and U.S. influence, 1946–59

PLDT's performance in the first decade and a half after independence provides further evidence for implications 1 and 5, and for 9 as well. The continuity in institutions, the strong leverage of the United States, and the concessions granted to U.S. citizens created a predictable and safe investment environment for both Filipino and U.S. businesses. These factors contributed to a stable and robust economy. Philippine Long Distance realized high profits and performed well under foreign ownership based on the commitment powers of the U.S. government. Control of the company's network was taken over by the U.S. army in 1945, and after some preliminary rehabilitation, was transferred two years later to General Telephone and Electronics Corporation (GTE), a U.S. company that acquired 28 percent of PLDT's common stock. Most of the remaining shares were held by other U.S. corporations, often as a means of portfolio diversification rather than control. The Filipino elite also acquired a small share of the company. Between 1947 and 1959 Philippine Long Distance rapidly increased its fixed assets and telephones in service (Figures 5.2 and 5.3).[19]

During this period the company enjoyed reasonable though declining, real rates of return on its assets and equity (Figure 5.4). Telephone charges had been set at relatively high levels after the war to attract the investment needed to rebuild the system. Rates were kept nominally constant throughout the 1950s (Figures 5.5–5.8), and real values eroded very slowly because inflation was low. Philippine Long Distance was ensured of receiving a reasonable return on its investments for several reasons. First, the U.S. influence in the company meant that it could count on the legal and political leverage at its disposal to prevent its profitability from falling too far below the competitive rate of return on capital. Second, the probability of a currency devaluation, which could have hurt PLDT, was low under the fixed exchange rate regime stipulated by the independence agreements between the Philippines and the United States. Moreover, any planned devaluation would have been known well ahead of the time because of the requirement for prior U.S. approval. Third, PLDT's customers were mainly foreigners and the Filipino elite. They were concerned about the availability and quality of service and were not interested in a confrontation with Philippine Long Distance that could jeopardize service expansion at a time when there was still a great deal of excess demand (Figure 5.9). Essentially, GTE's control of technology and rate of investment allowed it to capture part, though not all, of the surplus of PLDT's operations.

These same factors influenced the government's forthcoming attitude in meeting PLDT's foreign exchange needs in the second half of the

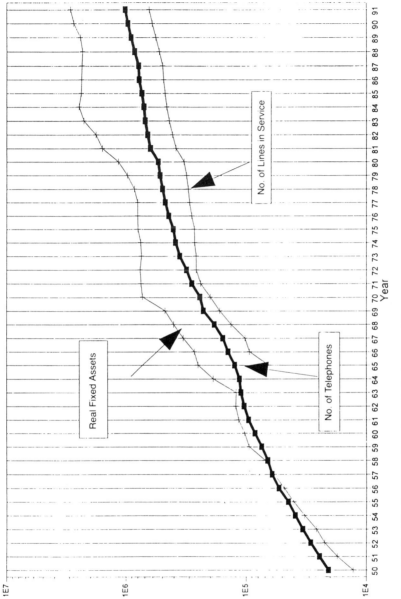

Figure 5.2. Real fixed assets and numbers of telephones and lines.

165

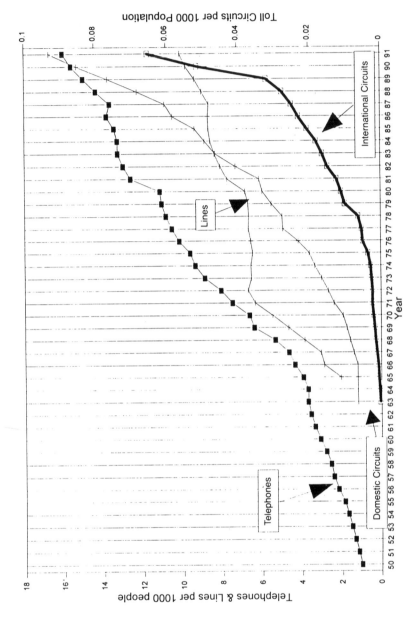

Figure 5.3. PLDT's telecommunication facilities, 1950–91.

166

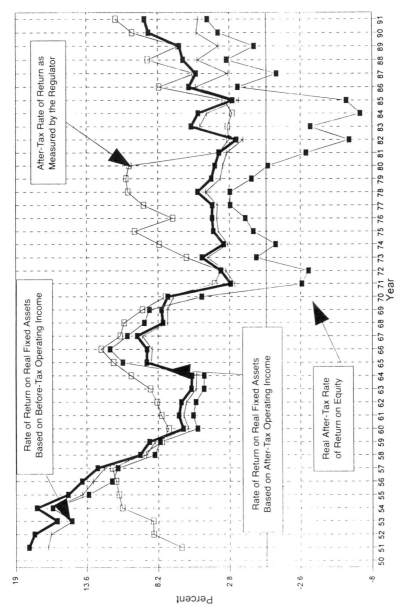

Figure 5.4. Rates of return on fixed assets and equity, 1951–91.

167

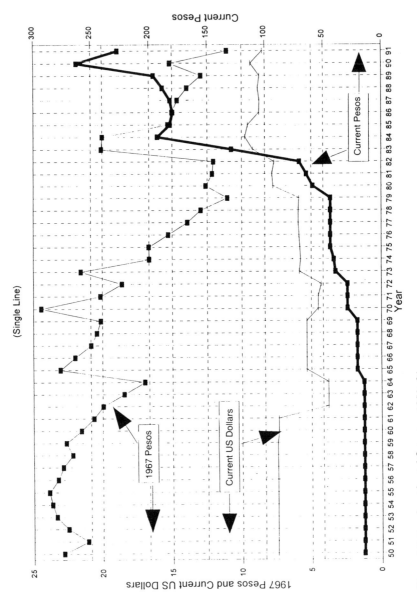

Figure 5.5. Local residential flat rates, 1950–91.

168

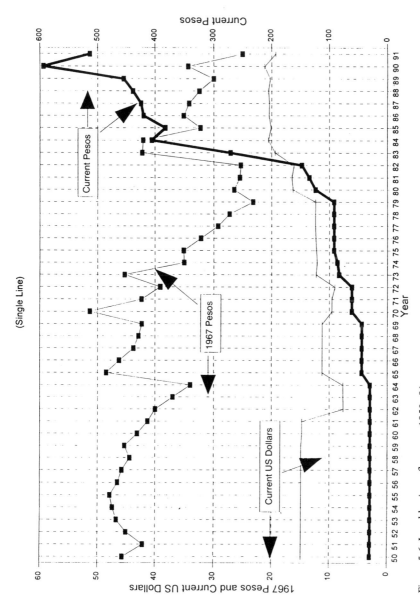

Figure 5.6. Local business flat rates, 1950–91.

169

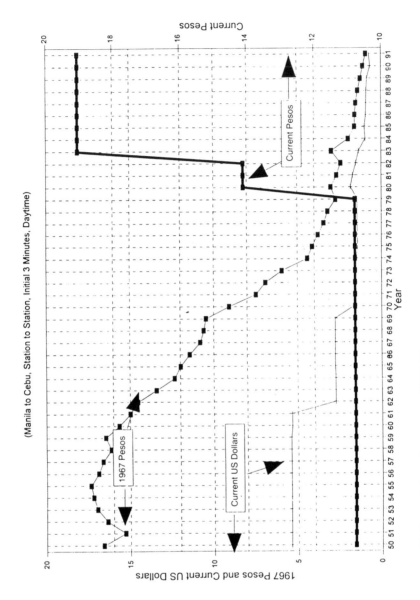

Figure 5.7. Domestic long-distance rates, 1950–91.

170

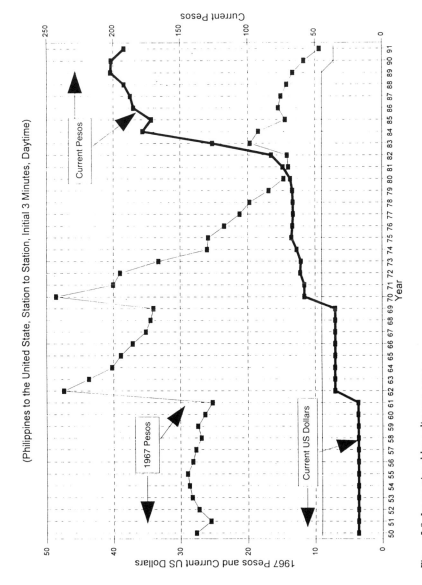

Figure 5.8. International long-distance rates.

171

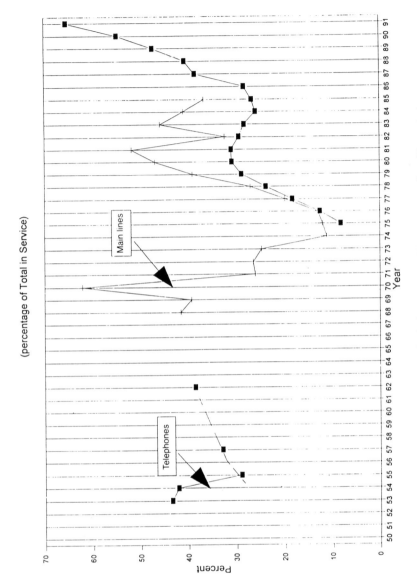

Figure 5.9. Unfilled applications for main line and telephones, 1953–91 (percentage of total in service).

1950s, when the country was experiencing balance of payments difficulties. Many other businesses faced foreign rationing.[20] The government did impose some restrictions on remittances of dividends to foreign shareholders, but that was a uniform policy affecting all businesses, and the fixed exchange rate imposed by the U.S. government meant that any losses due to the delay in remittance would be small. In addition, since the government did not restrict debt amortization, the company could easily circumvent remittance restrictions by increasing its foreign exchange debt in place of raising equity (Figure 5.10).

On the whole U.S. influence implied ownership security, institutional continuity, and economic stability, all factors that made the investment environment relatively safe. In addition GTE's control of technology and investment, and the excess demand for telephones among the elite, ensured the company that confrontation with the government was unlikely. Telephone service grew fast.

Currency devaluation and conflict, 1960–3

By the late 1950s the U.S. role in the Philippines had changed. As the Philippine elite grew more independent and established new relationships around the world, the U.S. government lost its influence as a source of commitment for domestic policies. PLDT's investment in the domestic telephone network declined during 1960–3, mainly as a result of this loss of commitment capability and the absence of a friendly relationship between the company and the government (implication 5). A balance of payments crisis exacerbated the problem, and open conflict between PLDT and the government surfaced when no price increase was granted despite a major devaluation in 1962 (implication 8). The conflict fully confirmed PLDT's perception of an impaired commitment mechanism in the new environment. On the international side of its operation, where the strength of commitment of domestic regulatory structures was not a serious concern, PLDT continued to invest without hesitation (implication 11).

As a major balance of payments crisis developed in 1960, the government negotiated with U.S. and IMF authorities on a stabilization plan. The IMF recommended a major devaluation and decontrol of the foreign exchange market, and the United States concurred. The decontrol would have little effect on PLDT because it had not faced much foreign exchange rationing. The devaluation, however, could be very costly for the company, which depended on imported equipment and foreign capital and whose controlling shareholders evaluated their profits in U.S. dollars. Had the government signaled a plausible commitment to adjust telephone charges in line with the devaluation, the company could have gone forward with the major expansion project it had prepared in 1960. But the

173

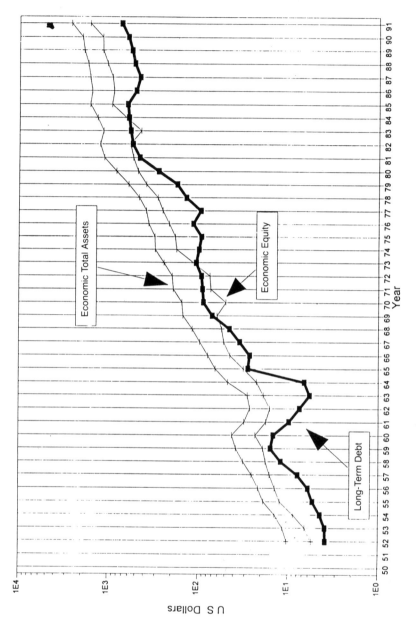

Figure 5.10. Economic assets, equity, and long-term debt, 1952–91.

company had little reason to believe that prices would be adequately adjusted. The government needed to keep inflation down to avoid further devaluations that could vitiate its stabilization efforts and holding down public utility prices was one way of doing so.

In 1961 Philippine Long Distance decided to postpone its expansion plan, even though the peso had not yet been devalued. Holding off on investment gave the company some leverage against the government. The company did not formally seek a rate increase before the devaluation, but when the new administration announced a 95 percent devaluation in January 1962, Philippine Long Distance and other public utilities immediately filed for rate increases. Utility owners argued that they would have difficulty financing expansion projects without a rate increase (Ronquillo 1965). The Public Service Commission was slow to respond. Philippine Long Distance announced publicly that it would not invest until a rate increase was approved (Ronquillo 1963). The confrontational tone of the company's *Annual Report* in March 1962 attested to the poor relationship between the company and the commission.

Unmet demand mounted as the telephone network grew very slowly after 1960, and the company hoped that further delays in investment would incite the elite to press the government to grant a rate increase. But the government, concerned that the stabilization plan was not working, found the cost of satisfying the demands of public utility companies too high. The Public Service Commission was instructed to take no action on the rate-increase applications until further notice. The government's stabilization policies began to take hold, and inflation remained relatively low, exports picked up, and GDP grew at a reasonable rate. However, the decline of import-substitution industries and the mounting deficiencies in infrastructure soon slowed GDP growth. The weakening economy, the pressures generated by shortages, and growing confidence in the stability of prices prepared the stage for approval increases in public utility charges in June 1964. PLDT received a 40 percent rate increase for its local services effective 1 January 1965. The company immediately launched its delayed expansion plan.

Had the owners of the major public utilities been close allies of the Macapagal administration that initiated the devaluation in January 1962, rate increases might have been granted earlier. PLDT's owners were mostly Americans, while the main supplier in the power sector was Meralco, which had been taken over from U.S. interests in 1961 by the powerful Lopez family, political opponents of Macapagal.

An important aspect of PLDT's investment withholding strategy during 1960–3 was its focus on the domestic side of operations. The company's international circuit investments were generally unaffected by the kinds of contracting problems it faced domestically, and it continued such

175

projects largely independent of the domestic regulatory situation. A submarine cable project from the Philippines to Guam, with links to Hawaii and the U.S. mainland, boosted the company's profitability far more than the 40 percent rate increase approved for local services. The share of long-distance revenues – in which international calls play an important role – in total revenue jumped from less than 20 percent in 1964 to more than 45 percent in 1967 (Figure 5.11).

Philippinization, 1964–70

The Philippinization of PLDT in the second half of the 1960s provides clear evidence for implications 1, 2, 3, 5, and 6. With the parity amendment set to expire and the absence of commitment remaining a serious problem, GTE would sooner or later have to divest its PLDT assets. Implications 1 and 2 suggest that under the Philippine political structure, allies of the president would be able to outbid others for the divested assets and that investment would be high in the first few years, with the company relying heavily on foreign debt financing. And since Philippine Long Distance was a corporation, with a large number of passive investors, the rate of return for stockholders would decline as those in control received large gains.

In the mid-1960s GTE was negotiating to sell its shares in Philippine Long Distance (GTE 1976; U.S. SEC 1977).[21] By 1966 GTE had found a group of interested Philippine investors headed by Jose Cojuangco, Jr., and negotiations reached an advanced stage. But soon after Marcos's inauguration high-level government officials urged GTE for political and security reasons not to sell its interest in Philippine Long Distance to the Cojuangco group – Cojuangco had been an ally of the Liberal Party leadership, which lost the 1965 election to Marcos. GTE was told to deal with another group of Philippine nationals, the Philippine Telecommunications Investment Corporation (PTIC) (U.S. SEC 1977).

The new group, led by Ramon Cojuangco (Jose Cojuangco's cousin), Luis Tirso Rivilla (Ramon's brother-in-law), Alfonso Yuchengco (a banker), and Antonio M. Meer (a lawyer), formed a holding company to take over GTE's shares in Philippine Long Distance. A deal was concluded in 1967, and a new board of directors took over in December of that year. GTE received a stake in the holding company (22.5 percent, as reported by Manapat 1993) that enabled it to appoint one director to the board. The terms of the contract provided that GTE's shares in the company would be bought for approximately $7 million in cash and $7 million in promissory notes (GTE 1976; U.S. SEC 1977). According to Meer (reported in Tiglao 1993c), the loan was guaranteed by the Development Bank of the Philippines. The notes were to be written off through a

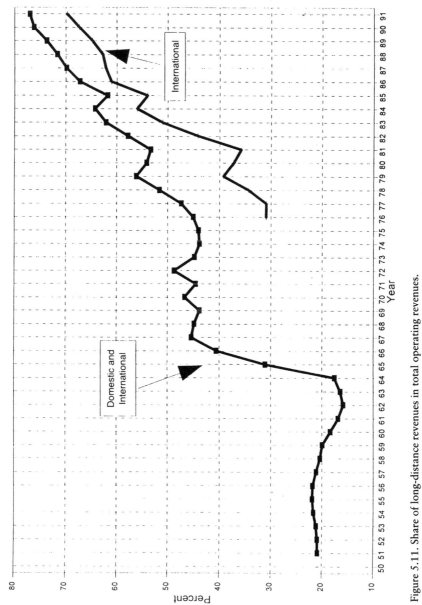

Figure 5.11. Share of long-distance revenues in total operating revenues.

5 to 7 percent commission on PLDT's purchases of GTE equipment "caused" by the PTIC group.

GTE also promised to pay cash commissions, amounting to $484,000 by 1976, to be delivered through the Stamford Trading Company, a Bahamian concern whose linkages the U.S. SEC could not trace. The commissions were paid "to provide [the buyers] with sufficient funds to pay back [the loans]. Neither the investment company [PTIC] principals nor a Bahamian company apparently controlled by them and used as a conduit for the GTE payments were expected to perform any services for GTE, the SEC suit contends" (*Wall Street Journal* 1977). Finally, GTE provided PTIC with an option to purchase 40 percent of GTE Industries, a subsidiary that manufactured telephone equipment in the Philippines. PTIC exercised the option in 1971 in exchange for a $468,459 "noninterest-bearing promissory note payable at the rate of $1 [sic] per annum" (*Wall Street Journal* 1977).

Further deals were made as Philippine Long Distance continued to purchase its equipment from GTE. According to Rosenblatt (1977)

The SEC said that GT&E made personal loans of $580,000 to Cojuangco, $280,000 to Rivilla, $100,000 to Yuchengco, and $40,000 to Meer in 1971 when their investment corporation needed cash to repay bank loans. The personal loans were made by GT&E "on the condition" that the telephone company "promptly sign a $20 million equipment purchase agreement with GT&E," according to the SEC suit. . . . The GT&E assigned the promissory notes to an independent escrow agent with the instructions to handle the notes "in accordance" with the wishes of the people who signed the notes, the SEC said. This means that the notes can be canceled without ever being paid.

The deals were clearly beneficial to the PTIC group and damaging to PLDT. According to the *Wall Street Journal* (1977), "GTE executives have testified . . . that one of the factors in setting the price for equipment purchase by PLDT was the amount of commissions GTE paid or credited through the Bahamas concern." Indeed, when the U.S. Securities and Exchange Commission filed suit in 1977, it had no difficulty getting the defendants to agree to the court injunction of a $1 million transfer from PTIC to PLDT.

After the GTE-PTIC deal other U.S. and Filipino shareholders in Philippine Long Distance remained by and large passive investors. The PTIC group came to dominate the PLDT board and insurance, construction, and many financing contracts went to enterprises held directly or indirectly by the PTIC group. This supply system made it possible for directors and management to transfer the company's profits to their own accounts rather than sharing them with stockholders. The Philippine Securities and Exchange Commission and the Public Service Commission never questioned these practices.

Although President Marcos held no interests in PLDT under his own name, revelations after his departure in 1986 show that he must have had a major stake in Philippine Telecommunications Investment, represented by the Cojuangco family. The attorneys investigating the case for the Presidential Commission on good governance found that in May 1978 Ramon Cojuangco and Luis Rivilla had transferred 46 percent of PTIC's shares with a current market value of 170 million pesos (P) to Prime Holdings Company, for P6.5 million (Sison 1986).[22] Prime Holdings had been formed by two of Marcos's financial advisers, one of whom admitted in 1986 to have acted as a Marcos front. Based on interviews with those involved and the evidence recovered, the attorneys concluded that the sale had not been forced, but that the shares had belonged to Marcos all along.[23] Why they were transferred to another front group in 1978 is not very clear. The transfer may have been prompted by Marcos's illness, as his family became concerned about securing his fronted assets after his death. Evidently, they had greater trust in the two financial advisers who did not come from elite families and owed their positions to the Marcoses (Manapat 1991, 353–66).

In 1969 PLDT's franchise was extended for twenty-five years beyond its 1978 expiration date. The extension generated some debate among those who believed that PLDT should be subject to corporate income tax and those who maintained that the franchise tax was sufficient. A final compromise raised the company's franchise taxes to 2 percent of its gross receipts and retained its exemption from other taxes.

Between 1964 and 1970 PLDT experienced one of its fastest growth periods. The transactions between the GTE and Filipino investors described above shed some light on why PLDT was investing so rapidly both before and after the transfer of ownership. The company's immediate rate of return had risen substantially as a result of telephone rate increases, the expansion in domestic and international long-distance revenues, and the decline in real wages in the mid-1960s (see Figure 5.4). For the longer term Philippinization promised stronger commitment because of direct government ties. GTE had other interests besides gaining immediate profits in starting the expansion early because immediate profits, a larger network, and an ongoing expansion project could help GTE obtain larger and longer-term equipment-supply contracts, thus allowing it to share in the surplus generated by the ownership change. PTIC's incentive to invest was also clear: after 1967 PLDT could count on supportive government policy at least as long as President Marcos remained in office. It invested with vigor particularly because major shortages in telephone service had developed following the investment stagnation of early 1960s. Moreover as the economy and the middle class expanded, demand continued to grow rapidly (see Figure 5.9). Most of the new telephones were installed in the

Manila metropolitan area, where demand was growing fastest and subscribers were more likely to use international long-distance services.

PLDT's profitability was also quite high in the second half of the
1960s. Although calculations based on declared profitability show real
rates of return lower than those in the 1950s (see Figure 5.4), the value
of the profits captured by Philippines Telecommunications Investment
through its contracts with GTE could alone cover the difference.[24] However, there were no further rate increases at the time, probably because
of increased political competitiveness, particularly middle-class activism
(implication 8).

PLDT was not the only telecommunications firm benefiting from a
close relationship with the administration in the late 1960s. In 1966 a
group of President Marcos's close associates led by Defense Minister Juan
Ponce Enrile formed the Philippine Overseas Telecommunications Corporation (POTC), which entered into a joint venture with the government to
create the Philippine Communication Satellite (Philcomsat). Philcomsat
was franchised as a carriers' carrier in 1969 to provide international
satellite services to the Philippines. Unlike other telecommunications enterprises, however, it was placed beyond the jurisdiction of the Public
Service Commission, purportedly because of the government's ownership
share.[25] Philcomsat has been a major supplier of international circuits for
all Philippine telecommunications companies, including PLDT. At the
same time POTC's owners have had interests in all the major telecommunications enterprises in the country (Isberto 1986). The company also
received handsome deals from GTE, similar to those provided to PLDT.
In fact, the bulk of POTC's equity was built in this way (Isberto 1986).
Again, after the fall of the Marcos regime, it was discovered that Marcos's front companies had obtained POTC shares amounting to 40 percent of the total in 1982 (Isberto 1986).

Devaluation and the end of Marcos's second term, 1970–2

PLDT's experience in the early 1970s demonstrates the problem of commitment beyond a president's term in office in the Philippines and clearly
supports implications 5 and 6. As the end of Marcos's second term
neared, investment declined, capital flight picked up, and the debt-equity
ratio stayed high. In 1970 PLDT's costs shot up, primarily because of a
65 percent devaluation. The company had borrowed heavily in foreign
markets, and the higher value of the dollar made repayment difficult (see
Figure 5.10). In addition, the tighter labor markets of the late 1960s and
greater labor militancy had substantially increased real wages and
PLDT's labor cost. However, in contrast to events following the 1962
devaluation, the Public Service Commission gave provisional approval

for rate increases for public utilities almost immediately after the devaluation in 1970. Meralco, the power company owned by the family of the vice president, received an automatic 3 percent adjustment for every P0.30 change in the peso-dollar exchange rate (which had jumped from P3.90 per dollar to P6.44). PLDT received a 40 percent rate increase on all its local telephone services. Permanent approval of the rate adjustments came more than a year later, delayed by challenges from business user groups. Although the opposition failed to get the approved rate increases rescinded, it did manage to postpone consideration of additional increases in the following two years. The liberal attitude toward rate increases was not accidental; events would have transpired differently had the companies not had patrons in the administration. Indeed, as events under martial law demonstrated, Meralco received very different treatment once its owners were expelled from the ruling coalition.

Although the rate increases in 1970 enabled PLDT to remain profitable for the year, the impact was short-lived. The real rate of return on equity fell significantly, becoming negative in 1971–2. Investment dropped sharply, and real capital stock stopped growing (Figure 5.12). The decline in PLDT's profitability during 1971–2 could have been due to undercompensation in the face of high inflation following the 1970 devaluation, while slow investment could have been a consequence of the low profitability and the high cost of foreign exchange, which caused difficulties for foreign financing. But the company's annual reports do not make such claims.[26] The relative stability of the peso after the 1970 devaluation and the slow growth of nominal wages also suggest that the sudden drop in profitability could not all have been due to continued significant cost increases.

An alternative explanation based on weak commitment seems to better fit the facts. In the early 1970s the main contender for the presidency after Marcos was Senator Benigno Aquino, whose relationships with the Marcos group were adversarial. The Lopez family, which could have put forward a candidate promising continuity with the Marcos regime, broke with Marcos in the early 1970s. As a result the probability of adverse regulatory action after 1973 was quite high. In this situation it makes sense for a business to transfer its assets abroad and turn from equity to debt, a response that would simultaneously explain declining in investment, continued borrowing, and low declared rates of return. In this regard it is important to recall that in 1971 PTIC owners had signed a new $20 million dollar contract with GTE, on behalf of PLDT, receiving an immediate $1 million in U.S. bank accounts (U.S. SEC 1977). At the same time they borrowed another half a million dollars to gain a stake in GTE Industries, Inc. Of course, GTE was only one of PLDT's suppliers. Dealings with others have not been documented.

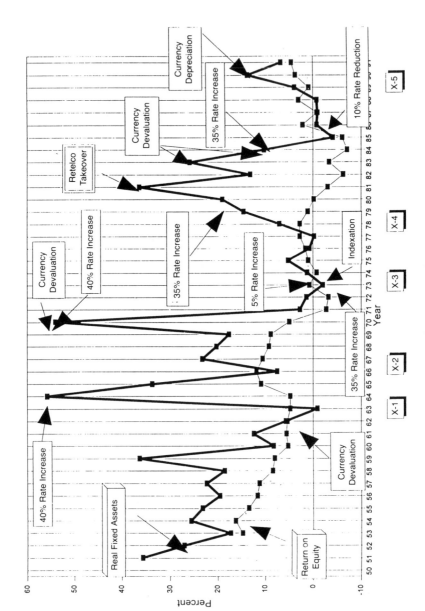

Figure 5.12. Growth rate of fixed assets real after-tax rate of return on equity.

Martial law and international scrutiny, 1973–8

Barring other overriding effects, the first few years of martial law should be times of high real prices and increased investment for sectors controlled by government associates (implication 5 and 9). Other sectors would also be expected to follow suit, giving in to the tremendous pressures unleashed by the broad presidential powers under martial law. Indeed, many sectors of the economy did display these patterns, and economy-wide investment mounted, GDP grew rapidly, and real wages declined sharply in the mid-1970s. PLDT also received rate increases and regulatory support, but made no net investment (see Figure 5.12). This seemingly contradictory outcome can be explained by two factors: a decline in the demand for telephones, and the U.S. SEC's suit against PLDT, which implied termination of the company's relationship with GTE. The first factor made it unprofitable for the company to expand during 1973–6, and the second closed off its channels of borrowing and equipment supply during 1976–7.

Soon after the declaration of martial law, the Public Service Commission was broken up into specialized regulatory agencies.[27] The new agency for the telecommunications sector (except radio) was the Board of Communications. No change in the regulatory framework accompanied this organization reform, which had little impact on the telecommunications enterprises. One of the board's first acts was to approve a 35 percent increase for PLDT's local tariffs in 1973 supplemented by an additional 5 percent increase the following year. The impact on the real prices of telephone services seems to have been small and short-lived (see Figures 5.5 and 5.6). However, the increases were accompanied by a subscriber investment plan instituted by presidential decree. Each subscriber was obliged to purchase 180 shares of PLDT's preferred stock (at a par value of P10 per share) to finance part of the line installation costs and, according to the presidential decree, to achieve widespread corporate ownership. The stock yielded annual dividends of P1 and could be converted to common stock one year after issue at a 10 percent discount. Considering the lack of interest among telephone subscribers in holding PLDT's common stocks and the high rates of inflation in the 1970s and 1980s, these terms implied negative real rates of return on these funds. More important, the funds provided PLDT with some nonvoting equity that it could use as a basis for securing larger foreign loans, without giving up any control.[28]

Another important change in regulations under martial law was the indexation of local telephone rates to the exchange rate. For every P0.10 increase in the peso cost of the U.S. dollar, telephone rates were automatically adjusted by 1 percent. Although this rule did not help much during the 1970s, when the exchange rate was maintained at a constant level, it provided PLDT with security against currency depreciation and boosted its foreign borrowing capacity. (Note that the rule allows the rates to increase geometrically when the exchange rate depreciates arithmetically.)

On the surface, it seems that during the mid-1970s PLDT's profitability was low and it had little incentive to invest (see Figure 5.4). However, the situation is far more puzzling than it appears. The company's third expansion plan (X-3), which it was implementing slowly between 1973 and 1978, was designed in the early 1970s as a very small project (less than half the size of the previous expansion plan in terms of installations). Though the mid-1970s were boom years for the Philippine economy, the company made no attempt to expedite or enlarge the expansion project. To the contrary. The expansion was largely completed by 1976, yet PLDT did not start its next project until two years later. During this time the government's supportiveness was clearly demonstrated through rate increases, the indexation of local rates to the foreign exchange rate, and the mandatory subscriber investment plan.[29] Though real local service rates were allowed to decline in the second half of the 1970s, that seems to have been part of a strategy to hasten PLDT's takeover of smaller operators.[30]

A clue to understanding PLDT's stagnation in the first few years of martial law is provided by the trend in excess demand (see Figure 5.9). Unmet demand fell sharply during the early 1970s, and by 1974 a 10 percent increase in the number of lines would have eliminated it. This was hardly a situation that would induce large expansion plans. But in a booming economy, what factors lowered the demand for telephones? For one, the boom benefited only those few who controlled the economy and enjoyed monopoly profits. For nearly everyone else, real income was falling. Between 1970 and 1980 the average real wage rate declined steadily by 8 percent a year. Thus, fewer and fewer households could afford telephones. PLDT's customers were essentially the elite and the upper-middle class, and most of them already had telephones.[31]

However, these arguments do not explain why investment continued to drag until 1978, though demand had begun to pick up in 1976. The delay is significant, because it seems to have been the root cause of the telephone shortages and quality deterioration of the late 1970s and early 1980s (see Figures 5.9 and 5.13). The difficulties that arose in PTIC's dealings with GTE seem to be at the root of much of the delay.

During the mid-1970s the U.S. public was becoming increasingly concerned about honesty in business and politics. In response, the U.S. Securities and Exchange Commission began investigating business misconduct and asked publicly traded corporations to carry out internal audits to identify inappropriate trading practices. GTE's audit uncovered its shady deals with Philippine Telecommunications Investment, and in February

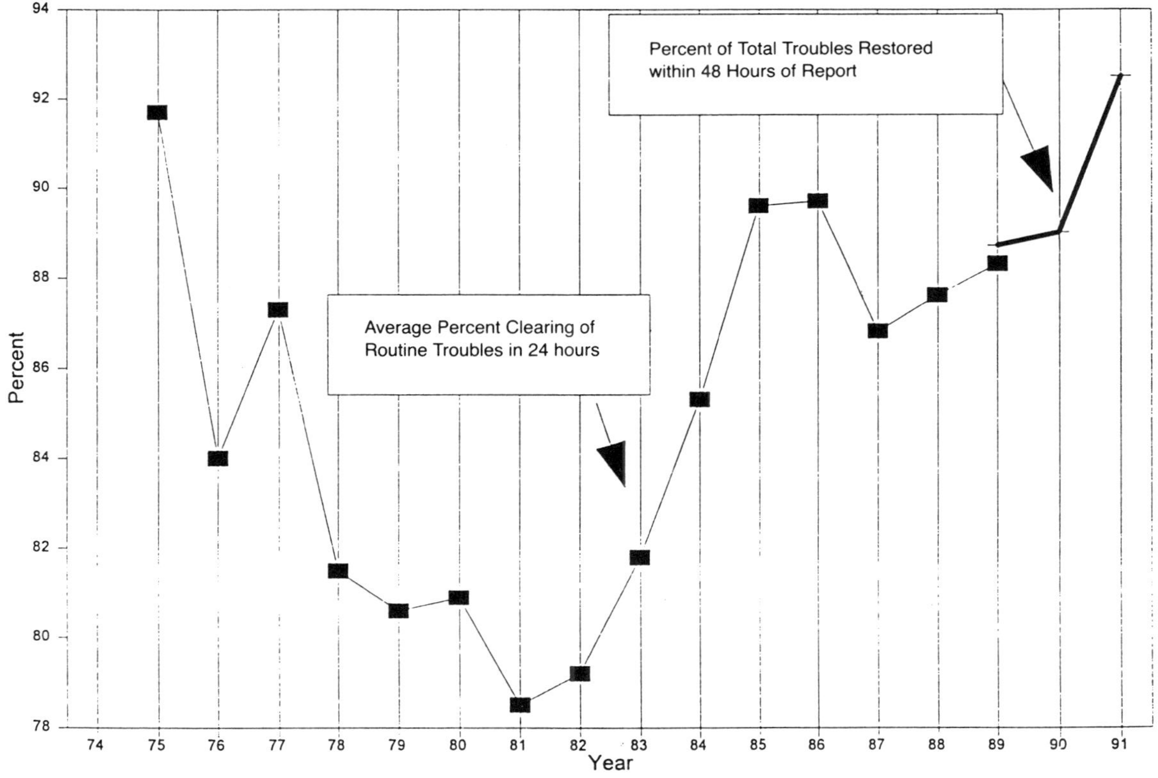

Percent of Total Troubles Restored within 48 Hours of Report
Average Percent Clearing of Routine Troubles in 24 hours
Percent
94
92
90
88
86
84
82
80
78
74
75
76
77
78
79
80
81
82
83
84
85
86
87
88
89
90
91
Year

Figure 5.13. Quality of services, 1974–91.

1976 GTE halted its arrangements with the Cojuangco group, informing them that commission payments would stop. It also refused to pay some $1.7 million that the group had earned under the existing arrangements (General Telephone and Electronics Corporation 1976, 22). GTE maintained its stake in PTIC, however. In January 1977 the U.S. SEC filed a complaint against the PTIC group. PLDT would find it difficult to borrow and invest while its contracts with GTE were being terminated and the U.S. Securities and Exchange Commission was preparing an indictment against it. Although the case was quickly settled out of court, the conflict with GTE continued until December 1977, when the GTE quietly "abandoned" its PTIC shares.[32] This resolution of the matter freed PLDT to resume its investments.

The only visible improvements in the network during these years were in the number of domestic and international long-distance circuits (see Figure 5.3). Many of the circuits were rented from related telecommunications companies – firms that were franchised as carriers' carriers. An important supplier for the domestic long-distance network was Domestic Satellite Philippines (Domsat), a company chaired by Ramon Cojuangco and directed by a number of well-known Marcos cronies (De Luna 1986). The main suppliers on the international side were Philcomsat, Philippine Global Communications (PhilCom), and Eastern Telecommunications Philippines (Eastern Telecom), all highly profitable firms owned largely by the same group of Marcos associates and front companies. They also had close interlocking interests with PLDT (De Luna 1986).

Philcomsat's background has already been discussed. The history of the other firms is similar. PhilCom began in the 1920s as a subsidiary of Radio Corporation of America (RCA), providing international telegraph and telephone services. By 1974 it was 60 percent Filipino owned, with Defense Minister Enrile's family corporation, Jaka Investments, and some PLDT directors as major shareholders (De Luna 1986).[33] Eastern Telecom was established in 1974 by more or less the same group that had formed Philcomsat, with the British firm, Cable and Wireless, holding a 40 percent stake. The verified share of President Marcos in these companies was about 40 percent of the Filipino-owned capital (Isberto 1986).

This interrelated structure of enterprises provided an important channel for directing PLDT's profits. For example, Philcomsat's profits over the 1966–89 period was far larger than those of PLDT (Isberto 1986). This structure also permitted investment in long-distance services unaffected by PLDT's troubles. The demand constraint in the earlier years affected only local telephone service, not long distance. The greater concentration of income during the period implied rising demand for long-distance services, an opportunity quickly seized by the elite with interests in the sector. With the backing of the administration, they launched new projects, including two new firms, Domsat and Eastern Telecom. Thus, PLDT's behavior seems to be an anomaly, a consequence of the decline in local-service demand and an intensification of international scrutiny. In all likelihood, then, growth and investment in the telecommunications sector would have moved into the expansion pattern predicted by the political-economy analysis had these two factors not intervened.

Entry into the telecommunications sector increased after martial law (implication 10). Previously, entry had been restricted because obtaining a franchise from the Congress was politically costly. Under martial law President Marcos could grant franchises at will, and he used this power to arrange for entry into the growing long-distance telecommunications markets for firms to which he had ties. To avoid conflict among his associates, particularly, between PLDT and the newly established firms, Marcos restricted the new franchises to message or data communications. They were, of course, allowed to lease their circuits to PLDT for voice transmission.

An endgame effect, with abundant supplies of foreign credit, 1978–85

The events in the Philippines between 1978 and 1985 clearly exposed the fundamental flaw in the country's underlying institutional structure. The weakness of the government in committing itself as an institution transcending individuals meant that members of the ruling elite would be compelled to cut back sharply on investments inside the country as soon as they sensed an imminent change in the political balance, even though they still had access to ample supplies of foreign credit and could ensure profitability in their businesses. The experience of the telecommunications sector in 1978–85 conforms to this pattern (implications 3–7, 9, and 11). PLDT received favorable treatment from the government that helped boost real telephone rates and provide access to enormous foreign loans. Yet PLDT's net investment in local service was modest, and its real rates of return were negative.

Indications of a crack in Marcos's authoritarian regime started to appear in the late 1970s, with rumors of his illness. In hopes of institutionalizing the extraordinary powers of the president under the 1973 constitution and resolving the succession crisis, Marcos launched a "normalization" process. Reforms were introduced in several areas, but to little substantive effect. Cronies used every arm of government to squeeze as much as possible from the economy. They were not interested in investment. The economy slowed, inflation mounted, and foreign debt and capital flight soared (see Figure 5.1). Opposition leaders saw an opportunity to bring down the Marcos regime and intensified their efforts. When Senator Aquino was assassinated in 1983, foreign lenders, worried that they might be unable to

187

collect on loans to Marcos's cronies should the regime collapse, quickly cut off new loans. The country entered into economic as well as political crisis.

Meanwhile, the authorities in the telecommunications sector were providing favorable treatment to PLDT and other firms with ties to Marcos. The National Telecommunications Commission, the new regulatory agency formed in 1979 by merging the Board of Communications and the Radio Control Bureau, approved major discretionary rate increases in 1980 and 1984. These increases, along with the automatic adjustment provision, reversed the downward trend in local and domestic long-distance tariffs (see Figures 5.7 and 5.8). Also, under a policy of sectoral integration and rationalization, PLDT was encouraged to take over several smaller telephone companies. These companies had been denied access to PLDT's network and, with real local rates falling, had become losing operations. The most important was Republic Telephone Company (Retelco), the second largest telephone firm in the Philippines, with a local network approximately one-tenth the size of PLDT's and bordering PLDT's area of operation on the outskirts of Manila. When the initial negotiations for the sale of Retelco stalled in 1980, President Marcos appointed a special committee to resolve the matter. Soon after the takeover agreement in early 1981, local rates were increased by 35 percent.

To enable PLDT to borrow more in international markets than its equity warranted, state-owned banks were directed to purchase nonconvertible, nonvoting preferred shares in PLDT (Gonzaga 1982). In the early 1980s such purchases supplied about 10 to 16 percent of PLDT's real equity without affecting PTIC's control of the company.

Given the ample availability of credit, PLDT's volume of investment and its debt-equity ratio rose substantially as it embarked on a new expansion project (X-4) in 1978 (Figures 5.2 and 5.14). However, the increase in investment spending did not translate into a commensurate expansion of the local telephone network: during the rapid expansion phase of 1978–83 real capital stock measured at cost grew at an average annual rate of 19.3 percent, the number of main lines in service by only 6.7 percent (Figures 5.2 and 5.12).[34] In contrast, during the earlier expansion phase of 1965–70, growth rates of capital stock at 26 percent and main lines at 23 percent were more in line with each other.

The investments of 1978–85 seem to have gone mainly into expanding domestic and international long-distance networks (see Figure 5.3) and improving the quality of service, especially for long-distance-related services such as direct dialing and digitalization. Indeed, these investments helped shift the composition of revenues toward long-distance services by leaps and bounds (see Figure 5.11), even though real prices of local services were rising while those of long-distance services were not (see Figures 5.5–5.8). Thus, the pattern of investment seems to conform to implications 5 and 11.

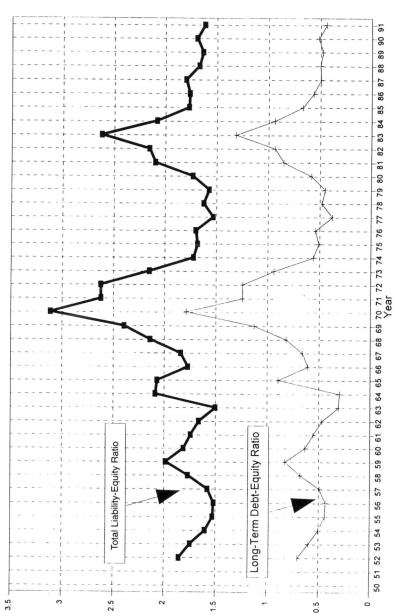

Figure 5.14. Liability-equity ratios (based on real values in 1967 prices).

Considering the increases in real local service rates and the rapidly rising long-distance revenues, PLDT's real rates of return should have improved after 1978. Instead, they worsened (see Figure 5.12). The increase in PLDT's franchise tax from 1 to 2 percent of gross revenues that took effect in 1978 does not seem to account for the decline, as a comparison of before- and after-tax rates of return shows (see Figure 5.4). The substantial increase in interest rates during the late 1970s and early 1980s may have played a role. But if so, why did PLDT accelerate its rate of borrowing during 1979–83 despite consistently negative rates of return? It could be that the owners were anticipating large returns in a more distant future, but that they would maintain such a high level of investment in the face of continued losses on equity over several years strains credulity.

More plausibly, perhaps, profitability really was high, but it surfaced elsewhere. That would explain the high rate of borrowing and investment in long-distance services while the company was losing money. Some implicit evidence supporting this hypothesis was given in the previous section, in the discussion of PTIC's connections with carriers' carriers and with PLDT's equipment and service suppliers. Sison (1986) and De Luna (1986) offer further evidence of business dealings with companies related to PLDT's directors and managers and suggest that these companies were quite profitable. An example of such a company was Electric Telephone Systems Industries, established in the Philippines as a joint venture between Siemens of Germany (30 percent share), Independent Realty (a Marcos front company, 42 percent share), and two other companies related to PLDT directors (De Luna 1986). This venture served as PLDT's main conduit of equipment purchases from Siemens, which after 1978 replaced GTE as PLDT's main equipment supplier. The extensive powers of Marcos exercised under martial law made it easier for his cronies to carry out more of their transactions inside the Philippines and thereby evade damaging international scrutiny.

The picture that emerges for the period 1978–83 is that of a telecommunications company with friendly ties to the administration that is given the opportunity to earn high profits, take over the assets of other companies, and borrow heavily. Because it is a publicly traded company controlled by minority shareholders, its profits are channeled to more exclusive accounts. And because the company is concerned about the stability of the administration, it hesitates to expand the local network, except where the expansion facilitates long-distance services.

As the disintegration of the Marcos regime accelerated in 1984–5 and the economy collapsed, PLDT's investment came to a complete halt, and attempts to secure capital abroad intensified. The evidence on capital flight in this period is extensive (Sison 1986), and there is no disputing that PLDT's managers deliberately failed to remit foreign exchange earnings in 1985 (Friedland 1988).[35] This effect is also reflected in the sudden decline in international long-distance revenue as a share of total revenues in 1985 (see Figure 5.11).

Regime shift, political turmoil, and regulatory activism, 1986–9

The anti-Marcos coalition that took over in 1986 included a broad range of interests with many differences to settle. During the period of turmoil that ensued, political activism among the nonelite increased. Regulatory conflict would be expected to arise between PLDT and the new government (implication 8) and investment to come to a halt in the local network (implication 5), though not necessarily in international circuits (implication 11). In fact, these are precisely the events that transpired in the early years of the new Aquino administration.

PLDT's first skirmish came less than three weeks after the inauguration, shortly after the establishment of the Presidential Commission on Good Government. The commission moved quickly to sequester PLDT's assets and to appoint a supervisory committee, headed by attorney Luis F. Sison, to oversee its management. A few days later, the committee's task was specified as the investigation of the company's connections with Marcos and its past business practices. Numerous allegations were leveled against those in control of the company. In particular, Marcos's holdings in Philippine Telecommunications Investment Corporation were identified and expropriated.[36] The sequestration was lifted on 2 May.

On 18 June, with the commission representing the sequestered Marcos shares, PLDT shareholders elected new members to the board of directors. Oscar Africa, from a prominent family with significant interests in other Philippine telecommunications firms, retired as president and was replaced by Antonio Cojuangco, Ramon's young son and a relative of President Aquino. The commission placed two of its members, Benjamin Guingona and Mario Locsin, on the PLDT board. Over the following months, they reexamined the company's business practices and issued a more positive report about its management. Eventually, the commission set the whole matter of PLDT "anomalies" aside.[37]

Meanwhile, in mid-April, the Philippine Bureau of Internal Revenue filed income tax deficiency claims against all telecommunications firms in the country for the period 1969–85. The firms maintained that the franchise tax had been intended to replace all other taxes. In a case involving Radio Communications of the Philippines, the Supreme Court disagreed, arguing that the tax code of June 1968 had implicitly repealed the income tax exemption of the franchisees because it made no exceptions for this purpose (*Business Day*, 12 June 1986). PLDT, acting more cautiously, dealt with the matter on a case-by-case basis, eventually convincing the

191

bureau to withdraw most of the tax deficiency assessments against the company. It was unable to evade Executive Order 27 of 25 November 1986, which assessed a 35 percent corporate income tax on all franchise holders and increased the franchise tax from 2 to 3 percent of gross revenue. These new taxes seem to have captured about 10 to 11 percent of PLDT's gross revenues and reduced the real rate of return on economic assets by about 4 percent (see Figures 5.4 and 5.15).

During the same period the National Telecommunications Commission ordered a 10 percent cut in PLDT's local residential tariffs "to make telephones more affordable" (Friedland 1988), but there was no change in other service rates or in the automatic foreign exchange adjustment provision.[38] Later, the commission became active in regulating PLDT's interconnection with the small local operators, setting a minimum share of long-distance revenues for the small operators to help them expand and improve their services. These changes probably cost PLDT about 3 to 4 percent of its gross revenues – much less than the cost of the new taxes.

In the first few years of the Aquino administration, the wide range of represented interests impeded the development of clear policy objectives and left individual government officials with broad discretionary authority. The new government seemed to prefer expropriating PLDT's assets through tax increases rather than rate reductions. The main common interest in these actions was to increase government resources. Explicit expropriation of PLDT was ruled out by the president, as the failed sequestration attempt in March 1986 made clear. PhilCom and Philcomsat also managed to avoid sequestration, because their patron, Defense Minister Enrile, who had participated in the coalition against Marcos, succeeded in retaining his post for a while (Isberto 1986). But Philcomsat lost its unregulated status and was ordered by the regulatory commission to cut its rates. Other Marcos-related firms, such as Domsat and Eastern Telecom, were less successful in evading penalties: their Filipino-owned shares were sequestered and new directors were appointed.

The presence of new interests represented in the government were also reflected in the desire to reverse the Marcos administration's policy of sectoral "consolidation," by allowing new entry into the sector. Ironically, this reversal was largely based on the entry authorized by Marcos. The regulatory commission began issuing Certificates of Public Convenience and Necessity for firms with franchises that could be interpreted as relevant. In particular, the commission authorized a number of small operators to establish new services, such as cellular telephony and paging, in competition with PLDT. In 1989 the commission approved applications by PhilCom and Eastern Telecom to establish their own direct international telephone service (gateway). The idea was to give these firms an incentive to develop local networks in less developed regions and to spur PDLT to expand as well. PLDT chal-

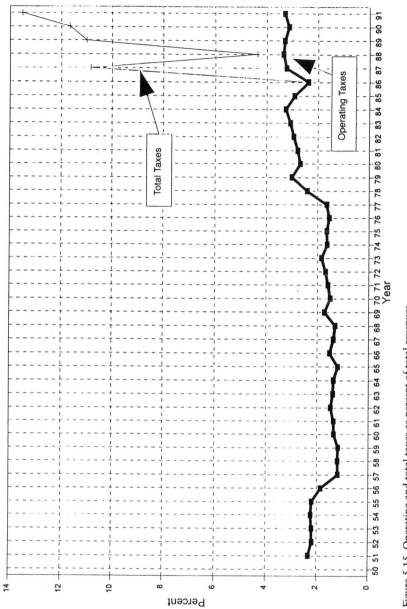

Figure 5.15. Operating and total taxes as percent of total revenues.

lenged most of these authorizations, and though it was initially unsuccessful, it managed to get some of the key decisions of the regulators reversed.

Another policy initiative based on similar concerns was the National Telecommunications Plan, developed by the Department of Transportation and Communications. Under the plan the government would use official development assistance funds to build telecommunications facilities in areas where they would not be in competition with the private sector. Once established, the projects would be transferred to the private sector through a competitive process. PLDT would be eligible to participate in the privatization process, but it would have to compete with other firms. Around the same time PLDT was denied access to a concessional loan offered by West Germany's export credit agency on the grounds that the company was too profitable to receive access to scarce development funds (Friedland 1988).

In addition to changes in the regulatory environment, PLDT faced difficult foreign borrowing conditions because of its own accumulated debt and because of debt rescheduling negotiations between the government and foreign creditors. Although the company benefited from a temporary debt service moratorium and rescheduling, new credit was difficult to obtain. The controlling PTIC group decided to let the domestic network stagnate until the dust had settled, though investment in international circuits continued. A major fiber-optic submarine cable project was completed in 1989. The group also used its capital to expand its activities in sectors and service areas where policy commitment was less problematic. For example, PLDT's related company, Piltel, broke into cellular telephony service.

PLDT's financing problems and slow growth were viewed by many in the government as stemming from the PTIC group's fear of losing control – the group could increase its equity in the company at only a limited rate and did not want to share control with new investors who would be willing to contribute more. This view, however, ignores the fact that PLDT had managed to borrow heavily before (far more than its real equity would have justified) whenever it was confident of government support for a few years (see Figure 5.14). As the company's history suggests, the financing problem is a consequence more of the weakness of government commitment capacity than of a shortage of funds or equity that the PTIC group could commit to PLDT. Members of the PTIC group have substantial assets outside the telecommunications sector and continue to make new investments elsewhere.[39] If they were assured of a comparable rate of return in the local telephone network, there would be no reason not to invest at a more rapid pace.

"Normalization" and entry restrictions, 1990–2

The events of 1990–2 show that under the country's settled, nonauthoritarian political institutions, entry into the telecommunications sector is difficult (implication 10). Also, increased political competition and influence by the nonelite can keep prices down (implication 8). But under the existing institutional structure this mainly gives rise to excess demand since entry barriers remain strong (implication 10). Finally, events in this period show that the government tries to privatize the telephone systems it has developed before the end of the president's term in office (implication 4).

By 1990 the new competitive political system had weathered several crises and become more settled. The leadership also had become more cohesive, as the elite regained control and reestablished the institutions through which they exercised control, although nonelite groups, especially the middle class, had more influence than in the past.

The PTIC group managed to improve its political standing with the elite groups that finally won out in the leadership struggle. The influence of the Cojuangco family in the legislature and the bureaucracy and its control of a major newspaper turned government policies toward PLDT more favorable and ensured that the representatives of the Good Government Commissions on the boards of PTIC and PLDT would remain inactive (Tiglao 1933a). However, the increased competitiveness of politics kept a lid on telephone rates (see Figures 5.5–5.8), and the uncertainty about the post-Aquino administration slowed PLDT's investment in its local network. The number of unfilled applications for new lines soared, and many undeveloped areas remained without telephones (see Figure 5.9).

Some in the government had hoped that the competition stimulated by the authorizations of new gateways and services would bring about a fundamental change in the sector and enable it to meet the growing demand. But the road to competition proved a rough one, thanks largely to the reinvigorated franchise system whose strong antientry bias flourished once again under the more normal political conditions of 1990–2.

PLDT's appeals to the Supreme Court also threw some obstacles in the way of greater competition. The court agreed with PLDT that Eastern Telecom's franchise allowed it to carry only "messages," not "voice." Supporting the decision was the argument that PLDT had "sufficient" international circuits and so there was no "necessity" for another company to operate additional circuits (*Manila Bulletin*, 29 August 1992). This was in sharp contrast with the court's earlier decision that the mobile telephony authorization granted to Extelcom was valid because competition would be in the public's interest (Gavino 1992, section IV.B6.). Curiously, PLDT did not challenge PhilCom's gateway in the courts and even granted it interconnection, apparently because of common interests between owners of the two companies.[40] Also, Eastern had established a partner company, Digitel, to invest in a system of local networks in areas not covered by PLDT, whereas PhilCom had been less ambitious in that respect. Digitel has been unsuccessful, however, in gaining a national franchise. Without it, establishing an efficient-size network in a contiguous area is nearly impossible. Even Extelcom, which had won out against PLDT, had a hard time getting interconnection until its major shareholder, Ruby Tiong-Tan, sold her shares to an undisclosed buyer.[41]

When the government moved to privatize two projects developed under the National Telecommunications Plan, initially those who favored a strong competition policy prevailed. Companies without franchises were permitted to bid for the projects on the assumption that the companies could operate the systems on a lease basis for five years while their franchise requests were pending. Thus, Digitel, which still had no franchise, was allowed to participate, and it submitted the highest bid. Soon after the results of the bidding were announced, the Secretary of Justice issued the opinion that it would be illegal for Digitel to run the projects without a franchise. The Department of Transportation and Communication decided to cancel the results and called for new bids. Digitel filed suit and managed to get the rebidding postponed, but its managers realized that pursuing the case would involve a protracted court battle.

By the time the post-Marcos regime had settled in, the Aquino administration was approaching the end of its term. Although PLDT had gained strong support within all branches of government, it invested slowly. Profitability could not have been the problem. The company's profitability was on the rise, and a number of firms were pushing hard to enter the market. PLDT even fought to reserve for itself underdeveloped regions and services in which it had no plans to invest any time soon. Clearly, all the parties involved considered the investment opportunities in the sector to be highly profitable. Those in control of PLDT succeeded in restricting entry, but they did not risk their own investment resources. They must have been seriously concerned about the government's inability to guarantee them a competitive rate of return beyond the end of the Aquino administration.

Events took a new turn under the administration of Fidel Ramos, who took office in June 1992. Ramos decided to support the entry of new telecommunications firms and to dismantle PLDT's monopoly (Tiglao 1993a). In February 1993 he presided at the signing ceremony for a joint venture between Globe Telecom of the Philippines and Singapore Telecom International, which hoped to take over a big part of the market from PLDT (Tiglao 1993b). The president's office also reversed the decision by the previous administration on rebidding the disputed privatization projects and allowed Digitel to operate them (Tiglao 1993c). The administration asked the Supreme Court to reconsider its ruling against Eastern Telecom, a request made shortly after the author of the decision, Justice Hugo Gutierrez, resigned following allegations that the ruling had been written by a PLDT lawyer (Panaligan 1993).[42] More recently, President Ramos replaced the representatives of the Good Government Commission on the boards of directors of PTIC and PLDT, who had been accused of failing to vigorously represent the government's interests (Tiglao 1993c).[43] PLDT now seems to be financially hard pressed, and financial analysts predict that its profitability may decline sharply in the next few years.

LESSONS AND APPROACHES TO REFORM

The political structure in the Philippines has been shaped by the desire of a small elite to maintain political and economic power by concentrating power in the executive, leaving the legislature and the judiciary relatively weak. Since the president can modify or reinterpret laws secure in the knowledge that the judiciary is unlikely to rule to the contrary, specific regulations to limit rent extraction by the government are not very effective. Getting such constraints in place is a difficult task, with little political payoff. The formal restrictions that do exist are effective mostly when they take the form of congressional veto power, for example, Congress's role in controlling entry into public utilities through the franchise system. Other constraints on executive power are largely informal, exercised through personal relationships.

The regulatory system in the Philippines is weak and ineffective and lacks specific and transparent rules as a result of the same forces that have weakened the judiciary. With the elite maintaining control over the professionals who are supposed to serve as "referees," the government as an institution cannot commit itself to hold to certain policies and to rule out opportunistic regulations. This environment induces a cyclical movement in the investment of telecommunications firms, characterized by short periods of expansion and long spells of stagnation. Firms grow mainly during the early years of administrations with which they have close ties. At other times they grow slowly or stagnate, because of concern about the possibility of opportunistic regulations.

The most fundamental way to bring about improvements in the Philippine regulatory system is to shift the balance of power toward the legislature and the judiciary, institutions with inherently greater stability and continuity than the executive branch. The need for such a broad institutional realignment has long been recognized in the Philippines and, indeed, in the late 1960s and early 1970s a constitutional reform of this type became the main item on the agenda for the political movements in the country. Unfortunately, that attempt backfired, and the Philippines was put under unchecked authoritarian rule for a decade and a half. The system put in place after years of martial law is more open to the nonelite than was its premartial law predecessor and may eventually evolve toward a more balanced structure. However, short of such a fundamental institutional change, what are the prospects for the telecommunications sector?

197

A number of important reform opportunities emerged under the new political coalition that came to dominate the government after the fall of Marcos. This group had strained relationships with the telecommunications firms, most of which had fallen under Marcos's circle of influence. The members of the new government were interested, at least initially, in increasing the flow of resources through the government. They also favored increased entry into the sector by private firms. These interests were manifested in two developments after 1986: the government began to invest in underdeveloped areas using official development assistance funds, and entry by new firms was facilitated by a liberal interpretation of the franchise rules. The cost-effectiveness of most of the investments has been low, and the projects have been earmarked for privatization.

Though PLDT still has enough clout in Congress to stem any incipient tidal wave of new franchises, many firms already held specialized franchises that allowed them to operate in narrow fields without effectively competing with PLDT. This system of franchises proliferated under Marcos, who allowed his associates to divide the surplus of the sector among themselves. After 1986, when some of the firms with ties to Marcos were placed in new hands, the National Telecommunications Commission, liberally interpreting the scope of their existing franchises, allowed the firms to expand into areas controlled by PLDT.

The regulators hoped that investment by the expanding firms and the response to this competition by PLDT would invigorate the sector. They also expected that privatization of government assets would provide opportunities for the expanding firms to gain a foothold in their new fields. It is not clear whether these policies are working. Until recently, PLDT managed to hold back some of the expanding telecommunications firms by challenging the new interpretations of their franchises in the courts. In other cases, conflicts with new entrants were resolved largely through interlocking interests among firms (for example, PhilCom, the new entrant into international telecommunications service, shares common directors and stockholders with PLDT).

Despite disappointing results so far, current policies show a new potential for reform in which international organizations like the World Bank may be able to play important roles. Among these potentials for reform are the following.

More specific rules

In the absence of a strong judiciary, getting specific regulatory procedures in place to control rent extraction may not be worth the effort, especially in the case of complex rules requiring expert judgment, whose impartiality is often questioned. A few simple and transparent rules might prove effective, however. Indexation to inflation with a limited range of adjustment toward the end of each presidential term is one example. Although such rules are typically rigid and create inefficiencies of their own, they are likely to lead to better outcomes than the current discretionary system.

Other, specific rules can also be applied to improve allocative efficiency, though they do not restrict rent extraction. Making the cross-subsidization from international long distance to local services more explicit can improve incentives for investment in the local network. Under the current system, cross-subsidies are implicit: local rates are kept low and PLDT is allowed to earn its profits from long-distance services. This system induces heavier investment in long-distance services and neglect of local services. One way to ameliorate the problem is to explicitly subsidize local telephone rates, say by assigning the proceeds from a specific tax on international calls to a fund that can be drawn on only if the company invests in local services. This mechanism can improve allocative efficiency and channel more investment to the sorely neglected local network.

Greater independence of regulatory agencies

A bill has been introduced that would grant greater independence to the National Telecommunications Commission through self-financing and fixed tenure for the commissioner. These changes could reduce the risk of implicit expropriation by relieving political pressures on the regulators. A regulatory body that is financially and politically independent could more successfully withstand changes in the political climate. Such reforms could also provide greater resources and incentives for developing the regulatory capabilities required to foster efficient operation in a field as technologically dynamic as telecommunications. Independence may raise the possibility of easier capture of regulators by the regulated firms, but a more severe problem of capture already exists under the current system, when the firm has ties with the executive. Capture cannot be a serious problem when the regulated firm lacks close ties with the executive because, in that case, the government will press the regulatory body to keep service prices down and, indeed, it is more likely to be successful if there is overpricing. Separation of the regulatory commission from the executive makes it difficult for either of them to unilaterally implement grossly one-sided policies, strengthening the system's checks-and-balances mechanisms.

A major benefit of regulatory independence is that it offers stronger incentives for developing the agency's expertise and capabilities since important regulatory policies will be made by the commission rather than being dictated from above. An example of the benefits of greater granting of independence can be seen in the case of the Commission on Elections which moved to reduce ballot box fraud after gaining increased independence and helped to legitimize elections.

Another argument in favor of regulatory independence is that once the regulators begin to act independently of the government, Congress will find it necessary to design more specific rules to restrain the commissioners. A combination of regulatory independence and specific rules can greatly improve the quality and stability of regulations and make policies more credible. Getting a bill of this kind through Congress may not be an easy matter in the current political economy of the Philippines, although the new active forces in government may present the opportunity for effective regulatory reforms.

Increased competition

Pressures for relaxing entry barriers have intensified, although progress has so far been mixed. Under the Philippine institutional setup an important advantage of having multiple firms is that at a point in time at least some of the firms will find the government supportive and will have an incentive to invest. And to the extent that discriminatory treatment can be challenged in court, favorable treatment for some is likely to mean at least reasonable treatment for all. That is all the more likely to be the case since cancellation of franchises and authorization certificates is not easy for the government for the same reasons that getting them in the first place is difficult. As a result, there can be greater hope of policy continuity since each administration will have some incentive to maintain existing regulations. Greater diversity of interests in the sector would thus enhance policy stability and private sector confidence in the system.

In the context of the political-economy of the Philippines, a greater number of firms does not necessarily mean increased competition since the possibility of collusion is not ruled out. Indeed, there are reasons to believe that collusion rather than competition would be the outcome of freer entry: firms that manage to enter the market are likely to be associated with the coalition in control of the executive branch. While political turnover may modestly increase the number of firms in the sector over time, unless powerful new political forces gain influence in the government having a larger number of firms does not imply removal of entry barriers that allow incumbent firms to block competition by the new firms. As a result, successful entrants firms have an incentive to cooperate rather than compete. This tendency may explain why the entry of new firms in cellular and international long-distance telephone services has not provoked the kind of vigorous competition expected in these highly profitable areas. Thus, entry by itself may not generate the arms-length competition that is conducive to efficiency and growth.

Of course, over time the entry of more and more firms may by itself establish a new norm, and competition may eventually emerge, especially if political coalitions continue to shift and the threat of rent extraction by unfriendly administrations diminishes. But establishing new norms in this way may take a long time. A more immediately effective reform would be to regularize and ease the process of awarding franchises, in order to reduce the ability of incumbent firms to keep potential entrants out. Easing entry for new firms will have greater impact if combined with more extensive use of transparent specific rules and increased political and financial independence for the regulatory agency.

Besides the official impediments, an important obstacle to the growth of competition is PLDT's domination of local networks and control of interconnections. The weaknesses of the regulatory agency allow PLDT to evade interconnection and stifle other firms with limited local networks. Although PLDT recently agreed to open its facilities to competing phone companies through interconnection (Tiglao 1993c), the problem may not go away easily since there is no guarantee that disputes over details will not arise in the future. However, the problem is likely to diminish if other operators gain control of large local networks. Of course, the most effective solution is to establish and enforce reasonable interconnection rights.

International commitment mechanisms

International political and financial institutions, which have been relatively effective in enforcing the country's foreign borrowing contracts, might be able to substitute to some extent for missing domestic institutions in providing assurances to investors, perhaps through conditions attached to loans. For a long time after the Philippines gained independence, the United States government played a similar role for U.S. investments in the Philippines. Exactly how foreign institutions become involved in a country's domestic policy concerns in a productive way is a complex and subtle issue. As the analysis here has shown, the enforceability of foreign lending contracts has sometimes been used by the ruling elite to facilitate capital flight, to the detriment of the country. Similarly, an administration with friendly ties to telecommunications firms may want to use the power of international institutions to guarantee monopoly profits for the firms during future administrations. To prevent such abuses, international commitment mechanisms need to be combined with carefully crafted rules verifiable by outsiders (an example might be a simplified version of Chilean-style price regulation based on long-run marginal cost pricing for a putatively efficient firm).

6

Argentina: The sequencing of privatization and regulation

ALICE HILL AND MANUEL ANGEL ABDALA

Argentina is a very recent entrant to the small group of countries with privately owned telecommunications firms – and, given its history, an unexpected one. Argentina entered this group in November 1990 when the government sold the Empresa Nacional de Telecomunicaciones (ENTeL) to private investors. Although it is too early to definitively assess the impact of this sale, the sequencing of the privatization and the development of a regulatory regime present some interesting issues.

The political situation during the transition from the administration of

The authors are grateful to the many individuals in Argentina and at the World Bank Group who were so generous with their time. They are responsible for most of the insights in this paper; the errors are all ours. In Argentina we would like to thank Ing. Maria Julia Alsogaray, Intervenor for ENTeL; Dr. Alberto Abad, Sindicatura General de Empresas Publicas; Dr. Henoch Aguiar; Dr. Jose Luis Baranda Leturio, Telefónica de Argentina; Ing. Raul Barido, Sindicatura General de Empresas Publicas; Lic. Roberto Cappa, Sindicatura General de Empresas Publicas; Dr. Rinaldo Colome, Comision Nacional de Telecomunicaciones; Lic. Hebe Franciulli de Zumaran, Impsat; Dr. Roberto Garasino, Compañía Argentina de Teléfonos; Dr. Jorge Grinpelc, Coopers and Lybrand Harteneck Lopez; Dr. German Kammerath, Subsecretary of Communications; Dr. Hector Mairal; Ing. Hugo Marias, Impsat; Ing. Juan Carlos Masjoan, Telecom Argentina; Dr. Jose Palazzo, Comision Nacional de Telecomunicaciones; Ing. Raul Parodi; Dr. Federico Pinedo, Comision Nacional de Telecomunicaciones; Dr. Adolfo Rinaldi, Telecom Argentina; Dr. Jose Miguel Romero, Coopers and Lybrand Harteneck Lopez; Dr. Rodolfo Terragno, Fundación Argentina Siglo XXI; Dr. Ricardo Tomaselli, Telefónica de Argentina; Dr. Edgardo Volosin, Telecom Argentina; and Dr. Ricardo Zinn, Fundación Carlos Pellegrini. We would also like to thank the following individuals in the World Bank and the International Finance Corporation: Mr. Stefan Alber-Glanstaetten, Ms. Myrna Alexander, Mr. Guillermo Argumedo, Mr. Lewis Boorstin, Mr. Ahmed Galal, Ms. Maria del Carmen Campollo Palmer, Mr. Carlos Corti, Ms. Maria Dakolias, Mr. Alfredo Dammert, Mrs. Mahyar Eshragh-Tabary, Mr. Brian Levy, Mr. Paul Meo, Mr. Peter Scherer, Mr. Mihkel Sergo, Ms. Mary Shirley, Mr. Eloy Vidal, and Mr. Bjorn Wellenius. We would also like to thank Professors Hadi Esfahani and Pablo Spiller of the University of California at Berkeley and Mathew McCubbins of the University of California, San Diego. Manuel Abdala would also like to acknowledge the invaluable assistance of Santiago Cunco, Enrique Neder, and Marcelo Schoeters.

President Raúl Alfonsín to that of President Carlos Saul Menem in 1989 presented the Menem government with a brief opportunity to introduce radical economic reform. Privatization was a central component of this reform program, and ENTeL was the first company put on the block. The sale became a test of the Menem government's ability and resolve to reform the economy. Rapid completion of the sale was the overriding concern, and development of a regulatory regime initially was neglected.

Regulation plays an important role in the private provision of telecommunications. Portions of the sector are characterized by economies of scale, making an argument for limiting entry in the interests of efficiency. However, inadequate competition can lead to abuses of monopoly power and to demands from customers and suppliers for regulatory protection from these abuses. Standards and interconnection rules affect the efficiency of the sector. High sunk costs and asset specificity make telecommunications firms especially vulnerable to the risks of expropriation. This problem is compounded by the temptation for opportunistic regulatory behavior that would enable the government to provide benefits for its other constituents by expropriating the sector's assets, whether outright, as in the case of nationalization, or gradually, through service requirements or low rates.

A credible and stable regulatory environment reduces the risk attached to investment and reduces the expected rate of return that private investors would require to induce them to participate.[1] The government's ability to provide a credible and stable regulatory environment depends largely on a country's institutional arrangements, particularly those that provide safeguards against opportunistic government intervention. The design of new regulatory institutions or the reform of old ones can create new safeguards, but existing institutions will constrain the options available.

Privatization adds another dimension to the role of regulation in reducing investment risk. Having a stable and credible regulatory regime in place *before* privatization increases the value of a firm to potential purchasers by reducing the risk associated with the purchase and therefore increases the price the selling government will receive. Failure to establish such a regime first will depress the sale price and increase the probability that the buyers will capture windfall profits if a stable regulatory regime is introduced after the sale. In addition, the privatization process can itself create new safeguards. Widespread domestic shareholding in the privatized company can create a new constituency that would resist government attempts to expropriate assets for the benefit of other constituencies. Transparency and predictability in the privatization process are important signals of the government's later intentions.

In the case of ENTeL the Argentine government used the privatization to establish its reform credentials. The need for a postprivatization regulatory regime was given lower priority and as a result, a well-defined regulatory regime was not in place before the sale. Nonetheless, the privatization appears to have had a net positive impact on Argentina's reputation and its welfare. In this instance it seems that the reform program generated its own virtuous cycle, creating and reinforcing credibility in the short run. Neglect of the regulatory regime appears to have been costly, however, in terms of the sale price obtained by the government and the rate structure demanded by investors. This neglect may also have a negative impact on performance of the sector in the long run.

This examination attempts to answer several questions. First, why and how did the economic reform program and the privatization of ENTeL come about? The dynamics of Argentine politics help explain why government policies have often undermined Argentina's economic development. Why this pattern changed during the presidential transition from Alfonsin to Menem is explored in the context of Argentina's institutional heritage and the problems that institutions posed for ensuring the credibility of the new reform program. Second, has Argentina avoided regulatory failure in the privatization process and in the subsequent definition implementation of its regulatory regime? Has the government demonstrated its commitment to an environment that will support private investment, and are the newly privatized companies responding by investing and improving services? The privatization of ENTeL is dissected to determine whether the process itself enhanced the government's credibility as a regulator. Third, what lessons does Argentina's experience with privatization and regulation have to offer and what additional actions might the government consider taking? Finally, what impact has the privatization and subsequent establishment of a regulatory regime had on welfare?

ARGENTINA'S POLITICAL AND INSTITUTIONAL HERITAGE

Political volatility has taken its toll on Argentina's economy. Decades of destructive factional competition have undermined economic and political development. By the late 1980s Paul H. Lewis observed in *The Crisis of Argentine Capitalism* that "Argentina fascinates students of development because, in so many respects, it seems to be going backward. Although it possesses many modern institutions, they are decaying rapidly" (1990). The liberal, market-oriented economic policies introduced by the Menem government are a departure for the country, and they resulted in rapid economic growth (8.5 percent in 1990, 9 percent in 1991), a substantial reduction in inflation, and an increase in investment. To understand how this change came about and whether it will continue requires an examination of the underlying political and economic forces.

Argentina: Privatization and regulation

The dynamics of Argentine politics

Since World War I Argentina has experienced a reversal of political development paralleled by a reversal of economic development.[2] The country appeared to be developing a broad-based participatory democracy in the first three decades of this century, but since the 1930s control of government has fluctuated between authoritarian or exclusionary regimes and populist-corporatist ones (Table 6.1). Since 1930 there have been five military coups and numerous military interventions, resulting in military rule for nineteen of the past sixty years. "Restrictive democracy," in which constitutional niceties were "observed" but major parties were banned, was imposed for an additional nineteen years during this period. Changes of regime have been accompanied by radical changes in policy designed to serve the constituents of the new regime. Successive governments have followed a type of beggar-thy-neighbor strategy, where the "neighbor" has been the constituents of the party out of power. Instead of cooperating to increase economic growth in Argentina, rival parties have competed in a zero-sum or negative-sum game.

This political discontinuity has been accompanied by a downward spiral of economic performance. Before World War I Argentina's per capita income was similar to that of Germany and higher than that of Austria, France, Italy, Japan, and Sweden. Before World War II it was still higher than that of Austria, Italy, and Japan. By 1965, however, per capita income was only one-quarter that of Japan and by 1982 it had fallen to a level comparable to that of Brazil, Chile, and Mexico (Taylor 1992; Waisman 1987).

Argentina's political instability results from interactions among three underlying conditions. First, industrial development has been limited. The economy has long revolved around export-oriented agriculture, the only sector that could generate an economic surplus to support industrial development. Yet government policies have penalized agriculture to the benefit of other sectors, leading to a decline in the surplus generated by agriculture, reducing the country's growth potential, and exacerbating the tensions between the urban working classes and the agrarian elite and urban middle class. The conflict over stagnant or shrinking real income has carried over into the political arena.

Second, the economy of Argentina is split regionally. With a few exceptions, what industry exists is concentrated around Buenos Aires, while agriculture is the dominant economic activity in the rest of the country. This economic split has produced a political split: the interests of the industrialized region, which is highly dependent on import substitution, are at odds with those of the agrarian regions.

Third, and perhaps most important, is the instability created by Argen-

Table 6.1. *Political regimes of Argentina, 1930–92*

President	Period	Means of accession
José F. Uriburu	1930–2 Military revolt	
Augustín P. Justo	1932–8 Election	
Roberto M. Ortiz	1938–40	Election

Ramón S. Castillo
  vice president
	1940–3	Delegation of authority
		  by president

Arturo J. Rawson	1943 Military revolt	
Pedro Pablo Ramírez	1943–4 Coup d'état	
Edelmiro J. Farrell	1944–6	Coup d'état
Juan Domingo Perón	1946–55 Election	
Eduardo Lonardi	1955 Military revolt	
Pedro E. Arambru	1955–8 Coup d'état	
Arturo Frondizi	1958–62 Election	
José M. Guido	1962–3 Coup d'état	
Arturo Illia	1963–6 Election	
Juan Carlos Onganía	1966–70 Military revolt	
Roberto Marcelo Levingston	1970–1 Coup d'état	
Alejandro Augustín Lanusse	1971–3 Coup d'état	
Héctor J. Cámpora	1973 Election	
Juan Domingo Perón	1973–4 Election	
María Estela (Isabel) Martinez de Perón (vice president)	Jul 74–Mar 76	Death of president
Jorge Rafael Videla	May 76–Mar 81	Coup d'état
Roberto Viola	Mar–Dec 81	Resignation of president
Leopoldo Galtieri	Dec 81–June 82 Resignation of president	
Reynaldo B. Bignone	Jul 82–Dec 83	Military revolt
Raúl Alfonsín	Dec 83–Jun 89	Election
Carlos Saul Menem	June 1989–	Election

tine national political institutions and election rules. Argentina is a federal republic with a constitution that provides for federal and provincial levels of government. At the national level executive power is vested in a president, elected by an electoral college to a six-year nonrenewable term, who serves as both chief of state and head of government. The bicameral Congress includes a Chamber of Deputies, whose members are elected by universal adult suffrage from a closed party list, and a Senate, whose members are elected by the provincial legislatures by plurality, with two from each province.

Two features of the congressional electoral rules undermine the potential for cohesive, national party coalitions and increase the probability that the electorate will produce divided partisan governments. First, deputies are elected provincially, not nationally. Candidate lists are controlled by provincial party organizations. As a result same-party deputies from a single province tend to have similar political views, but the views of provincial organizations and the national organization of a particular political party can vary considerably. Second, the timing of elections reinforces the provincialization of the political system. Deputies are elected for four years, senators for nine, so only half the deputies and a third of the senators are elected at the same time as the president. Thus, there is little incentive to nationalize and unify the federal and provincial party organizations. In addition, the staggering of elections means that the composition of any coalition will be constantly changing. A national election involving half the seats in the lower house occurs every other year, while every third year a third of the seats in the Senate are at stake.

As a result, in addition to a diversity of parties, there are significant divisions within parties. The two largest parties today are the Radicals and the Peronists. While the Radicals generally represent the middle class, there are both moderate and extreme factions within the party, and in various periods there has been more than one Radical party. The same is true for the Peronists. While their base is the urban, unionized working class the Peronists have been represented by more than one party, and the party has been segmented into moderate and extreme factions. The effective number of parties in the recent Argentine elections has been more than three, but none of them cut across regional and class divisions (Shugart and Carey 1992).[3]

This destructive pattern of politics began to change after the restoration of democracy and the elections of 1983, when the Radical party won control of the presidency and the Chamber of Deputies, but the Peronist party gained control of the Senate. The stalemate that resulted brought an end to the beggar-thy-neighbor behavior, since the Radicals were unable to pursue their own interests at the expense of the Peronists, but it did not result in cooperative behavior that might have allowed Argentina to improve its economic performance. The economic situation continued to decline, threatening the viability of democratic government. Army rebellions confronted President Alfonsín in April 1987 and December 1988.

The stalemate ended with the elections of 1989 in which the Peronists won control of the presidency and both houses of Congress. This time, however, rather than returning to politics as usual, the Peronists embarked on a program of economic reform. This change seems to have been made possible by a conjunction of events. The Argentine constitution provides for a long transition period between the elections in May and the swearing in in December. During this period in 1989 the economy deteriorated rapidly. Hyperinflation raged for the first time in Argentine history, raising fears of a collapse of economy and the political system.[4]

Faced with the possibility of a return to military rule, the lame-duck Radical party concluded an agreement with the incoming Peronists that allowed President Menem to take office in July, five months ahead of schedule, while in return the Radicals in Congress agreed to support his economic initiatives. This agreement effectively created a coalition between the moderate factions of the Peronist and Radical parties and permitted the introduction of new economic policies to improve the performance of the economy.

Privatization of ENTeL was one of the first actions of a comprehensive reform program that included fiscal reform and tax enforcement, monetary reform, and deregulation. The program sought to fundamentally alter the roles of government, labor, and the private sector. The Menem administration set out to change the reputation of the government and, by extension, the country. The success of the program depended on the government's improving its reputation as an economic actor, and speed in implementing the reform program was critical in establishing and maintaining this reputation. The reform program created its own dynamic, which served to offset Argentina's institutional weaknesses.

Institutional heritage and implications for the credibility of reform

For economic reform to succeed private investors must believe that the reforms will endure over the medium-to-long term. Otherwise, concern about the expropriation of their assets – either directly through nationalization or indirectly through regulation, price controls, or high taxes – will drive private investors to demand high-risk premiums or keep them from investing at all.

The Menem administration inherited Argentina's poor record and reputation for economic policy. Privatization of ENTeL presented the challenge of changing the country's reputation and boosting its credibility.

Argentina's institutional heritage offered few tools for credibly committing the government to refrain from arbitrary behavior. Its political cul-
ture lent little credence to informal norms of behavior: informal norms
have not restrained political actors from acting punitively toward their
antagonists as they have, for example, in the United Kingdom. Similarly,
confidence in the judicial system was low. The judiciary was nominally
independent – judges are appointed for life by the president with the
approval of the Senate – but in practice, judicial turnover has typically
accompanied changes in government. The Menem government, while not
undertaking a wholesale replacement of the judiciary, did pack the Supreme Court (with the agreement of Congress) by increasing the number
of justices from seven to fifteen.

The structure of Argentina's legislative and executive institutions offered greater promise of commitment. Because of the division of powers
between the two branches and the frequency with which they have been
controlled by different parties, any law enacted by the unified government under President Menem would be difficult for future governments
to reverse. In the case of the privatization of ENTeL, however, and implementation of the first stage of the general reform program, the Menem
administration chose to take the more expeditious route, using the power
to act by executive decree conferred under the State Reform Law.

Two additional mechanisms enhanced the government's credibility in
the ENTeL case. Both are transitory, however, and unrelated to institution building. The ENTeL privatization was one of the first and most
visible components of the Menem government's reform program. To
avoid sabotaging its own reform program, the government has an incentive *not* to act opportunistically toward the newly privatized telecommunications firms, lest it undermine the credibility of the entire program. In
addition, the reform program has led to an improvement in Argentina's
economic performance, strengthening the incentives for political actors to
continue to support reform. Should Argentina's economic performance
falter, however, cooperation may cease and politics may revert to its
previous mode.[5]

TELECOMMUNICATIONS SECTOR BEFORE PRIVATIZATION

Argentina is a large and relatively affluent country with a strong demand
for telecommunications services and the resources to invest in providing
them. As a result, the country has a large telecommunications infrastructure. Compared to countries of similar development and income, Argentina had a higher than average number of lines per capita in 1988 (Figure
6.1). Initially, telephone services were provided by private companies

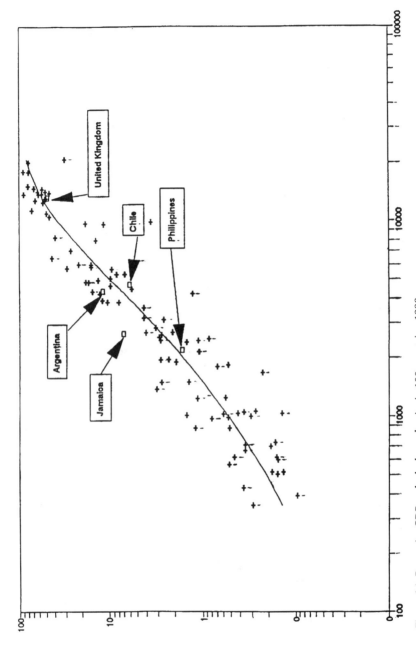

Figure 6.1. Per capita GDP and telephone density in 100 countries, 1988.

with minimal regulation by the federal government. Following the election of Juan Perón in 1946, the telephone companies were gradually nationalized. By 1990 some 90 percent of telephone lines were owned by ENTeL. While the level of telephone penetration has been high, problems arose with the backlog of unmet demand, the quality of service, and the level of corruption within ENTeL. In 1988 the administration of President Raúl Alfonsín attempted to reform the sector by partially privatizing ENTeL. That initiative failed because Alfonsín's party did not control both houses of the Congress. Just one year later, however, President Menem was able to initiate the privatization of ENTeL with the cooperation of Congress.

The early years

The first telephone company in Argentina, Société du Pantelephone de Loch, was formed in 1880, four years after Alexander Graham Bell invented the telephone, and it began operations in Buenos Aires in 1881. Two more companies started up soon after. In 1886 the three companies merged, forming the Union Telefónica del Rio de la Plata. Backed by British capital, Union Telefónica expanded to serve the more affluent provinces around Buenos Aires. Other small firms entered the market elsewhere in Argentina, operating under licenses granted by a province or city. There was no federal regulation until 1904, when the central government required all private operators to report their activities to the executive. In 1907 the federal government set the tariffs for telephone services in Argentina (Decree 4408/1904).

In 1929 the U.S. company International Telephone and Telegraph (ITT) entered the Argentine market by buying Union Telefónica. At about the same time the Swedish group Ericsson took up equity in Compañía Argentina de Teléfonos, which operated in the provinces of Mendoza, San Juan, Santiago del Estero, Salta, Tucaman, and Entre Rios. Ericsson had originally been an equipment supplier to Compañía Argentina, which had run up large unpaid bills; this debt was exchanged for equity in the company. By 1935 forty-three telephone companies were operating in Argentina.

During this period domestic integration of telephone services was very poor. A subscriber in the northernmost province of Jujuy could place a call to Europe without much difficulty, but found it virtually impossible to call Buenos Aires. In 1935 the federal government instructed the telephone companies to arrange for interprovincial connections, and in 1936 telephone services were declared national services under federal jurisdiction. All private telephone companies would operate under "precarious permit" status. The federal government would grant no formal concessions, and operating permits could be canceled at any time. The decree also gave the government the right to acquire the assets of operating companies (Decree 91,698/1936).

Nationalization and state control

By the end of World War II Argentina had accumulated foreign capital reserves of nearly US$1.7 billion as a result of its exports of raw materials to the combatants. The Perón government used the reserves to buy out several large foreign-owned domestic firms, including railways, ports, power companies, and telephone companies. ITT's holding in Union Telef!nica was purchased in 1946 for US$95 million. By 1948 the new firm was wholly owned by the Argentine government. A year later the government acquired companies in four northeastern provinces. This process of geographic expansion continued until 1969, encompassing thirty-one private companies in seventeen of Argentina's twenty-three provinces (Crawley 1984; Lewis 1990; Scobie 1971).

An exception to ENTeL's expansion was Compañía Argentina de Teléfonos. Although Ericsson was prepared to sell its shares, it wanted a price comparable to that paid to ITT. From 1948 to 1959 Compañía Argentina was prohibited by executive decree from investing in its system while the sale was being negotiated. Sale to the Perón government was virtually completed in 1955 when the military revolt intervened. Finally in 1959 the government of President Arturo Frondizi decided not to buy the company. Compañía Argentina was allowed to raise its rates and expand its network, but it continued to operate under provincial, and therefore precarious, licenses until 1992. It operated under the same rate structure as ENTeL; rates were negotiated between the government and ENTeL and Compañía Argentina was required to apply them in its territory.

Throughout the period telecommunications policy was the responsibility of the Secretary of Communications. With telecommunications declared a national service, the federal government had the right to set prices, define investments, and grant precarious permits to private firms. The 1936 decree was succeeded by the National Telecommunications Law of 1972 (Law 19,789/1972), which reflected the growing nationalism and protectionism that preceded the return of Perón to power in 1973. The law gave the government a legal monopoly of all telecommunications activities, now defined to include telex, radio, and television as well. The federal government could provide the services itself or grant permits with precarious status to other providers. The government was responsible for policing the sector, encouraging research, promoting development of domestic industry, and coordinating all activities in the sector.

Despite the discontinuities in Argentine politics, there was a consistent theme in telecommunications policy, which was to foster the development of a domestic telecommunications equipment industry. The government promoted import substitution in the sector, forcing ENTeL to source its equipment in Argentina. ENTeL was thus restricted in its access to technology and burdened with the cost of buying equipment at prices well above those in Europe or in the United States.

Despite the high costs imposed by Argentine industrial policy, ENTeL was one of the largest telecommunications carriers in the world by the late 1950s. In 1956 it was one of the ten largest firms in terms of the number of lines installed and seventh in number of calls placed. In 1957 Argentina had 43 percent of the telephones installed in South America, and telephone density in Buenos Aires was almost twice as high as in any other major urban area in Latin America. But even as the system grew, so did backlogs in the supply of lines (Figures 6.2–6.4). Local cooperatives sprang up in many areas where ENTeL failed to provide service (ENTeL *Annual Reports* 1958–60). ENTeL also experienced managerial and labor problems: the quality of service was poor (Figures 6.5–6.7), unions sometimes took over managerial activities, strikes were accompanied by sabotage, phantom workers collected salaries, and clandestine telephone connections were made, with payments going to ENTeL staff rather than the company.

The 1988 attempt to privatize ENTeL's management

Under the Megatel Plan of the mid-1980s the civilian government of President Raúl Alfonsín first tried to improve the level of service and reduce backlogs, using dramatically higher connection charges to finance an increase in investment (Table 6.2 shows ENTeL's investments during the 1980s). When that failed the government tried to partially privatize the firm in a bid to improve management and attract more capital.

By 1985 the backlog represented 1.3 million lines or 52.7 percent of the lines in service (see Figure 6.4). To finance the installation of 1 million lines between 1986 and 1989, connection charges were raised 486 percent for residential users and 629 percent for businesses. Payment had to be made in advance to get on the waiting list for a new telephone line. Though only 650,000 customers subscribed to the plan, the installation of subscribed lines was still unfinished in 1990, and these liabilities were carried over into the privatized companies.[6]

The appointment of a new minister of public works in October 1987 marked a turning point in the government's attitude toward ENTeL. Seeing a need for additional investment that neither ENTeL nor the government could finance and widespread corruption and irregular practices within ENTeL, the new minister advocated opening up the market,

Thousands of lines

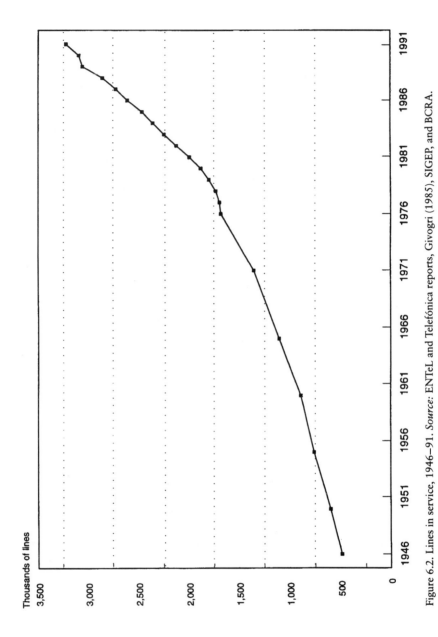

Figure 6.2. Lines in service, 1946–91. *Source*: ENTeL and Telefónica reports, Givogri (1985), SIGEP, and BCRA.

214

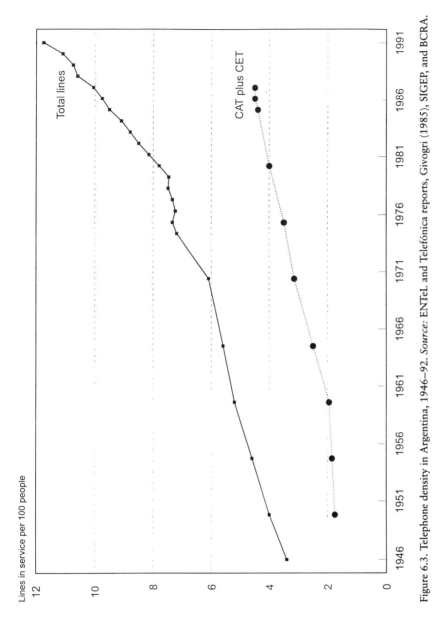

Figure 6.3. Telephone density in Argentina, 1946–92. *Source:* ENTeL and Telefónica reports, Givogri (1985), SIGEP, and BCRA.

215

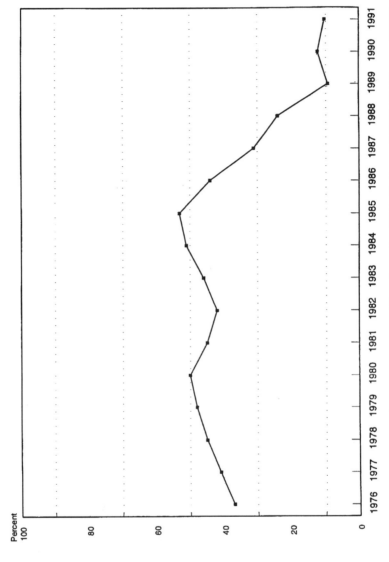

Figure 6.4. Unfilled line orders as a percentage of lines in service, 1976–91. *Source*: ENTeL 1985 Report, SIGEP, Telefónica and Telecom reports.

216

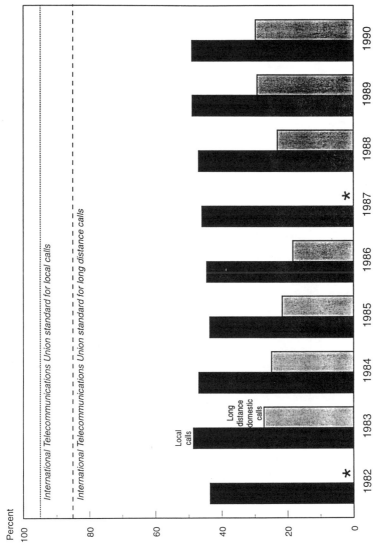

Figure 6.5. Call completion rates, 1982–90. *Note:* *indicates data is unavailable. *Source:* ENTeL, SIGEP, Telefónica and Telecom reports.

217

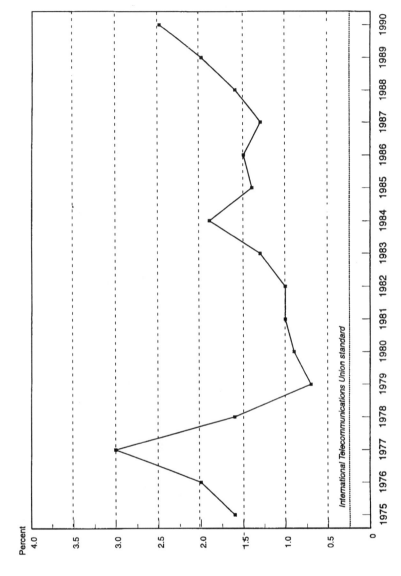

Figure 6.6. Pending repair orders as a percentage of lines in service, 1975–90. *Source:* ENTeL, SIGEP, Telefónica and Telecom reports.

218

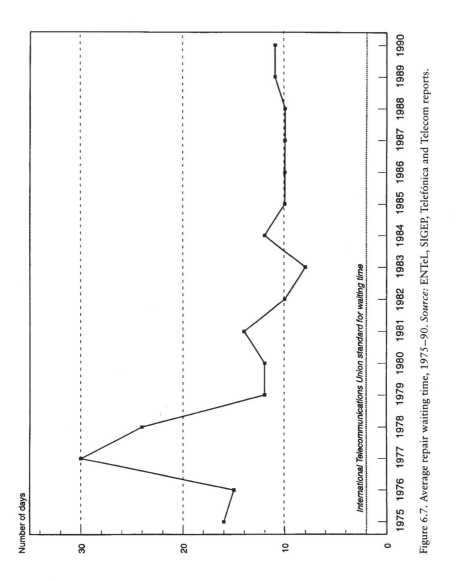

Figure 6.7. Average repair waiting time, 1975–90. *Source:* ENTeL, SIGEP, Telefónica and Telecom reports.

219

Table 6.2. ENTeL's profits, losses and investment 1980–90
(millions of australes)

Year	ENTeL's profits and losses (current prices)		ENTeL's share in GDP amount (1970 australes)	ENTeL's share in GDP (percent)	ENTeL's share in gross investment amount (1970 australes)[b]	ENTeL's share in gross investment percent (percent)[b]
	SIGEP	PEPIS[a]				
1980	0.006	0.004	105.1	0.930	3.24	3.07
1981	0.020	0.047	106.9	1.014	1.69	2.00
1982	0.028	−0.321	116.7	1.165	2.07	2.74
1983	0.472	3.912	124.9	1.210	2.09	3.11
1984	−184.700	−181.000	131.8	1.245	1.14	2.12
1985	−77.105	−70.000	142.5	1.443	1.92	3.06
1986	−536.479	−438.000	152.5	1.431	3.92	5.34
1987	531.945	753.000	160.0	1.480	7.94	12.12
1988		−6481.000	169.6	1.592	3.36	7.30
1989			151.7	1.550		

[a] Profits and losses from ENTeL's reports have been adjusted to correct for inflation accounting procedures and extraordinary items.
[b] Data for 1981–6 include Post Office.
Source: Columns 1, 5, and 7, SIGEP (various years); column 2, PEPIS (various years); columns 3 and 4, IADE (various years).

introducing new private management, and partially privatizing ENTeL. Liberalization of the sector was initiated by three executive decrees that allowed the secretary of telecommunications to issue permits to private telecommunications service providers (Decrees 1651/1987, 1757/1987, and 1842/1987).

Taking into account the high level of political uncertainty and ENTeL's administrative problems and corruption, the Alfonsín government decided to sell the company through negotiations, inviting a potential investor to evaluate the company and discuss terms. The government planned to keep control of the company (51 percent of the shares), to transfer 9 percent of the shares to workers, and to sell 40 percent to a new investor who would be responsible for managing the company. To this end the government entered into a preliminary agreement with Telefónica of Spain that granted the partially privatized company a twenty-five-year monopoly on all types of telecommunications services, including cable television but not cellular telephony, with an option to extend for another ten years. This monopoly was to include the regions served by Compañía Argentina de Teléfonos, which would lose its licenses. The proposal left the company enormous discretion in many areas, including accounting standards, rates, interconnection, and the definition of which value-added services came under its exclusive license.

Despite popular support for the partial privatization of ENTeL, Congress opposed the government's proposal.[7] Some members objected on ideological grounds and some objected to the specific terms of the deal, particularly the lack of competition and regulation. More important, the Peronists, who held a majority in the Senate, were unwilling to support any action that would help the Radical Party candidate in the 1989 election. Ultimately, the government ran out of time. The Peronist presidential candidate, Carlos Saul Menem, was elected in May 1989 and Minister of Public Works Rodolfo Terragno was tapped as the liaison between the outgoing and incoming governments, ending his efforts to partially privatize ENTeL.

PRIVATIZATION OF ENTEL

One of the most remarkable aspects of the 1990 privatization of ENTeL is that it happened at all. The unheralded shift from adversarial to cooperative politics provided a window of opportunity. The Menem government seized on this opportunity to reduce the scope of government activity and the level of government indebtedness. Completing the privatization would enable the Menem government to demonstrate early in its term that it had the resolve and ability to fundamentally change the economic role of government. The fact that the completion of the sale was central to the government's attempt to establish its credibility imposed a discipline on the actors involved and diminished the influence of the sale's critics. While the privatization team recognized the importance of the sale conditions and the need for a regulatory regime, these issues were secondary to completing the transaction. All these decisions sent signals about the future conduct of the Argentine government.[8]

The process of privatization

Following passage of the State Reform Law on 17 August 1989, the Menem government moved quickly on the privatization. The executive decree initiating the process was issued on 12 September 1989. Drawing on the powers delegated to the executive by the State Reform Law, the decree modified portions of the 1972 National Telecommunications Law that were incompatible with the privatization, striking out provisions that had reserved for the government the exclusive right to provide and control telecommunications services. An intervenor was appointed to oversee the privatization, and preparation of the company for the sale began at once (Decrees 59/1990, 60/1990, 61/1990, and 62/1990).

Early in the process the government approached the World Bank for technical and policy advice. The privatization of ENTeL became one of the conditions for the Bank's Public Enterprise Reform Loan, strengthening the government's incentives to complete the transaction and providing the privatization team with leverage against opponents.

In anticipation that political resistance to the sale would grow, a very tight timetable was set for the bidding process and the accompanying institutional reforms. For the same reason the privatization was implemented through executive decrees, as provided for in the State Reform Law, rather than through new legislation. While these decrees were easier to implement, they were also easier to reverse than legislation.[9] The conditions for the sale of ENTeL were laid out in the Document of the Terms and Conditions for the Privatization of Telecommunications Services (referred to hereafter as the Terms and Conditions) contained in an executive decree of 5 January 1990 (Decree 62/1990). ENTeL was to be split into two companies, with different geographic coverage, and each was to be granted an exclusive license to provide basic telecommunications services in its area. The first 60 percent of the shares in these companies was to be sold by competitive international bidding. The remaining shares were to be disposed of in a public flotation (25 percent), sale to cooperatives (5 percent), and sale to ENTeL employees (10 percent). In addition the Terms and Conditions laid out the timetable (Table

Table 6.3. *Original schedule for the sale of ENTeL*

Date	Event
10 January 1990	Publication of the call to bid
22 January	Opening of the consultation period
2 March	Last date to carry on consultations on the document
21 March	Deadline for prequalification presentations, and the opening of the presentations
28 March	Notification of the results of the prequalification
5 April	Opening of the period of access to information
22 May	Closing of the period of access to information
11 June	Deadline for the presentation of the proposals of the prequalified bidders, and opening of the proposals
14 June	Notification of the preaward
22 June	Deadline for the presentation of objections to the preaward
28 June	Deadline for the award by decree of the executive branch and resolution of the objections to the preaward
6 August	Deadline to sign the transfer contract
8 October	Deadline to take possession

6.3) and principles of the regulatory regime for the sector. The bid was to be announced almost immediately, and the transfer to the new owners was to take place on 8 October 1990.

The Terms and Conditions presented two licensee companies for sale, a "northern company" and a "southern company," created by decree and given exclusive licenses to provide basic telephone services for a limited time. Also created by decree was a new company with an exclusive license to provide international services for a limited period and a new company to provide services open to competition (such as data transmission, naval radio transmission, and telex). Ownership of these two companies was split equally between the northern and southern companies.[10]

The licensee companies were granted exclusive licenses for basic telephone services for seven years, provided they met a set of minimum performance requirements for investment and quality of service. They were also granted an option to extend the exclusive license for an additional three years if they met a higher set of performance targets. After this period the companies would continue to have a license to operate, but it would no longer be exclusive.[11] The Terms and Conditions also laid out the obligations the licensee companies would have to fulfill to retain their licenses, including the basic service goals.[12] To prequalify to bid for either licensee company, a consortium had to meet a detailed set of criteria designed to ensure that the winning consortium had the technical

Table 6.4. *Bids for the northern and southern regions*

Component	Telefónica	France cable and Radio/Stet	Bell Atlantic
Bids for southern region			
Cash	114	114	–
Argentine debt	2180	1944	–
Interest on debt	540	389	–
Total	2834	2447	–
Bids for northern region			
Cash	100	100	100
Argentine debt	1850	1750	1856
Interest on debt	458	350	371
Total	2408	2200	2337

ability to run the company and the financial depth to make the purchase and meet the obligatory investment goals.[13]

The minimum prices for the licensee companies, set by decree on 28 February 1990 (Decree 420/1990), included a cash component (US$114 million for the southern company and US$100 million for the northern) and a debt component, paid through the cancellation of part of the Argentine government's debt (no minimum was set). In addition, the government would assume ENTeL's existing debts, replacing them with debt in the form of notes payable to the government. This level of corporate debt was set at US$202 million for the southern company and US$178 million for the northern.

Of the fourteen potential purchasers who bought the bidding documents for US$20,000 apiece, seven submitted applications for prequalification by the 19 April 1990 deadline. The seven consortiums were headed by Cable and Wireless, Nynex Corporation, Telefónica of Spain (with Citicorp and Inversora Catalinas), Stet of Italy (with J. P. Morgan), GTE Corporation, France Cables and Radio, and Bell Atlantic Corporation (with Manufacturers Hanover and Cititel). All seven qualified to submit bids, but only three did so: Telefónica of Spain, the consortium headed by Bell Atlantic of the United States, and a merged consortium headed by France Cable and Radio with Stet of Italy. Telefónica and France Cable and Radio with Stet submitted bids for both the northern and southern regions; Bell Atlantic bid only for the northern region (Table 6.4).

The Telefónica consortium submitted the highest bid for both regions, but the Terms and Conditions did not permit two awards to the same consortium. Telefónica was awarded the southern company, and Bell

Atlantic was awarded the northern company, once it had matched Telefónica's bid.

As a regional operator in the United States, Bell Atlantic was constrained to 4.9 percent of the consortium by U.S. regulations governing the size of its foreign investments. To enable Bell Atlantic to qualify for the bidding, the Argentine government revised the Terms and Conditions to reduce the minimum size of the operator's share from 10 percent to 4.9 percent. This adjustment allowed Bell Atlantic's higher bid to stay on the table, but Bell Atlantic had other difficulties. The Argentine members of the consortium wanted Bell Atlantic to carry their share of the consortium's investment, first at 40 percent and then at 15 percent. Also, Bell Atlantic's banker, Manufacturers Hanover, had problems raising enough Argentine debt to fulfill Bell Atlantic's bid (see Table 6.4). The government gave Bell Atlantic additional time to complete its financing arrangements, but Manufacturers Hanover failed to amass enough sovereign debt. Bell Atlantic had to withdraw its bid in early October.[14]

Following the procedures outlined in the Terms and Conditions, the privatization team formally invited the France Cable and Radio/Stet consortium to enter negotiations for the northern company. The consortium mobilized to deliver a bid of US$100 million in cash and US$2,309 million in debt and interest, an increase of US$209 million in debt and interest over its original bid and nearly matching the failed bid of Bell Atlantic. The government accepted the bid and extended the deadline for taking possession of the northern and southern companies by one month to 8 November 1990.[15]

The contracts signed on 8 November 1990 transferred 60 percent of the shares in the northern company, henceforth known as Telecom Argentina, to the Nortel consortium operated by France Cable and Radio and Stet and 60 percent of the shares in the southern company, now known as Telefónica de Argentina, to the Cointel consortium operated by Telefónica of Spain. (The shareholding of the two consortiums is broken down in Table 6.5.) The government retained 40 percent of the two companies, 25 percent of which was to be sold to the general public, 5 percent to telephone cooperatives, and 10 percent to ENTeL employees. Responsibility for liquidating this holding remained with the intervenor for ENTeL.

The international and domestic public offerings of Telefónica's shares were made the week of 12 December 1991, and those of Telecom the week of 23 March 1992. The shares reserved for cooperatives were included in the offering, with cooperatives given priority in the allocation of the shares. Both offerings were oversubscribed and both brought in far more than the US$300 million the government had anticipated: US$830

Table 6.5. *Shareholding in the Cointel and*
Nortel consortiums
(percent)

Investor	Ownership share
Shareholding in Cointel consortium	
CVC (Citicorp Venture Capital)	20.00
Banco Rio de la Plata S.A.	15.26
Telefónica International	10.13
Inversora Catalinas	8.13
Banco Central de Espana S.A.	7.04
Sociedad Comercial del Plata S.A.	5.14
Banco Hispano Americano S.A.	5.00
Telarg Investment Corp.	4.33
Southtel Equity Corporation	4.22
Zurich Ltd.	4.16
The Bank of Toyko Limited	4.16
The Bank of New York	4.16
Other Investors (each with less than 7.16 percent)	7.99
Total	100.00
Shareholding in Nortel consortium, Telecom	
Stet	32.50
France Cables	32.50
Perez Companc	25.00
J. P. Morgan	9.75
Morgan Capital Corporation	0.25
Total	100.00

million in the case of Telefónica and US$1,227 million in the case of Telecom.

The cash value of these 30 percent shareholdings turned out to be higher than the cash value of the first 60 percent of shareholdings the government had sold by tender, which was US$214 million plus US$5,029 million of Argentine debt and associated interest at face value.[16] At the time of the transaction this debt traded in the secondary market at 19 cents on the dollar or US$955 million.[17] Thus the equivalent cash value of the price paid for the first 60 percent of ENTeL was US$1,169 million: US$630.8 million for the southern company, Telefónica, and US$538.7 million for the northern company, Telecom.

The arrangements for the 10 percent of the shares reserved for ENTeL employees were finally put in place in December 1992. The price was set at US$16.6 million, to be paid out of the dividends associated with the shares. Until payment to the government is made in full, the shares will be held by a trustee, the Banco de la Ciudad de Buenos Aires.

Privatization as a commitment mechanism

Both the process of privatization and the resulting pattern of ownership can serve as commitment mechanisms. The degree of transparency and predictability in the sale process is an important signal of a government's willingness and ability to commit itself to providing a stable regulatory environment after the privatization. The resulting pattern of ownership may strengthen the government's commitment by creating new political constituencies that identify with the privatized firms.

The signals generated during the privatization of ENTeL were mixed. The bidding process was straightforward and well publicized. Rules governing all steps of the bidding process were laid out, and the bids were opened in public. Not surprisingly, the haste in which the privatization was undertaken necessitated some technical clarifications of the bidding Terms and Conditions and revisions in the bidding schedule, although ultimately the sale was completed just one month after the original deadline.

More seriously, some of the terms of the bid were modified during the bidding process or were not resolved until after the final bids had been submitted. For example, one week before the deadline for prequalification applications, the minimum asset levels for membership in the bidding consortiums were changed. The effect of the modification was to reduce the number of eligible operators – thereby reducing the number of consortiums that could qualify to bid – and increase the number of nonoperator members eligible to join the bidding consortiums. The reason for these changes was not clear, but they signalled an increase in risk and uncertainty.[18] Another example was the status of Compañía Argentina Teléfonos, whose provincial licenses had expired. The territory that Compañía Argentina served was included in the new exclusive licenses that would go to the two new private telecommunications companies. The Ministry of Public Works had been charged with negotiating the purchase of Compañía Argentina's assets, but failed to do so before the final bids were submitted. Negotiations for the purchase of these assets did not take place until after the award.

Even though the bidding and the public offerings were open to foreign bidders, the resulting ownership structure includes substantial participation by Argentines. Once the transfer of shares to workers has been completed, the division of shares (percentages) between Argentine and foreign shareholders will be as shown in Table 6.6.

227

Table 6.6. *Division of shares (percentages)*

	Telecom	Telefónica
Domestic	43.0	47.4
Diverse	18.0	17.4
Concentrated	15.0	20.0
Employees	10.0	10.0
Foreign	57.0	52.6
Diverse	12.0	12.6
Concentrated	45.0	40.0
Total	100.0	100.0

The concentrated domestic shareholders are the members of the consortiums – banks and influential industrial groups. The diverse domestic
shareholders are mostly individuals; together with the workers, they form
a large bloc. The substantial participation of Argentines in these two companies provides additional insurance against regulatory expropriation of
the companies' assets. Such an action would not only be costly to the
government's credibility as a regulator, but it would also generate political
pressures that would reduce the incumbents' chances of being reelected.

In addition, the operators of the two companies are either partially or
entirely state-owned, Telefónica by the government of Spain, Stet by the
government of Italy, and France Cable by the French government. The
operators, therefore, have direct links with their home country governments and the capacity to call on their support.

REGULATION AS A COMMITMENT MECHANISM

In the privatization of ENTeL the most serious shortcomings were in the
implementation of the regulatory regime. During the bidding phase, regulatory clarity was sacrificed to speed and politics. The Terms and Conditions outlined the basic rights and obligations of the privatized companies
and provided for the general regulatory principles and the establishment
of a regulator. However, little was done to implement the regime. Not
until more than a year after the privatization did the government focus on
the problems of regulation.

The definition and implementation of regulation
before privatization

Before privatization the design and implementation of regulation affects
perceptions of risk and therefore the price that potential buyers are will-

ing to offer. The weakest part of the privatization was the failure to define the regulatory regime until the end of the bidding process and the substantial revisions that were made during the bidding process. These problems were not entirely accidental. The Argentine government explicitly chose to emphasize rapid completion of the sale over development of the regulatory regime. This was an important strategic decision that recognized the potential for resistance to the privatization. However, the Terms and Conditions did lay out the basic rights and obligations of the privatized companies and the basic principles and general concepts for regulating the sector. An initial set of pricing rules was also set out, and regulatory authority for the sector was assigned to the Secretariat of Communications in the Ministry of Public Works.[19]

The Secretariat of Communications was also responsible for developing a comprehensive regulatory decree based on the principles in the Terms and Conditions. Believing that the privatization would fail, the secretariat was slow to act. Although the Terms and Conditions committed the government to issue details of the regulatory framework by 28 February 1990, the secretariat did not issue the decree until 22 June, just before final bids were to be submitted.[20] The decree had been circulating for some time in draft form, so its contents were no surprise to the bidders, but the government did not commit itself until the last possible moment. The delay also meant that no steps had been taken to implement the regulatory regime defined by the decree. Bidders had no information about who would run the regulatory agency and how it would be staffed. Not until after the privatization did the Secretariat of Communications move to transform itself into a regulatory agency. The same cast of characters that had run the secretariat and had chosen not to support privatization would now run the agency.

Additional uncertainty was introduced by a change in the original pricing rules limiting the rate base on which the minimum rate of return was guaranteed for the first two years. The original pricing rules had been based on the privatization team's estimate that together the licensee companies would need at least US$500 million a year to fund the obligatory investment program. The team was concerned that the companies would have difficulty raising that much capital, so they planned a rate structure that would provide at least that much net income. Based on the minimum rate of return of 16 percent promised in the original Terms and Conditions, achieving this outcome would require a combined rate base of US$3.2 billion.

However, the National Development Bank's independent valuation of ENTeL's assets set their value at US$1.9 billion, leading to opposition in Congress to allowing a rate base of US$3.2 billion. President Menem was pressured by his party to issue decrees limiting the rate base to US$1.9 billion plus the licensee companies' additional investments and to increase the minimum bid to include US$3.5 billion of Argentine government debt. The executive decree increasing the minimum bid was announced on 28 March 1990 (Decree 575/1990) and another reducing the rate base on 11 April 1990 (Decree 677/1990), one week before the deadline for prequalification submissions.[21] The privatization team opposed the changes, and speculation arose that President Menem would dismiss the intervenor. Her chief adviser resigned in protest. However, as the bidding process neared completion, it became evident that the few remaining bidders were far more concerned with actual rate levels at the time of the transfer than with the minimum level of return provided for in the original Terms and Conditions.

The issue of the effective rate level was still unresolved at the 25 June 1990 deadline for final bids and may have been a factor in the small number of bids received. Indeed the issue of rates was not resolved until after the awards were made. On 7 March the intervenor had announced the base rate and the indexing mechanism. As with most indexing formulas in Argentina, adjustments were to begin the following month. However, inflation for the current month was running at 95 percent, and the bidders wanted this accounted for in the rate level. The government resisted, but the bidders persisted. The government's formula gave 193 australes per pulse (about 3 U.S. cents) as the price of the basic unit for calculating telephone charges; the bidders' formula gave a price of 293 australes per pulse. The companies argued that the higher rate was necessary to ensure their profitability. They threatened to withdraw if it was not approved. The Minister of Public Works threatened to resign if the government allowed the increase. The government had very little bargaining power since it was running up against its self-imposed deadline and had no bidders waiting in the wings should the two consortiums withdraw. Holding firm could have doomed the privatization.[22]

The final agreement on an indexing formula for the pulse price, which was incorporated in the two transfer contracts, produced a rate of 247.9 australes per pulse (about 4.8 U.S. cents). This change had a large impact on consumers, since it resulted in a real increase in the per pulse rate of 96.57 percent over previous bills. In return the two consortiums gave up their rights to a minimum return of 16 percent on their rate base – not much of a sacrifice, since the definition of the rate base had been dramatically narrowed.[23]

The regulatory framework after privatization

The problems with definition and implementation of the regulatory regime before the privatization were followed by more implementation problems after privatization. The 22 June 1990 regulatory decree set out a well-designed legal framework. The decree also created a telecommunications regulatory agency, the National Telecommunications Commission. Five commissioners were to be appointed for five-year terms by the president, who also had the powers to remove them. Commission decisions could be appealed only to the executive. The commission's primary sources of funding were to be a tax of 0.5 percent on telecommunications revenues and charges for use of the radio spectrum.

The commission's functions were defined as administrative and technical regulation, control, supervision, and verification. Its objectives were to ensure the continuity, regularity, equality, and broad availability of service; to promote universal basic telephone service at a fair and reasonable price; and to foster development of competitive services.[24] The commission could grant and revoke licenses, authorizations, and permits; decide whether to extend the exclusive regimes granted in the privatization; verify that conditions were being met; review and approve investment plans for operational compatibility, quality of service, and interconnection of networks; resolve consumer complaints; prevent anticompetitive behavior; and approve prices in cases where rates must follow license guidelines. The commission could apply sanctions including warnings, fines, and cancellation of licenses, authorizations, or permits.

New entrants were regulated through the license requirement. Supply was regulated by the need for authorization before installing or operating new facilities. While the commission had the power to grant competitive licenses, only the executive branch had the power to grant exclusive licenses.

Licensees were required to publish prices and to supply accounting and cost information to the commission. The two companies with exclusive licenses were required to establish interconnection between regions and with independent operators. The licensees were also required to provide nondiscriminatory access to their networks to providers of data services and other value-added services, on terms negotiated between the interconnecting parties. The commission could be invited to intervene in the case of disputes or could intervene of its own accord to set prices or conditions of service.

Although in its details the regulatory framework was well-designed, its implementation was problematic. In the beginning the regulatory agency did little to put the regulatory framework into action, creating uncertainty for all participants in the sector. After more than a year of inactivity and mounting uncertainty, the Menem administration replaced the management of the commission.

In its first incarnation, the commission was staffed entirely by former employees of the Secretariat of Communications and ENTeL, including the former Secretary of Telecommunications. This group had no experience in regulation and had neither supported the privatization nor expected it to succeed. Not until the first phase of the privatization was completed did the secretariat, in November 1990, set about transforming itself into a regulatory body.

In early 1991 the Ministry of Public Works was merged with the Ministry of the Economy, bringing the Telecommunications Commission under the purview of the new minister of the economy. The new minister's priority was to restore economic stability, which he tackled by introducing a currency convertibility plan on 20 March. The commission's functions and reorganization of the merged department received little attention. The commissioners were clearly not members of the minister's economic team, and as outsiders they were denied full and direct access to the funds raised by the special tax established to support the commission's activities.

Although charged with enormous regulatory responsibility, the commission did little from the end of 1990 to the end of 1991. It established no regulatory procedures, and a backlog of decisions began to pile up. The commission lacked experienced staff and the resources to hire additional staff or even to regularly pay existing staff. The commission's failure to perform hurt the telecommunications sector. On issues on which it should have played an active role it seems to have played none. The most significant example was the revision of the rate formula following introduction of the inflation-fighting convertibility law at the beginning of 1991. The law introduced a new currency, the peso, valued at 10,000 australes and fixed at one peso to the U.S. dollar, and banned all price indexing formulas linked to Argentine price indexes. The indexing formula for telecommunications rates was voided, freezing the nominal prices of telephone services and subjecting them to erosion by inflation. Under the transfer agreements, any modification of the terms of the exclusive license was subject to indemnification. Yet the commission did nothing. Its president was quoted in the press as saying that the frozen rates were high enough.[25] The failure to replace the indexing formula severely diminished the credibility of the commission's commitment to the rule of law.

Eventually the issue was resolved because the companies refused to help prepare the prospectuses for the public sale of the government's remaining shares. The government was forced to the negotiating table, but it was the Ministry of the Economy and not the Telecommunications Commission that did the negotiating. The new formula, agreed to on 28 November 1991, fixed the rate levels in U.S. dollars and permitted adjustments every six months based on the U.S. consumer price index (CPI). The formula allowed for price adjustment, but it exposed the companies to the risk that the inflation rates in the United States and Argentina would diverge – as indeed occurred in 1992, when the CPI was 3 percent while the equivalent inflation rate in Argentina was 25 percent. Firms were also permitted to begin rebalancing rates between different classes of users in January 1992. Firms were allowed to keep the connection charge in force, which was to have been replaced with a debt instrument, but they were required to meet a schedule that would reduce the charge from US$900 for residential users and US$1,800 for commercial users to US$250 for all users by November 1997 (Decree 2585/1991).

The commission's paralysis caused problems in other parts of the telecommunications sector as well. The six-month delay in responding to Compañía Argentina Teléfonos's request for a rate increase greatly complicated negotiations for the sale of Compañía Argentina's assets. The commission also failed to address imbalances in local, long-distance, and international service rates. Cross-subsidies of local services by long-distance and international services created artificial incentives for new firms to enter the long-distance and international markets. U.S. telephone companies were alleged to be selling their international credit calling cards door-to-door illegally in Argentina. The commission's failure to police the sector left the two licensed operators vulnerable to the loss of a significant portion of their international revenue to these illegal sales.

The commission's failure to develop standards and processes for issuing licenses also retarded the availability of new telecommunications services. A pricing policy that treated providers of these services as end-user business customers, even though they made little use of existing telephone company infrastructure, further stunted their development and made most of these services economically inviable. Facing license delays and little or no policing of operations, a number of radio operators and telephone cooperatives started to operate without licenses.

Consumers also suffered from the commission's inability to act effectively. The failure to address customer service complaints undermined the reputations of the companies, which relied on the commission to arbitrate complaints.

The two licensee companies claimed to have exceeded the performance targets set for them under their contracts, but the commission had no way to verify the claims. That opened the door to the possibility of cheating by the companies and increased the risk that the companies would be unable to prove that they had met the targets, as required for retaining their licenses. The situation was further complicated by the commission's lack of involvement in the development of the telephone companies' internal information systems, making it more difficult to review and verify whether the companies had met their performance targets.

The commission's methods of decision making were also problematic. Personal relations and other nonobjective criteria were applied rather than a clear set of rules based on public analysis and comment. Even with

233

a clearly defined range of responsibilities and powers for the regulatory agency, the effect of this type of unpredictable behavior was to increase the risk for capital investment in the sector.

By undermining the credibility of the government's privatization program, the commission's poor performance also had implications outside telecommunications. The privatization of ENTeL was intended to demonstrate the government's commitment to transform the economy. The first phase, the transfer of ownership to the private sector, met that objective. The second phase, implementation of an effective regulatory regime, did not. This failure to put in place clear, universally applied rules for the conduct of business was a bad signal to private investors. And without a regulator to safeguard the interests of consumers, Argentines would oppose the privatization of other government monopolies.

By the end of 1991 nearly everyone agreed on the need for a more effective regulator. New consumer advocacy groups viewed regulation as an avenue for improving the quality of telephone service and ensuring fair pricing. New service providers needed clarification of the ground rules. Even the two licensee companies, which might have been expected to profit from inefficient regulation, realized that the legal and political uncertainties associated with ineffective regulation could be costly.

In December 1991 the Subsecretariat of Communications was reestablished in the Ministry of Economy and Public Works and a new subsecretary of communications was appointed. In January 1992 the government intervened officially in the National Telecommunications Commission, replacing its commissioners with an intervenor and four subintervenors. Although the executive branch had the power to dismiss the commissioners outright, it chose not to do so because of the bad precedent that would create. It chose instead to use administrative intervention to signal that the situation was an exceptional one. The catalyst for the intervention was a World Bank report highlighting the deficiencies of the regulatory agency. Unlike the commissioners the intervenors were associated with the political coalition supporting economic reform and, perhaps more important, with the minister of economy and public works.

In collaboration with the World Bank, the Subsecretariat for Telecommunications formulated a plan for developing the commission's regulatory capacity. Through international competition the government selected an independent consulting team to collaborate with the staff of the commission in formulating an explicit set of regulatory policies, functions, and procedures and in implementing, evaluating, and fine-tuning them.

Two competing tasks faced the commission's new management: addressing the pressing backlog of regulatory decisions and charting out a strategy for the long term – and obtaining the human and financial resources needed to implement it. In the first six months of the intervention, the short-term issues dominated the agenda. Though not surprising considering the backlog of decisions that had accumulated in the commission's inactive first year, this strategy generated concern that the commission would revert to its old ways once the intervenors departed.

By October 1992 the commission had issued licenses regularizing the status of 140 of the 300 independent telephone cooperatives and expected to complete the balance by the end of the year. It had initiated bidding for mobile telephone service in the regions outside of Buenos Aires and established norms for domestic data transmission, video conferencing, and private mobile radio, all provided on a competitive basis. To promote competition in the provision of cellular telephones, the commission dropped regulations requiring partial fabrication in Argentina and allowed the use of any equipment approved by the U.S. Federal Communications Commission.

The commission also established norms for the use of the radio spectrum and resumed compliance monitoring. It dramatically improved collection rates for use of the radio spectrum: through the end of 1991 the commission had collected the equivalent of US$2.9 million; in the first eight months of 1992 the intervenors collected more than US$10 million. The commission signed a contract with a consumer advocacy group (Adelco) to facilitate the collection, processing, and monitoring of consumer complaints. A decree defining the rights and obligations of consumers was drafted in collaboration with the licensee companies and went into effect in September 1992.[26]

Despite the commission's progress on many fronts, the legal and political uncertainty created for the licensee companies by a weakly specified regulatory regime was not eliminated. Indeed, the intervenors added to the uncertainty through actions motivated, it seems, by a firm belief in the value of economic liberalization and competition. While respecting the core of the exclusive licenses for the provision of the basic telephone service, the commission took steps that eroded the companies' rights at the margin. In one instance, the commission issued decrees permitting new competition in long-distance service linked to the future cellular licensees (Decrees 506/1992 and 663/1992). The decrees were issued without warning or discussion with Telecom and Telefónica, which appealed them to the executive. The government appointed an arbitrator to resolve the dispute.

In another instance the licensee companies argued that the Terms and Conditions entitled them to a second cellular license, but the commission disagreed. Instead the granting of the second cellular license was linked to reductions in off-peak long-distance rates and acceleration of the schedule for reducing connection rates that had been negotiated in December

1991. The decrease in the rates ranged from 9 percent to 17 percent. The approximate cost to each company, calculated as a net present value of the reduction over a five-year period, was US$145.6 million.

Still unresolved is the technically difficult and politically awkward issue of rate rebalancing. Cross-subsidies of local services from long-distance and international services are large: local calls account for 75 percent of calls in Argentina but only 25 percent of revenues. Such large imbalances create pressures from firms seeking to enter the market for long-distance and international services and incentives for illegally bypassing the network. The original Terms and Conditions permit the operators to rebalance their prices as long as the overall price level is not increased. Telecom and Telefónica are anxious to initiate this process so that by the time their exclusive licenses end, their rates will more accurately reflect the costs of providing service.

Meanwhile, the long-term development of the commission needs to be addressed. Its top staff are political appointees and could leave at any time. To ensure continuity the commission needs to create permanent positions, improve compensation, and recruit and retain skilled staff. It also needs to develop its internal systems and procedures. Strategies and procedures have been developed, but implementing them will require permission from the executive branch to exempt commission staff from civil service pay restrictions.

The commission's long-term effectiveness will also depend on its access to financial resources. Its budget of approximately US$27 million is only a fraction of the revenues it generates. According to the decree creating the commission, it is supposed to control its own revenues. Revenues not used to fund commission activities are to be applied to development of the telecommunications sector, but in practice the Ministry of Economy and Public Works controls access to funds, and any surplus is applied to the public debt.

Despite these unresolved issues, the prognosis is good. The current management of the commission has begun to implement the legal framework for regulation. Staff and processes are in place and should continue to function. Although incremental change may take place over time, dramatic change in the commission's character seems increasingly unlikely.

AN EVALUATION OF REGULATION AND COMMITMENT

Argentina's success in establishing a credible and sustainable regulatory regime in these first few years has been mixed. Uncertainty about the reform and privatization process was initially very high, and investors demanded high-risk premiums, which reduced the benefits the government received from privatizing ENTeL. These risk premiums appear to have declined as the government made progress in implementing its regulatory regime and the rest of its economic reform program.[27] Though it is too soon to tell what the implications of the regulatory regime are for performance in the telecommunications sector, there is some evidence to suggest that uncertainty has diminished since the privatization. Indeed, Argentina's reputation seems to have improved generally, and both foreign and domestic investors seem more optimistic about the country's economic future.

One way to explore perceptions about the credibility and sustainability of reform in the telecommunications sector is to examine evidence on bidder interest in the first stage of privatization, the returns earned by investors in the privatized companies, and the investment behavior of the companies. Evidence from the stock market, the secondary market for Argentine sovereign debt, and new foreign investment flows gives a sense of perceptions about the continued success of the government's economic reform program and Argentina's economic future.

Buyer interest in ENTeL was initially strong, but dropped off rapidly during the bidding process. Though fourteen groups bought the bidding documents, only seven applied for prequalification on 19 April 1990. In the end only three consortiums submitted bids (one consortium was a merger of two others), and one of the three later dropped out. This attrition was correlated with modifications to the bidding process and uncertainty about the rate structure at the time of ownership transfer. The drop from fourteen to seven potential bidders came just after the rate regime and the prequalification criteria were changed. The drop from seven to three – then to two – bidders came at the end of the bidding process, after the regulatory framework had been clarified but before the starting rate level (which affected potential profitability) was defined. The drop in the number of bidders reduced competition and the government's leverage in the final round of bargaining; presumably, it also reduced the price offered for the two companies.

Changes in the prices offered for the two companies between the first round of bidding and the general public offerings reflect changes in buyers' assessments of the risks involved in the purchase. The Telefónica consortium paid the cash value equivalent of US$630.8 million for the southern company, and the Telecom consortium paid the equivalent of US$538.7 million for the northern company.[28] By the time of the public offerings of stock the market's assessment of risk seems to have diminished dramatically. Investors paid US$830 million for 30 percent of Telefónica and US$1,227 million for 30 percent of Telecom. Adjusted for the size of the two blocks of shares, the price paid in the public offering was 3.6 times the price paid by the operating consortium for Telefónica's shares and 4.5 times that paid for Telecom's shares. Accordingly, the return to investors who bought shares in the secondary offering is lower than the return earned by investors in the first round of the privatization, implying a drop in the risk premiums demanded by investors and more positive perceptions about credibility and sustainability.[29]

The investment behavior of Telefónica and Telecom seems to confirm the improved outlook. Both companies have exceeded the investment levels required under the terms of their licenses (Table 6.7). Telefónica invested US$208.6 million in its network in the eleven months up to 30 September 1991, and an additional US$615.2 million the following year. Telecom, which started with a slightly smaller network, invested US$132.0 million in its first eleven months and US$609.0 million the following year.[30] Most of the funds were internally generated, but both companies have borrowed to finance investment and working capital. Telecom increased its debt by US$74.9 million in 1992 and Telefónica by US$218.6 million. Their ability to borrow is an indication of lenders' optimism about the future of the sector.

Their investment went to improving services. Telefónica added 66,176 lines to its network in the eleven months up to 30 September 1991 and 276,364 lines in 1992. Telecom added 50,809 and 221,941 lines in the same periods.[31] In the 5 years preceding the privatization, ENTeL had added an average of 98,000 lines a year to the entire system. Both companies have also invested in digitalizing their systems. Of the 420,370 lines Telecom installed in 1992, 401,272 were digital. Telefónica increased the digitalization of its network from 18.1 percent in September 1991 to 24.0 percent in September 1992.

Private investors in Argentina seem to be optimistic about the country's economic prospects, as demonstrated by the performance of the stock market and the increase in foreign direct investment. The market index increased from 23.7 at the end of May 1989 to 13,279.43 on 19 March 1993 (Figure 6.8). Changes in the stock prices of Telefónica and Telecom have roughly paralleled the movement of the market. Foreign direct investment in Argentina more than doubled between 1989 and 1992, rising (according to IMF statistics) from US$1 billion in 1989 to US$2.5 billion in 1991 and an estimated US$2.4 billion in 1992.

The value of Argentine sovereign debt in secondary markets has also improved since implementation of the reform program, again signaling positive perceptions about the health of the economy. The value on the dollar of Argentine debt rose from 13 cents on 22 May 1989 to 46 cents by 1 March 1993 (as quoted by Salomon Brothers). The conclusion of the Brady plan arrangements on 7 April 1993 gave another boost to confidence.

Thus, perceptions about risk seem to have fallen considerably over time as the privatization was implemented and the regulatory regime moved

Table 6.7. *Telefónica and Telecom investment, 1991–7*

	1991	1992	1993	1994	1995	1996	1997	Total
Telefónica								
Network investments (millions of U.S. dollars)	208.6	615.2	549.2[a]	558.5[a]	596.3[a]	639.0[a]		3166.8
Lines in service added in fiscal year ending 9/30 (unaudited)	66,176	276,364						
Lines in service to be added per calendar year								
For seven-year exclusivity	70,000	105,000	154,000	136,000	85,000	69,000		619,000
For ten-year exclusivity	91,000	137,000	200,000	176,000	111,000	89,000		804,000
Telecom								
Network investments (millions of U.S. dollars)	132.0	609.0	771.4[a]	688.0[a]	600.8[a]	596.5[a]		3,97.8 (1991–6)
Lines in service added in fiscal year ending 9/30 (unaudited)	50,809	221,941						
Lines in service to be added per calendar year								
For seven-year exclusivity	60,000	90,000	135,000	121,000	87,000	72,000	12,000	577,000
For ten-year exclusivity	79,000	117,000	175,000	160,000	114,000	92,000	15,000	752,000

[a]Company projections.
Source: Annual Reports. Document of the Terms and Conditions for the Privatization of Telecommunications Services.

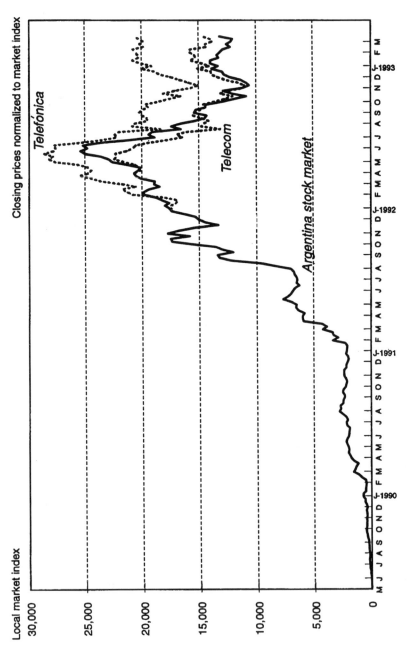

Figure 6.8. Argentina stock market index and closing prices for Telecom and Telefónica, May 1989–March 1993. *Source:* IFC Emerging Markets Data Base – weekly index data.

into action. The reduction in risk has been accompanied by substantial investment by the two privatized companies. At the same time the economic reform program has succeeded in improving Argentina's economic performance and expectations about the country's economic future.

While all these factors point to the success of the privatization of ENTeL and the eventual establishment of a regulatory regime for the sector, hindsight points to certain other actions that the Argentine government might have taken – and some that it could still take – to improve the outcome of the privatization.

One way to improve the credibility of the existing regulatory system would be to formalize it in legislation. The government chose to use executive decrees to define and create the regulatory regime because that was easier and faster at a time when easy and fast were positive attributes. They are now liabilities since they threaten the stability of the regulatory framework, which could easily be changed by a new administration. Legislation is more difficult to reverse because cooperation between Congress and the executive is required. The current administration could take advantage of its majority representation in both chambers of Congress to enact regulatory legislation.

Budgetary independence is probably not a realistic expectation for the National Telecommunications Commission, but the current budgetary arrangement is unacceptable since it implies that the government does not abide by its own rules. Under provisions of the regulatory decree, the tax on telecommunications services is to fund the commission's activities and the commission is to control the revenues from this tax. In practice, the commission depends on the Ministry of the Economy and Public Works for its funding. These budgetary arrangements should be regularized.

Argentina may eventually wish to modify the appeal mechanism. Appeals are made to the executive rather than to the judiciary, an arrangement that reflects a lack of confidence in the judicial system. However, appeal to the executive has a number of drawbacks. It circumvents a system of checks and balances among the branches of government. It presumes a level of executive expertise that may be unwarranted.[32] And in theory the executive is a far more transitory institution than the judiciary, since judges are appointed for life (though in practice they rarely serve beyond the term of the executive that appointed them). Argentina has begun to reform its judicial system, and once the reform has taken hold, judicial review might well be substituted for the existing appeal mechanism.

Argentina's experience suggests some guidelines for other countries that are contemplating privatizing their telecommunications systems. A clear lesson is the importance of establishing a well-defined regulatory regime early in the privatization process and of adhering to a transparent

241

and predictable process. Argentina seized a rare, opportune moment to privatize ENTeL and so chose not to wait until a regulatory regime was in place. Had it tried to do both at the same time, it might not have succeeded with either. The price of this approach appears to have been an increased risk premium for investors and lower returns to the government from the privatization.

By selling shares in public enterprises in stages, the government may be able to capture higher returns as credibility improves, a useful strategy when there are doubts about the government's ability to provide stable regulation. A country may have to tolerate high risk premiums in the initial sales, but the premiums will drop in subsequent sales if the country's reputation improves. However, the first offering must be large enough to give a reliable signal of a change in regime. In most cases that would mean selling a controlling interest in the firm. Widespread distribution of share ownership can also reduce the likelihood that the privatization will be reversed.

Finally, when choosing a strategy for price regulation, caution is recommended in setting a price-cap formula. Superficially, a formula based on a price index minus some X factor seems to require little effort to monitor. A starting level of rates is set, and increases are held to the rate of inflation less some amount X, which is intended to reflect technological innovation. However, the effect of this type of regulation depends on the starting price level. Setting the initial level is extremely problematic when the government lacks the information to calculate the sort of return this level would generate. The disadvantages mount if buyers do have the information, because that gives them a significant advantage in bargaining with the government. The government might agree, without full knowledge, to an initial rate level that is very profitable to buyers at the expense of consumers.

CONCLUSION

Expectations for Argentina's economic future seem to have improved enormously since the beginning of the Menem administration, and the net welfare impact over time of the privatization of ENTeL looks promising. If Argentina succeeds in putting in place an effective regulatory regime along the lines outlined in the regulatory decree and if the telecommunications companies meet their performance targets, the direct gains to the country should be substantial. A partial equilibrium analysis, which is described in more detail in the annex to this chapter, shows a net benefit to Argentina over the next ten years of US$1,946 million (in 1991 dollars, expressed in net present value terms). Some US$2,853 million in benefits go to the government, most of it from the higher taxes it will be able to collect. The gain to government is essentially a gain to taxpayers, whose liability is reduced.

This gain to taxpayers is partially offset by a loss to consumers. Because of the large increase in unit rates, consumers will be US$1,164 million worse off. Consumers will gain from a greater availability of services, but not until 1996 does the improved supply outweigh the effects of the price increase. These welfare projections do not consider changes in quality, but consumers should receive an additional unmeasured benefit if the two companies meet their agreed performance targets. It is also important to note the income distribution changes that accompanied the privatization. ENTeL's rates before privatization did not reflect its costs of operation – its losses were large and growing (see Table 6.2) – which meant that Argentine taxpayers had been subsidizing consumers of telephone services. Because the poor and rural inhabitants generally lacked telephone services, that meant that the taxpayer subsidy to ENTeL represented a transfer from these poorer groups to better-off urban groups.

Benefits of US$69 million are projected to accrue to domestic nonlabor shareholders, US$174 million to ENTeL's former employees, and US$13 million to telephone cooperatives and other suppliers. In addition to the net domestic benefits, foreign shareholders are projected to receive benefits of US$3,245 million – US$3,214 million of it going to the foreign members of the operating consortiums. (Some US$31 million of the benefits to domestic shareholders were received by Argentine members of the consortiums.)

The high level of rents accruing to the consortiums raises a question about the competitiveness of the bidding process. In theory, the prices paid in a competitive bidding process should already incorporate future rents. That does not seem to have happened. One possibility is that the successful consortiums had access to inside information during the bidding; however, there is no evidence for that. Another explanation is that the consortiums used higher discount rates than those we used in our estimates. Uncertainty about the country's policies and risks of future regulatory changes or renationalization are among factors that would lead foreign purchasers to arrive at a higher discount rate. After the fact, the consortiums might have discovered that they had overestimated the risks and were therefore enjoying higher than anticipated gains. Finally, perhaps the bidding process should not be thought of as fully competitive. Only three groups submitted bids, and one of the three dropped out. The government was left with very little leverage, and Telefónica and Telecom were able to hold out for higher base unit prices after the bidding process was over. In that way, rents were transferred from consumers to the telecommunications firms (and to the government in taxes).

Thus, transparency and predictability are important in the sequencing of privatization and regulation and in the process of privatization. Had it been feasible to develop a regulatory regime earlier and had the privatization process been more predictable, the government would probably have been able to capture more of the gains of privatization for its citizens. That being said, however, it nonetheless remains that the privatization of ENTeL appears to have generated large and positive gains for the country. More important, the reform program seems to have shifted the balance of the Argentine economy from the public to the private sector and altered its underlying structure.

ANNEX. PARTIAL EQUILIBRIUM ANALYSIS OF THE NET IMPACT OF THE PRIVATIZATION

One would expect a change from public to private ownership to result in changes in technical and allocative efficiency and in income distribution. These effects of privatization can be estimated in a partial equilibrium context using cost-benefit methodology developed by Jones, Tandon, and Vogelsang (1990).[33] Projections for the flows generated by a firm are developed for the case of private operation and then for the counterfactual case of the firm continuing to operate in the public sector. Comparison of the two cases permits estimation of the change in benefits accruing to different groups as a result of the change in ownership. Since the focus is on the difference between the two cases, estimation is less problematic than in the case of estimating the absolute value of the flows in each case.

The estimate of relative change in welfare was broken down into the following components: the domestic purchaser of the firm, the foreign purchasers of the firm, the employees of the firm, the firm's competitors, its suppliers, consumers of the firm's services, the government, and citizens.

The analysis focuses on the present value of the flows for ten years after ENTeL's transfer in November 1990 – the maximum period for which the government will grant monopolies to Telecom and Telefónica. It is not clear how much competition in basic services will take place after the year 2000. In any case, flows after this ten-year period will have a minimal impact on present values.

Flows for Telecom and Telefónica are combined and treated as though they were those of a single firm to facilitate comparison with the counterfactual projections. This consolidation is feasible since both Telecom and Telefónica face the same regulation and enjoy identical monopoly licenses.[34] All flows are projected in constant U.S. dollars. Real discount rates used are 16.5 percent in 1990, 14 percent in 1991, and 11.5 percent from 1992 onwards, reflecting the fall in the country risk premium and international rates in general since 1990. Real deposit rates of 4 percent a year and loan rates of 12 percent are used. The spread between the two is high, but reflects current conditions for dollar-denominated finance in Argentina.

The projections for the combined Telecom and Telefónica case are based on the valuation report by the National Development Bank; the investment targets and pricing regime laid out in the regulatory framework; the accounts of the two companies through March 1992; and the business plans and quantitative information in the prospectuses for the firms' public offerings. The actual pulse price is used until August 1992. Thereafter the pulse price is assumed to follow the new pricing formula and vary with the U.S. consumer price index on a semiannual basis. Inflation has been higher in Argentina than in the United States, meaning that there is a fall in the real pulse price. This relative decline is assumed to continue. Firms are expected to meet the quantitative investment targets necessary to extend their exclusive licenses to ten years. Intermediate input prices, mainly for equipment, are exogenous and are assumed to grow at a rate linked to wholesale prices and the exchange rate. Real average wage levels for the private firms are projected to stay at the same level as in 1991. Based on actual data productivity, gains are estimated at 14 percent in 1991 and at 8 percent for Telecom and 1.5 percent for Telefónica in 1992. In accordance with current managerial expectations in the firms, an 8 percent productivity improvement is projected for 1993. After 1993, labor productivity improvements are assumed to be 4.2 percent a year, 1 percent higher than ENTeL's historical rate of increase of 3.2 percent.

The projections for ENTeL are based on the firm's performance from 1980 to 1990 and information on ENTeL's condition before privatization provided in the National Bank for Development's valuation of the firm. The assumptions in the counterfactual projection are different for the pricing regime, the treatment of labor, the level of investments, and the conditions of the sale. The basic assumption on the pulse price is that, without the privatization, the price would not have increased as much but would have been adjusted to compensate for the high inflation in the first quarter of 1991 and then remained at the same real level for the duration of the period. Growth in labor productivity is estimated to continue to increase at the historical rate of 3.2 percent, lower than in the private firm case. New investment is projected to continue at the average annual level achieved in 1980–9. Without the debt restructuring that took place before the privatization, ENTeL would have continued to operate with a higher level of debt and its associated expenses.

Based on these assumptions, the transfer in ownership is estimated to have increased the value of the firm to society by US$5,209 million in constant 1991 dollars. (Table 6A.1 presents the base case reflecting the

Table 6A.1. Partial equilibrium
analysis of the impact of ENTeL divestiture
(millions of 1991 dollars)

	Base case			Discount + loan rate 5 percent lower			Discount + loan rate 5 percent higher		
	Private	Public	Difference	Private	Public	Difference	Private	Public	Difference
Government									
Taxes	6,247	4,061	2,186	7,709	5,396	2,313	5,186	2,995	2,192
Net quasi-rents	636	1,331	-695	668	2,813	-2,145	607	383	224
Net sale proceeds (cash)	1,883	0	1,883	1,972	0	1,972	1,803	0	1,804
Debt takeover	-2,013	0	-2,013	-1,936	0	-1,936	-2,093	0	-2,093
Government Subtotal	6,753	5,393	1,360	8,413	8,209	204	5,504	3,378	2,126
Debt canceled at market value	955	0	955	955	0	955	955	0	955
Debt canceled at excess market value	538	0	538	141	0	141	984	0	984
Government total	8,246	5,393	2,853	9,509	8,209	1300	7,443	3,378	4,065
Employees									
As shareholders	466	0	466	693	0	693	319	0	319
Labor rents	0	292	-292	0	351	-351	0	248	-248

Private domestic shareholders									
Diverse shareholders	43	0	43	434	0	434	−204	0	−204
Concentrated shareholders	45	0	45	61	0	61	32	0	32
Foreign shareholders									
Consortia	3,214	0	3,214	4,723	0	4,723	2,203	0	2,203
Diverse shareholders	31	0	31	305	0	305	−143	0	−143
Competitors	123	110	13	169	152	17	91	81	10
Providers	0	0	0	0	0	0	0	0	0
Citizens									
Via shadow increments	0	0	0	0	0	0	0	0	0
Subtotal	12,168	5,795	6,372	15,894	8,712	7,181	9,741	0	6,034
Consumers	64,574	65,738	−1,164	79,619	80,357	−739	53,735	55,158	−1,422
Total	76,742	71,533	5,209	95,512	89,070	6,443	63,476	58,865	4,611
Welfare result									
Net change in welfare within Argentina	1,965		1,965			1,414			2,552

Source: See text.

assumptions outlined above and the outcomes for discount and loan rates that vary by plus and minus 5 percent. The general results are robust.) Of this amount, US$2,853 million accrues to the government. The most important effect comes from the change in tax revenue, which brings in an additional US$2,185 million. With the privatization the government loses the indirect tax it levied on telecommunications, but this is more than outweighed by the increased revenues from the value added and corporate taxes. The cash proceeds from the sale, less transaction costs, are the second most important contribution to government benefits, totaling US$1,883 million. Also given up are quasi-rents on the order of US$695 million, which the government would have earned as an ENTeL shareholder. While external debt worth US$1,493 million was canceled, the government took on debt of US$2,013 from ENTeL as part of its financial restructuring.

Consumers as a group are estimated to be US$1,164 million worse off as a result of the privatization. Higher prices in the private firm scenario reduce consumer surplus, particularly in the first half of the 1990s. This loss is offset in the second half by benefits deriving from the increased quantity of services available as a result of increased investment. Externalities created by the growth of the network also benefit consumers, by making telephone services more valuable to new and existing users. Aside from this network externality, changes in quality have not been included in the calculations.

Once discounted, the early costs to consumers resulting from the higher per pulse price dominate the results. Different categories of consumers will be affected differently by the change in prices. As prices are rebalanced, residential customers and those who make intraurban calls are likely to experience the largest price increase, while business customers and long-distance users should experience a relative decrease in prices.

Telephone cooperatives, together with other competitors providing private circuits and other miscellaneous goods, should register a net gain if they behave as price takers and increase their prices to the same level as Telecom and Telefónica. The gain is small, US$13 million, because this segment of the industry is small.

The impact on Argentine suppliers of telecommunications equipment has not been calculated, though it appears to be mixed. The prices these suppliers have been able to charge has been dramatically reduced, but unlike ENTeL, the two private companies can actually pay for the equipment they purchase.

Provided the Argentine government fulfills its commitment to transfer 10 percent of the privatized companies' shares to former ENTeL employees, labor benefits from the transfer of ownership. After deducting the foregone rents associated with changes in labor contracts, employees gain US$174 million.

The value of the two firms' combined private earnings is US$6,753 million. Subtracting the US$466 million that accrues to the workers' shares leaves US$6,287 million in present value terms for the 90 percent of shares sold to the consortiums and in public offerings. This is much higher than the US$2,954 million that the private owners paid for the two firms together, but very close to the stock market value of the firms. Reexpressed in 1992 dollars, the projected value of the two firms together is US$8,423 million.[35] The stock market value for 100 percent of the firm has ranged from a low of US$5,789 million to a high of US$10,082 million and was US$7,419 million at the end of August 1992.

The domestic members of the holding companies enjoy a net benefit of US$45 million from their participation. The Argentine purchasers who bought approximately 60 percent of the stock in the public offerings enjoy a gain of US$43 million, even though Telecom's stock dropped from its initial offer price of 0.399 a share to 0.288 at the end of August 1992.

The foreign buyers of the two telecommunications firms, including those in the consortiums and those who bought shares in the public offering, are the largest beneficiaries of the transfer. The net benefit to this group is US$3,245 million, of which US$3,214 million accrues to the foreign members of the operating consortiums. Many of these buyers were financial institutions that swapped their holdings of Argentine government debt to make the purchase. This transaction appears to have been very profitable. Whatever the reason for the rents accruing to the members of the consortiums, the fact that many of these benefits accrue to foreigners means that the net benefit to Argentina of the transfer in ownership is US$1,965 million, or less than half the total social benefit resulting from the transfer. This share might have been higher if there had been more competition or less uncertainty in the bidding process.

Notes

1. A FRAMEWORK FOR RESOLVING THE REGULATORY PROBLEM

1 Institutional analysis has made major gains in recent years in accounting for the conduct of regulatory and other economic policies in the United States and elsewhere, but the empirical assessment of some key hypotheses has been constrained by the long periods of stability in core U.S. political institutions identified as key explanators of policy outcomes. (Several studies, however, have exploited electoral changes and their repercussions on the composition of the U.S. Congress and the executive in undertaking such assessments; for example, Spiller and Gely 1992 and Weingast and Moran 1983.) Cross-country comparative analyses provide one way to release this constraint. The country studies on which we base our analysis are part of a World Bank project on "Institutions, Regulation and Economic Efficiency," funded, in part, by a grant from the World Bank Research Committee. Because of the nature of the grant, we did not include the United States as a case study, though we refer to features of the U.S. system.

2 Weingast (1993) presents an interesting analysis of the role of central government discretion in determining incentives for private sector investment.

3 While McCubbins, Noll, and Weingast (1987) do not say it in those words, that is their main message concerning administrative procedures in the United States.

4 Multiple, distinct regulatory episodes within individual countries do, however, provide additional "degrees of freedom."

5 Financing requirements for sunk investments are not part of operating costs. The inability to repay debt acquired to pay for sunk investments will bring the utility to bankruptcy, but it will still not be worth liquidating. Asset liquidation will take place only when operating revenues fall short of operating costs, where operating costs include a return on the utility's nonspecific investments.

6 Pricing in sectors not characterized by large economies of scale and sunk investments may be political as well, but for utilities, politicization combined with asset characteristics brings about unique problems.

7 One way is to choose technologies that require lower levels of specific investments, at a tradeoff in lower quality and higher operating costs (for example, cellular rather than fixed-link telephony).

251

8 Public enterprises are also subject to the kinds of administrative expropriation considered here, though it usually takes the form of systematic underfunding.

9 For example, setting the prices of bananas below their long-run average cost will have at most a one year effect on banana prices. On the other hand, setting prices of water services below long-run average costs may imply a reduction in prices over quite a long period of time.

10 Williamson (1985, 35) would call such constraints on regulatory decision making "contractual governance institutions."

11 Commenting on the interaction among technology (institutions), governance, and price (regulatory incentives) Williamson (1985, 36) says, "inasmuch as price and governance are linked, parties to a contract should not expect to have their cake (low price) and eat it too (no safeguard)." There is no free institutional lunch.

12 Having different electoral cycles for the different branches of government tends to create electoral checks and balances (Jacobson 1990). For an in-depth analysis of the determinants of the powers of the executive relative to other branches of government, see Shugart and Carey (1992).

13 Electoral rules also influence the "effective number of parties" likely to emerge from an election and thus the extent of government control over the legislative process. For example, proportional representation tends to generate a large number of parties, while first-past-the-post arrangements with small district elections tend to create bipolar party configurations. This result has been coined Duverger's Law (1954). See also Taagepera and Shugart (1993); Cain, Ferejohn, and Fiorina (1987); and Cox (1987).

14 While parliamentary systems grant such powers in principle, whether they do so in practice depends on the electoral rules and the political party system. Electoral rules that bring about fragmented legislatures provide little scope for legislative initiative by the executive – usually headed by a minority party with a coalition built on a very narrow set of specific common interests. Electoral rules that create strong two-party parliamentary systems – as well as some other kinds of nonparliamentary political institutions – grant substantial legislative powers to the executive. For a discussion of the differences between parliamentary and presidential systems, and of the influence of electoral rules see Shugart and Carey (1992).

15 In the United Kingdom regulatory frameworks have traditionally evolved through a series of acts of Parliament. Gas regulation legislation was passed in 1847, 1859, 1870, 1871, 1873, and 1875; water regulation legislation in 1847, 1863, 1870, 1873, 1875, and 1887. Systematic regulation of electric companies started in 1882, only four years after the first public demonstration of lighting, followed by major legislation in 1888, 1899, 1919, and 1922, and culminating in the Electricity (Supply) Act of 1926, which created the Central Electricity Board. See Dimock (1933), Hormell (1928), Keen (1925), and Self and Watson (1952) for discussion of the evolution of utility regulation in the United Kingdom.

16 This has traditionally been the way administrative discretion has been restrained in the United States as regulatory statutes have tended to be quite vague. For an analysis of specificity in statutes, see Schwartz, Spiller, and Urbiztondo (1993).

17 Though a corrupt judiciary might side against the government on contract disputes (after all, government lawyers will have little incentive to bribe

judges, while private lawyers will have a lot), it becomes an easy hostage to the government on key issues. Unexpected press disclosures may trigger calls for judicial reform and sanctions.

18 The discussion that follows can be interpreted as either positive or normative. It is positive in that it predicts which combinations of background institutions and regulatory systems will lead to good performance, and which will not. It is normative in that it suggests what kind of regulatory design will be credible given the background institutions of the country in question.

19 When electoral laws are designed to return the same party to power in every election, complex party decision making may provide regulatory credibility, even in the absence of legally binding contractual arrangements or precise legislation. This seems to have been the case in Japan until the 1993 elections. See Baron (1992) for an excellent discussion of how decision making in the Liberal Democratic Party was structured to provide a large number of veto points.

20 The detailed case studies on which this book is based follow a research framework developed at the outset of this project. That framework emphasized, as this book does, the contracting problems endemic to utility regulation. It also required gathering detailed information about the regulatory structure (including information on regulatory proceedings and court cases) over time and a common set of information concerning investments, prices, and outputs.

21 Jamaica inherited British political institutions on independence in 1962. See Chapter 5 for a discussion of this point.

22 Britain's lack of a written constitution has not precluded the development of a large body of constitutional law.

23 See Salzberg (1991) for a discussion of the secondary role of the British judiciary in statutory interpretation.

24 For a discussion of the development of regulatory agencies and their procedures in the UK since the beginning of the privatization process, see Veljanovski (1991).

25 For example, "the Cable Authority is not bound to give reasons for its decisions, and it may well decide not to spell out its selection criteria in any detail in an effort to retain the greatest flexibility" (Baldwin and McCrudden 1987, 292). (See Baldwin and McCrudden 1987 for a discussion of procedures in various British regulatory agencies, including the Office of Fair Trading and the Monopolies and Mergers Commission.) The Jamaican Public Utilities Commission did, however, hold public hearings and was, in principle, subject to U.S.-style conditions for judicial review.

26 Judicial review can be initiated on procedural grounds or if the regulator's decision has been unreasonable. A claim of unreasonableness, however, rarely wins, because the regulator is not required to explain in detail the basis for a particular decision such as the granting of a cable license (Baldwin and McCrudden 1987, 292–3).

27 Major policy changes start with an ad hoc commission charged with analyzing the prospective policy change. The commission prepares a consultative green paper, a preliminary position paper that is circulated for public comment. (Telecommunications reform, for example, started in 1981 with the Beesley report that recommended unrestricted resale of leased lines, price flexibility on leased lines, and network entry.) Following this comment period, the government may decide to drop or to continue (with or without modifications) the

policy initiative. If the government decides to go ahead, it eventually publishes a white paper, which is the basis for the cabinet's legislative initiative. This process, which is also followed in Jamaica, has the virtue of providing interest groups with early warning of impending policy changes – a process similar to the advance warning features of the U.S. Administrative Procedures Act (McCubbins, Noll, and Weingast 1987; Spiller and Urbiztondo 1993). Interest groups, then, can attempt to influence the policy change by lobbying party members and legislators. See Miller (1985, 197–211) for a discussion of how this process provides opportunities for interested parties to participate in the legislative process in the United Kingdom.

28 Cox's (1993, 47) main point is that requiring joint and several ministerial responsibility increases "the power of the executive body by decreasing the chance that executive decisions will be challenged in any broader arena. Indeed, the convention of collective responsibility in the United Kingdom has been so effective in preventing internal Cabinet disagreements from spilling out into the Commons that many have questioned the independent importance of the legislature."

29 For a transactions cost analysis of the rise of the Westminster model of bureaucracy, see Palmer (1992).

30 Prime Minister Manley broke with political tradition and replaced many permanent secretaries. Since then, permanent secretaries have lost some of their influence and prestige, reducing the position's attractiveness to highly qualified individuals (Stone 1986). For a discussion of Britain's bureaucracy and a comparison with that of the United States, see Fesler (1983).

31 Shugart and Carey (1992, 173–4) refer to Chile's political system until 1970 as the "archetypal presidential system."

32 This respect for institutions persisted even during the military regime of General Pinochet. For example, the constitution was amended by a popular referendum. Similarly, the military regime's decision to return the country to a democratic system followed an electoral loss.

33 Concurrent elections provided for the development of bipolar coalitions that offered voters choices on national policies without the need to develop strong central parties (Shugart and Carey 1992, 174).

34 Shugart and Carey (1992, 183) call the system before the constitutional changes of 1958 and 1970 the "inefficient secret," as the regionalization of politics and weak presidential powers resulted in a dynamic legislature. Shugart and Carey (1992, 200) describes the post-1970 Chilean system as the strongest among presidential systems.

35 For example, both countries have separation of powers; a written constitution limiting legislative and executive power and to be enforced by the courts; two legislative houses and weak political parties; and a federal structure of power, with strong decentralization. The effective number of parties contesting elections is two in the Philippines, but higher in Argentina, reaching 3.4 in 1989 (Shugart and Carey 1992, 220–1). As in the United States, parties in the Philippines do not control nominations, nor do they use list ranks to control the order of elections or pool votes. As in the United States, Filipino legislators have considerable independence from their central parties.

36 Argentina's 1853 constitutional separation of powers remained in place for almost a century, until amended in 1949 by President Juan Perón to substantially expand the powers of the president. The military overthrew Perón in 1956 and restored the earlier constitution. Two other periods of military

power began in 1966 and in 1976. In the past, civilian governments have been fragmented, making it difficult to enact and sustain economic reforms, or have pursued zero-sum policies that reward their supporters. The administration of President Carlos Menem is an important exception. Not only did his Peronist Party win control of both houses of Congress in the 1990 elections, but when Menem took power Congress (including Menem's opponents) ceded him special powers to deal with the economic crisis.

37 There is as yet no theory explaining why arbitration of interest group conflicts is deferred to the judiciary and the legislature in some countries, rather than to the army. Calvert's (1992) view of constitutions as conventions is a beginning; coordination games have multiple equilibrium, with one equilibrium characterized by lack of coordination.

   In Argentina the disdain for constitutional legality appears even in the transfer of power following democratic elections. The transfer of power from the Radical Party to the current Peronist Party government was advanced several months before the legal date, arranged through an agreement between the two parties that required the incumbent Congress (not yet Peronist dominated) to pass an Economic Emergency Law granting the future president the power to implement a series of economic measures by decree. Members of the judiciary are appointed by the president (and confirmed by the Senate) and serve for life, giving them substantial formal independence. In practice, however, changes in government (whether constitutional or not) have been accompanied by turnover in the judiciary. In 1990 the new Menem government, with the agreement of Congress, increased the number of Supreme Court justices from five to nine. By 1993 President Menem was able to appoint six of the nine justices. The Menem Court has recently been plagued by corruption scandals (*The Miami Herald*, 12 October 1993).

   In the Philippines too, despite constitutional provisions for an independent judiciary, judicial scandal has been endemic. Under martial law, judicial independence was further constrained, and President Marcos was effectively empowered to remove any judge. Since 1986, the judiciary has regained some independence and influence, although corruption scandals continue. For example, in 1992 the Supreme Court blocked the entry of a competing international communications carrier (Eastern Telecom), and a few months later Justice Hugo Gutierrez, the author of the decision, resigned following allegations that the opinion had been written by a lawyer for the incumbent firm (Panaligan 1993).

38 Over the longer term, though, the multiplicity of parties in both countries suggests that government authority may be curtailed if current democratic episodes represent a clear break with unconstitutional transfers of power. U.S-style legislative and executive institutions were reasonably effective in constraining arbitrary government authority in the Philippines in its first quarter century of independence, although the Philippine constitution tilted the balance of power more sharply toward the executive than does the U.S. model (Abueva 1988). Ferdinand Marcos's declaration of martial law in 1972 (despite some modest reforms after 1978), further concentrated power in the executive. Since his overthrow in 1986, the country has reverted to a modified version of its former political institutions.

39 While British Telecom's license was specific on price setting, it was vague on quality regulation. The regulator, Oftel, has devoted most of its efforts – and applied most of its regulatory discretion – to quality control measures. Given

British Telecom's woefully inadequate internal quality control systems at the time of privatization, it might well be that such efforts by Oftel were in the interests of British Telecom's shareholders as well as its customers.

40 Jamaica's licenses have traditionally been granted for twenty-five years. British Telecom's license was also for twenty-five years, but its current price-cap feature expires after five years. Unless the license is modified before the price-cap regulation expires, British Telecom's pricing becomes unregulated. This sunset provision gives British Telecom a strong bargaining position since it can take up to a year to undertake a license modification against its will.

41 Spiller and Vogelsang report in Chapter 3 of this volume that following the failure at the Monopolies and Mergers Commission of the Director General's proposal for license reform in the marketing of 900-type calls, the Director General was advised not to proceed with his proposal because he would be successfully challenged in courts. Recently, however, Mercury, a rival telecommunications firm, filed a suit against British Telecom and Oftel, the telecommunications regulator, and won in the preliminary hearing. Mercury claimed that "Oftel had not offered it reasonable terms for the carriage of its traffic by BT, through a *consistent misinterpretation* of BT's government license. Mercury's victory . . . means there will be a full hearing of its application for a legal interpretation of that part of the license which deals with interconnection" (*Financial Times*, 1 March 1994, our italics).

42 Constitutional interpretation has traditionally viewed independent regulatory agencies in the United Kingdom as separate entities from their respective secretary of state. Laker Airways successfully challenged in the Court of Appeal the Civil Aviation Authority's revocation of Laker's Skytrain license to fly to the United States in 1976 following the issuance of the Secretary of State's guidance for the CAA (see *Laker Airways v. Department of Trade*, 1977 QB 643, cited in Baldwin and McCrudden 1987, 167). The court ruled that the Department of Trade's guidance "could supplement the CAA's statutory objectives; it could not replace them. . . . In issuing peremptory instructions to the CAA it constituted direction rather than guidance. . . . Parliament could not have set up an elaborate licensing code, subject to limited powers of direction, only to allow the Crown to render licenses useless by use of the prerogative power." This ruling did not, however, preclude ministerial influence. Indeed, since the statute provided for appeal of CAA decisions to the Secretary of State, what *Laker* shows is that the Secretary of State may use the powers given by statute and consistent with the constitutional view of the role of independent agencies. Since the *Laker* case eighteen appeals to the Secretary of State have been successful, in whole or in part; before *Laker* no appeal to the Secretary of State had been successful (Baldwin and McCrudden 1987, 168).

43 As mentioned, Jamaica's licenses have traditionally been granted for twenty-five years. At expiration time, the drawing of a new license agreement would also require the acquiescence of the company.

44 For example, Jamaica could not implement the flexible competitive boundaries used in the United States as a way of adapting the regulatory regime to new technologies (Knieps and Spiller 1983) without compensating the company for the loss in profitability. If new entrants were allowed, interconnection rates would have to be high enough to compensate the company for its profit loss. This is not altogether different from the position taken by New Zealand's High Court in its recent *Clear Communications* decision concern-

ing the interconnection of new entrants to New Zealand Telecom's network (Mueller 1993).

45 The politicization of the bureaucracy during the mid-1970s diminished its attractiveness to the middle class. Several commentators have noticed that since the 1980s secretaries have tended to depend less on the advice of their permanent secretaries and more on advisers outside the civil service.

46 Jamaica's rate-of-return system differs in important dimensions from that common in the United States or Chile before the 1970s and even from its own pre-1966 system. The regulator has little latitude to challenge capital investments, and the rate of return is based on stockholders' revalued assets rather than on fixed or operating assets.

47 For analyses of price-cap regulation, see for example, the *Rand Journal of Economics* symposium on price caps, vol. 20, 3 (1989).

48 Conversation with Richard Downer, Coopers & Lybrand, Jamaica, and consultant to the Jamaican government.

49 In Chapter 2, Spiller and Sampson provide evidence against the "capture" hypothesis by computing the value of Telecommunications of Jamaica under its license scheme and comparing it to the price paid by the private investors. The two are very close.

50 It could be said that Jamaica's regulatory system has a de facto price-cap feature, since a freeze has been imposed on the price of local calls since privatization, while changes in the price of international calls have been used to provide the necessary rate of return. At the time of privatization, Telecommunications of Jamaica informally agreed to a five-year freeze. The company has maintained the freeze since then.

51 Indeed, since the elimination of the Jamaican Public Utility Commission not a single regulatory agency has had substantial visibility and a reputation for independence.

52 We claim this to be the case in Argentina.

53 Following a commission decision to increase rates, Jamaica Telephone filed a case in the Supreme Court complaining that the increase was too small. A group of users filed their own case, arguing the increase was too high. The Supreme Court declined to hear either case. In 1974, the government amended the utilities act to specify a minimum rate of return (related to the yield on the government's foreign debt) for the regulated companies. The utilities commission interpreted the amendment as specifying a maximum rather than a "total entitlement" (see Chapter 2).

54 Consider what happened in a 1973 rate case. The utilities commission rejected the company's request for a price increase. So the government imposed a tax on telecommunications and gave the company a subsidy equal to the tax. The utilities claimed that the action was unlawful, but there was no legal challenge to the government's action (see Chapter 2).

55 At the end of the concession period the government could either take over the company, paying the value of its assets expressed in pesos-gold, or renew the concession for another thirty years (see Chapter 5).

56 In particular, we refer here to potential macroeconomic considerations arising from the second world war and its aftermath.

57 In Latin America's presidential systems, laws may be interpreted by the administration through regulatory decrees with the power of law. As a consequence changes in a regulatory decree may require specific new legislation,

unless the regulatory decree itself left open the need for its own modification (Shugart and Carey 1992).

58 The law requires the use of the capital asset pricing model in computing the allowed price levels. The law also stipulates the precise averaging procedure for recalculating the costs of the putatively efficient firm (see Chapter 5).

59 Chile imposes benchmark regulation only in market segments that are deemed not to be contestable and has an explicit procedure of public hearings for determining whether contestability exists in individual segments.

60 Several aspects of the regulatory regime remained to be interpreted by the antitrust commissions and the courts (interconnection agreements, the right of ENTeL – a long-distance company created in the late 1960s and privatized in the late 1980s – and CTC to enter into each other's lines of business) See Chapter 5.

61 All calls are priced according to the price of a pulse, with more expensive calls (long distance) incurring more pulses per minute.

62 Such disdain for rules is also evidenced by the granting of exclusive licenses that included the service areas of the main private regional telephone company, CAT, a subsidiary of Siemens. The licenses thereby took away CAT's legal standing, forcing it to agree to be purchased by the new licensees (see Chapter 6).

63 The current regulatory regime has few substantive restraints and there are no restraints on changing the system, so it is only a theoretical exercise to think about the enforcement of restraints in the Argentine and Philippines cases.

64 The quadrupling of additions to main lines in 1992 may simply reflect the use of available cash flows – it was politically impossible for the consortia to repatriate all the earnings generated by the telecommunications companies. By reinvesting their retained earnings now, the companies relax the constraints the license investment requirements may impose in future years, when cash flows may be smaller (see Chapter 6).

65 For example, even when the U.K. Labour Party denounced British Telecom's privatization in the mid-1980s, its platform called for renationalization without "speculative gains" rather than outright nationalization (see Chapter 3).

2. TELECOMMUNICATIONS REGULATIONS IN JAMAICA

1 For a similar interpretation of judicial power in the United Kingdom, see Salzberg (1990, 1991). For an analysis of the role of political institutions in determining the extent of judicial discretion, see Gely and Spiller (1990).

2 For example, more than three-quarters of Jamaica Telephone's customers are in the Kingston area, where the penetration rate is still less than 4 telephones per 100 residents.

3 The development of the data entry industry during the 1980s changed that, however, since data entry is highly dependent on telecommunications. Estimates of demand for international services show some minor increases in the elasticity around 1978–9.

4 Government employment rose from 4,500 in 1943 to 57,000 in 1968 and 110,000 in 1980. Similarly, public expenditure rose from 13 percent of GDP in 1950 to 17 percent in 1962, 21 percent in 1967, and 42 percent in 1977. Fiscal deficits as a share of GDP were less than 3 percent until 1970, increasing to 20.8 percent in 1981, before falling back to 13.7 percent by 1984.

5 By 1980 the small business sector had grown significantly in number of

enterprises and employment. By 1980 there were 50,000 small businesses (fewer than 50 employees) employing 31 percent of the labor force. In contrast there were only a thousand large enterprises employing 23 percent of the labor force. The petty commodity sector, though, employed the largest number (46 percent of the labor force) and had the largest number of enterprises (300,000). The growth of the small business sector is a result of the change in the structure of Jamaica's economy as agriculture fell from 36 percent of GDP to 7 percent by 1983 while manufacturing increased from 6 to 19 percent, and government and other services (apart from trade and commerce) from 18 to 41 percent (Stone 1986).

6 An interesting altercation developed following a 1950 rate review in which the company refused to pay the bill of the consultant because it disagreed with the consultant's methods. The company protested the consultant's separation of total costs into Kingston, All Island, and toll charges. Eventually, the government had to pay one-third of the consultant's bill.

7 The Public Utilities Commission Act established that the commission should set rates that will provide the utilities *no more* than 2.5 percent above the redemption yield of government long-term bonds issued in the United Kingdom. The Telephone Act, though, provided for an 8 percent return on the rate base, which the commission interpreted to mean "permitted" rather than "entitled." Responsibility for determining the rate base was not a trivial provision during periods of high investments. Whether works in progress are counted toward the rate base has important revenue implications, as it affects both the rate base and the total amount of depreciation.

8 Renewal and expiration need to be differentiated. Should the government decide not to renew, the license usually details how to dispose of the company's assets (through a sale to another company or through government takeover). Expiration requires a new license to be written, and the government may grant the new license to another company. The old license, though, usually stipulates how to dispose of assets. Licenses usually allowed for one renewal period.

9 Continental paid J$1.19 a share, implying an equity value at J$11.6 million. Our analysis of Jamaica Telephone's real assets in 1969 implied an equity value of J$8.8 million (at 1969 prices). Thus, either Continental assumed that operation of the domestic network was going to be very profitable or it valued Jamaica Telephone's assets at least $3 million over their real value. Since debts are usually more transparent than the value of assets, Continental may have valued Jamaica Telephone's fixed assets rather than its real assets. We valued Jamaica Telephone's fixed assets in 1969 at J$20 million, so Continental's overvaluation of fixed assets must have been at least 15 percent.

10 The commission claimed in a letter to Minister of Public Utilities Eric Bell (4 December 1972) that the stamp duty was against the law, because it was decided without public comment. At that time, the government also wanted to guarantee a specified return to Jamaica Telephone (comment on the notes of the Managing Director of Jamaica Telephone, by Ministry of Finance, December 1972).

11 Soon after the National Party came to power in 1972, the company expressed in a meeting with Minister of Public Utilities Eric Bell that it would not object to equity participation by the state (Notes of meeting between Minister Bell, Continental Telephone, and Jamaica Telephone, 30 March 1972). The Public Utilities Commission also objected to the issue of stocks to the government

as, it contended, such an issue will dilute the ownership shares of the minority shareholders.

12 The commission's main complaint was that the number of lines was not being expanded as fast as the rate base. Essentially, it seems that the company was replacing technically and physically obsolete equipment without expanding its network at the same rate.

13 Swaby, a consultant to the 1950 and 1953 rate boards, made a passing reference to the nontransparent procurement procedures, a complaint that was not confirmed by other sources. Essentially, the argument would be that given that Jamaica Telephone now faces a binding rate-of-return constraint, the majority shareholder would have an incentive to organize procurement through its own subsidiaries so as to transfer profits through overcharged transfer prices. This claim is not very convincing for the Jamaica Telephone case because Continental's initial holdings were just above 50 percent. The remaining shares were in local hands, possible among local board members. For the claim to be valid, Continental and the local board members would have had to devise a system whereby part of the profits from transfer pricing would be syphoned to the board members. No one has claimed that such a collusive arrangement was actually organized. Parris (1981) claims that such a transfer pricing scheme was organized by Continental for its Trinidad-Tobago investment, a 50-50 percent government-Continental joint venture.

14 Jamintel's accounting method did not revalue fixed assets. If Cable and Wireless had previously followed the same method, a difference of this size implies that Cable and Wireless contributed more than it was given credit for.

15 The government finished paying off its zero-interest debt to Cable and Wireless only in 1985–6. Thus in present value terms Cable and Wireless received less that J$1 million (in 1971 dollars) rather than the J$7 million (1971) that it had lent. Cable sold Jamintel half of its fixed assets, for a value of J$7 million and received dividends for a present value of J$1.5 million. Finally, in 1987 Cable contributed its shares in Jamintel to the creation of Telecommunications of Jamaica. Its shares were valued at about J$115 million in 1987, equivalent to J$12 million in 1971 dollars, which in present value is approximately J$3.5 million. Thus, in present value, Cable and Wireless received J$13 million, or just about what it contributed according to the accounting valuation – or J$3.3 million less (20 percent) according to our permanent inventory model. All present value calculations were done assuming a real rate of discount of 8 percent.

16 Jamintel's chairman of the board until the creation of Telecommunications of Jamaica was Mr. Barber, a senior civil servant, who was the financial permanent secretary at the time the company was created. He eventually became president of the central bank. To what extent Jamintel's board represented the interests of the minority shareholders is uncertain. Major changes in the regulatory setup, though, like changes in the license, required the consent of Cable and Wireless. The sharing agreement, however, was an operating decision left to the board.

17 Since the size of the domestic network clearly takes into account the amount of international communications, some of Jamaica Telephone's fixed assets may be directly related to the volume of international communications. Between 1979 and 1985, however, Jamaica Telephone's fixed assets increased

by less than 50 percent while those of international communications increased by 300 percent. Jamaica Telephone's domestic revenue also increased by less than 50 percent.

18 To demonstrate cross-subsidization we have to show that combined profits were normal and domestic revenues would not cover the incremental cost of domestic service. In 1984–5 combined real returns on fixed assets were around 14–16 percent (total costs minus the costs of operating the network only for international calls). Since most international calls arise from businesses, the size of the network could be substantially reduced without much of a reduction in international calls. Thus, the incremental cost of domestic service should be at least half the current costs. By 1984–5 domestic revenue was less than half of total revenues, so domestic revenue did not cover its incremental cost, suggesting cross-subsidization.

19 The company has recognized, however, that real prices of domestic services are too low, creating too much demand. It has tried to increase domestic prices by shifting customer billing from flat service fees to measured calls.

20 Initially, most Labor Party supporters and middle- and upper-income voters favored privatization, most National Party supporters and lower-income voters opposed it (Stone 1992, 119–20). Since then, public approval rates have risen – from 36 percent in March 1990 to 54 percent in July 1991.

21 Since changes in equity equal operating profits minus dividends, larger dividends imply that equity – and thus allowed total profits – grows less rapidly. Thus, by not distributing its earnings in the form of dividends, working capital should increase, enabling the financing of system expansion.

22 Customers could attach any equipment they want to the network, but they had to notify the company, which then added a rental charge or surcharge accordingly. A recent ruling by the Fair Trades Commission has put an end to Telecommunications of Jamaica monopoly over customer equipment.

23 Consider the case of cellular telephone services. When Telecommunications of Jamaica moved to prevent another company from establishing cellular services in Jamaica, the government sided with Telecommunications of Jamaica. Though the Telephone Law mentions only wire and communications, the license is silent about it. Both Telecommunications of Jamaica and the government contended that the license granted a monopoly over *all* telecommunications services. A second reason for government support relates to the cross-subsidization of the domestic services. If cellular services turn out to be very profitable, then extending the monopoly to cellular would allow Telecommunications of Jamaica to reduce the price of international communications, and thus the cost of the cross-subsidy.

24 The government received US$155 million for the shares after legal costs and excluding dividends during a period of two and a half years. After discounting (at 12 percent), this represents US$130 million, which is our valuation of the government's shares in Jamaica Telephone and Jamintel as of March 1987. Thus, the government seems to have received a fair value for its assets.

25 Calculated as follows (in U.S. dollars of equity per share) the price of a share is given by $P = \Sigma_{t=1}^{25} d_t/(1+\delta)^t + K_{25}/(1+\delta)^{25}$, where δ is the discount rate; K_t is the value as of period t with $K_t = K_{t-1}(1+.175) - d_t$, where d_t represents the dividend distribution in period t, with $d_t = K_{t-1}0.04$.

26 Slightly lower rates of discount imply substantially higher prices. For exam-

ple, a discount rate of 15 percent implies a price of US$0.37 in March 1988, almost 100 percent above the public sale price.

27 Government revenue includes indirect taxes (estimated) and company income taxes (from annual reports). Government's income from its share of the dividends distributed by Jamintel appears as part of the changes in the profitability of the companies.

28 This effect is simply the Slutzky effect and can be computed as $-\Delta P^* Q$, where ΔP reflects the increase in real price from year to year and Q reflects the previous year's quantity.

29 Because Jamaicans' access to the telephone network is constrained by the availability of lines, increases in lines represents an upward shift in the demand curve for the network. Consequently, holding constant the quantity of calls, an increase in the number of lines increases total consumer surplus by the area under the two curves. This area can be approximated (assuming a linear demand curve) by the change in the number of lines times the elasticity of the inverse demand for the service times the average revenue per line. Estimated log linear inverse demands for both domestic and international services for the period 1972–91 corrected for serial correlation, are as follows:

	International price	Domestic price
Constant	−10.42	8.75
	(4.96)	(4.30)
Log real international	−.64	–
output	(.24)	–
Log real domestic	–	−2.01
output	–	(.29)
Log lines	1.75	1.43
	(.58)	(.52)
Trend (post-1980)	−.007	−.008
	(.02)	(−.01)

Note: Standard errors in parentheses.

These estimated equations were used to compute the gains from changes in the number of lines from domestic and international service. Demand for international services is assured to be more elastic than the demand for domestic services because the growth in demand for international communications by households has increased since 1979 and because of the way international and domestic calls are charged. International calls are charged by the minute, while most households pay monthly flat service fees, plus intercity toll charges for domestic service. As a consequence, unless a substantial number of toll calls are made, the measured elasticity of the domestic demand would be lower than that for international services.

30 Conversation with Richard Downer, consultant to the government of Jamaica on the privatization.

31 For example, in early 1967 Jamaicans owned 9.1 percent of Jamaica Telephone. Shortly after Continental acquired shares, trading on the New York Stock Exchange of Jamaica Telephone shares increased and by the end of 1969 only 5 percent of the shares were held by local residents.

3. THE UNITED KINGDOM: A PACESETTER IN
REGULATORY INCENTIVES

1 *FPC v. Hope Natural Gas Co.,* Supreme Court of the United States, 1944, 320 U.S. 592, 64 S.Ct. 281, 88 L.Ed. 333.

2 This does not mean that U.S. utilities haven't had their share of regulatory difficulties. Inflation, oil price increases, and the environmental concerns that emerged in the 1970s required substantial changes in the regulatory process (Joskow 1974) – electric utilities were trading at 70 percent of their book value (Joskow and MacAvoy 1975). A legacy of this period has been an increase in the perceived risk of regulatory change, as capacity additions (mostly nuclear) undertaken during the oil shock period were challenged in courts by environmental groups and eventually withdrawn from the rate base. See, however, Gilbert and Newbery (1990) and Lyon (1991) for models that provide efficiency rationales for regulatory investment reviews performed with "regulatory hindsight."

3 This, however, does not mean that Members of Parliament will devote no time to servicing their constituency. Doing so still helps them get reelected, particularly in marginal districts (Cain, Ferejohn, and Fiorina 1987).

4 Compare this to the United States, where all senior staff at the federal level are political appointees. In the United Kingdom, permanent secretaries have traditionally been maintained following changes in party government (Deutsch, Dominguez, and Heclo 1981; Fesler 1983).

5 This role of white papers is similar to that of the Administrative Procedure Act in the United States (McCubbins, Noll, and Weingast 1987).

6 This issue was repeatedly mentioned in interviews with the directors general of telecommunications, fair trading, and electricity, and with members of the Monopolies and Mergers Commission.

7 Baldwin and McCrudden (1987, 57), quoting Sir Michael Kerry, the former Treasury Solicitor, observe that judicial review of administrative agencies has "increased from a handful a year in the 60s to 50–100 in the early 70s, to a rate of about 400 a year in the first six months of [1982]." Furthermore, "most of these cases come under two main heads, applications to quash planning decisions . . . and immigration cases" (Kerry 1983; Young 1985). Judicial review may also be effective in resolving disputes among branches of government (Baldwin and McCrudden 1987, 59).

8 In private conversation Acting Director General of Telecommunications Wigglesworth mentioned that Oftel lawyers recommended against unilaterally amending British Telecom's license in the *Chatlines* case because of the failure of the Monopolies and Mergers Commission to support Oftel's proposals. It was alleged that such a unilateral move could have been easily challenged in the courts.

9 See Spiller and Vogelsang (1993) for a more detailed analysis. See also Dimock (1933), Self and Watson (1952), Keen (1925), and Hormell (1928).

10 This section has benefited from the discussion in Doyle (1990).

11 Public enterprises have usually been organized as a department of a ministry, as a public corporation, or as a private company with the government as majority shareholder, and the level of involvement of ministers and parliamentary committees is strongest in the first type and weakest in the third. In the first two types, the government has substantial discretion in managing the

enterprise. Government discretion is slightly less for the private company form of organization.

12 The fiscal deficit (measured by the public sector borrowing requirement) exceeded 8 percent of GDP in 1974 and 1976 and reached 11.2 percent in 1975. The debt burden of public corporations exceeded 1 percent of GDP in 1974, 1976, and 1977. Inflation was high, reaching a peak of 24.22 percent in 1975, and the current account deficit reached an alarming 4.42 percent of GDP in 1974 (Select Committee on the Treasury and Civil Service 1981).

13 In 1975 the government established external financial limits to control annual changes in the net indebtedness of public corporations to the government. These were questionable devices, however, as they may constrain (postponable, but efficient) investment in favor of (necessary) current expenditures.

14 To handle the oversubscription the allocation mechanism was inversely related to the size of the application. Thus, for example, those who demanded fewer than 400 shares obtained their whole application, while those demanding more than 100,000 shares got nothing (Newman 1986, 167).

15 The Labour Party's conference of October 1984 nonetheless called for the renationalization of British Telecom, with compensation to be paid on the basis of "no speculative gain" (BT *Prospectus,* 1985, chap. 3).

16 The right to offer international switched services was not granted until 1983, and in November 1984 Mercury's license was modified to include full switched service. Mercury's license differs from British Telecom's in two major ways: Mercury is not subject to price regulation and it has no obligation to provide universal services throughout the United Kingdom. Mercury does, however, have to provide services in specified urban areas.

17 Because of its completely digital network, Mercury has some quality advantages over British Telecom. Beyond that, Mercury's success in the market is at least partly explained by its ability to underprice British Telecom, due partly to British Telecom's unbalanced rate structure. From the beginning Mercury priced about 12 to 15 percent below British Telecom, a difference that has remained fairly stable (Bradley 1992). On the other hand, Mercury suffers from unequal access. In particular, customers have to change their telephone numbers if they switch from British Telecom to Mercury. As a result Mercury has concentrated on high-volume customers.

18 Oftel lost its reference to the Monopolies and Mergers Commission in the *Chatlines* case. The commission did not agree to the unilateral modification of British Telecom's license as recommended by the Director General, even though the commission agreed that the current situation was against the public interest (Monopolies and Mergers Commission, "Chatlines and Message Services," January 1989, London: Her Majesty's Stationery Office.)

19 See Chairman's Speech at British Telecom's Annual Shareholders' Meeting, 1992, cited in Veljanovski (1992, 20).

20 For those used to the U.S. adversarial system of regulation, the notion of losing face and inappropriate behavior are difficult to understand though they are quite common among British public servants, regulators, and executives. The U.K. administrative system is based more on personal relations, informal contacts, and implicit agreements. The U.S. system prohibits substantive but informal contacts among commissioners, between commissioners and staff members, and between commissioners and representatives of regulated companies.

21 The only exception is the airline industry. Since the Civil Aviation Authority is

both the regulator of airports and a provider of services (air traffic control), the enabling legislation requires that airport license amendments be approved by the Monopolies and Mergers Commission. Apart from this work and the *Chatlines* case, the commission has yet to receive a regulatory reference (see commission reports and Veljanovski 1992).

22 The case of the electricity sector provides some conflicting evidence. While responsibility for granting licenses to electric companies moved from the Board of Trade, to the Electricity Commissioners, to the Secretary of Transport, the historical record gives no indication that the changes were undertaken to undermine the companies' performance. Yet at the time the companies were nationalized, their licenses did not stipulate any amendment procedures and the Board of Trade and its successors were in charge of licensing and setting prices (see Spiller and Vogelsang 1993).

23 During the summer of 1992 the British press was full of reports about the "obscene" profitability of the privatized utilities. Regulators were not immune to such popular pressure. The directors general of telecommunications, electricity, water, and gas all made statements about the need to bring the companies' profitability toward normal returns.

24 Initially after privatization, British Telecom's private circuit rentals remained unregulated, providing British Telecom with an opening to introduce steep increases. For a long time before, the prices of private circuit leases had been noncompensatory. Under a policy of general price controls by the Labour government in the 1970s the prices of the private circuits had been held down under the rationale that industries that were themselves price-controlled should not be subject to increasing prices of publicly provided inputs. After 1983 price increases for private circuits were moving British Telecom toward compensatory rates, but the steepness of the increases triggered political pressure from consumers. A separate price-cap basket for private circuits was established in 1989 with an RPI-0 constraint. Accordingly, private circuit rates on average could only go up with inflation, and rebalancing could occur only within the basket of private circuits.

25 British Telecom, in responding to the consultative document, noted "It is . . . expected that further discussions with Oftel will take place covering the detail of British Telecom's proposals and their financial impact" (British Telecommunications, 1992, 3).

26 While Beesley and Littlechild (1989) suggest that agreements are reached in negotiations between the Director General and the licensee, Director General Sir Bryan Carsberg has maintained that there have been no negotiations with British Telecom, only exchanges of information. The Director General presents his findings to British Telecom and "unless they reveal new information, they are then free to accept the findings or face the prospect that the case will be referred to the MMC" (Newbery's recording of a meeting with Sir Bryan Carsberg on 29 October 1991). Sir Bryan's shortcut in announcing his decision in June 1992 was not a change in procedure. The practice of coming out with a consultative document first and having interested parties respond was followed as before. Sir Bryan's experience with closed door negotiations with British Telecom, however, was not a happy one. During the duopoly review, such negotiations led the Director General to make public a set of policy recommendations. Mercury immediately complained about the process, particularly about not being consulted on key issues, forcing the Director General to revise the proposed license changes.

27 Personal interviews with BT representatives, London, July 1992.
28 Beesley and Laidlaw (1992) calculate the new coverage at 73.5 percent.

4. CHILE: REGULATORY SPECIFICITY, CREDIBILITY OF COMMITMENT, AND DISTRIBUTIONAL DEMANDS

1 The term "intervene" is used in Chile (and here) to refer to government taking control of a private firm without acquiring ownership.
2 For example, net fixed assets now exclude construction in progress, operating capital is estimated as one-sixth of gross annual revenue, interest on operating capital is estimated at 6 percent, and depreciation is 5 percent.
3 No information could be obtained for CTC before 1960 and for ENTeL before 1979.
4 For an analysis of these disputes see Coloma and Herrera (1990) and Paredes (1987). For a review of disputes under Chile's first antitrust law of 1959, see Furnish (1971).
5 These firms also suffered from inefficient plant size. The Economics Department of the University of Chile studied economies of scale in telecommunications in Chile in 1987 and found that elasticity of total cost with respect to output varies between 0.5 and 0.95 depending on plant size; described in Ale (1989).
6 According to Decree Law 211 of 1973, conflicts pertaining to anticompetitive behavior are resolved first by the thirteen Regional Preventive Commissions at the local level and then by the Resolutive Commission. Decisions of the preventive commissions can be appealed to the Resolutive Commission and to the Supreme Court. To ensure neutrality the five-member Resolutive Commission is made of the chief of the Supreme Court as chair, two government representatives (appointed by the ministers of economy and finance), and a dean of a law school and of an economics department (selected at random). The members of this commission remain in office for two years.
7 In retaliation, ENTeL's subsidiary, Global Telecomunicaciones S.A., applied for concessions to provide local service in specific business sectors in Santiago. CTC accused ENTeL of cream skimming, arguing that the telecommunications law does not allow a concession holder to carve out a specific area within an existing concession for a new concession. CTC also objected to the pricing system to be applied, arguing that the guidelines for pricing must be similar to CTC's. This dispute is still pending.
8 Two other constitutions followed in 1925 and 1980 (amended in 1989).
9 The Liberal and Conservative parties have historically represented the interests of the right, mainly landowners, industrialists, importers, and some professionals. The Radical party represented the interests of the center, whose constituency was drawn from civil servants, school teachers, and the urban middle class. The Communist and Socialist parties represented the left, whose main support came from miners, industrial workers, the lower-middle class, and the intelligentsia. Over time the Christian Democratic party grew partly at the expense of the Radicals, partly by attracting a large number of the middle class, and partly by incorporating new voters, particularly peasants and urban squatters. Election outcomes have largely depended on whether the center and right were united or split.
10 According to some analysts, the technocratic elite represented the political

counterpart of the emerging class of entrepreneurs. The new economists supported the private sector in numerous ways, including simplifying customs and providing the credit needed to start up businesses.

5. THE POLITICAL ECONOMY OF THE TELECOMMUNICATIONS SECTOR IN THE PHILIPPINES

1 Data on the performance of Philippine Long Distance are based largely on information provided by company representatives and in its annual reports. Additional information has been obtained from annual reports of the National Telecommunications Commission and from the 20K forms the company has filed with the U.S. Securities and Exchange Commission. The macroeconomic data are based on the International Monetary Fund's *International Financial Statistics*.

2 When six members of the communist-led Democratic Alliance were elected to the Congress in 1946, the Electoral Tribunal chose to disqualify them (Wurfel 1988, 101).

3 Shugart and Carey (1992, 175, 187) attribute the strength of the executive in the Philippines to the importance of local politics and the desire of the elite to bring benefits to their regions while "freeing themselves of direct involvement with broader national policy matters." However, facts such as the highly centralized nature of the Philippine government and the president's considerable control over local government do not support this view.

4 Indices developed by Shugart and Carey to gauge the relative legislative and nonlegislative powers of popularly elected presidents around the world place the Philippines in the group of countries with the most powerful presidencies (1992, 156).

5 The executive also exerted some control over cases being brought before the courts by having state prosecutors screen lawsuits before they are seen by a judge (Bacungan and Tadiar 1988, 178).

6 Several clearly excessive cases, however, were brought before the Supreme Court and struck down, among them President Quirino's attempt to ram the budget through by executive order in 1949 and President Marcos's creation of thirty municipalities by decree in 1968 (Wurfel 1988, 77).

7 The size of the group in power could not be very large, since once a support group got beyond a certain size, the marginal political gain from adding new members to the ruling coalition diminished while the marginal cost rose. For a discussion of this "minimum winnings coalition" principle, see Riker (1967).

8 The 1935 constitution prohibits heads of government departments and their assistants from intervening, directly or indirectly, in the control or management of private enterprises in any way related to or regulated by the government. The 1973 and 1986 constitutions have similar provisions.

9 The 1935 constitution had restricted these activities to Filipino-controlled enterprises. In other areas, only joint ventures with at least 60 percent Filipino equity were permitted.

10 The leverages also allowed U.S. politicians to mediate among the Filipino elite and thus contribute to the long-term stability of the system.

11 An important example of this difficulty concerned interpretations of how U.S. investments made under the Parity Amendment should be handled after

1974. U.S. corporations had assumed that they could maintain their owner-ship over the land they had purchased before 1974, but the Supreme Court disagreed, forcing them to sell their lands by the end of 1974.

12 In fact, with the consent of the U.S. government, a set of expanding import and foreign exchange controls was imposed on the economy beginning in 1950 (Wurfel 1988, 14–15).

13 The controversial reelection of President Marcos in 1969 also seems to have played a role in this decision (Abueva 1972).

14 The two justices wrote "if a new government gains authority and dominance through force, it can be effectively challenged only by a stronger force; no judicial dictum can prevail against it" (quoted in Wurful 1988, 117).

15 For detailed and well documented accounts of how the crony system worked and its extent of activity see, among others, Manapat (1991) and Hawes (1987).

16 For example, the composition of Electoral Tribunals has been changed to proportional representation of parties in Congress. Also, in the case of mar-tial law, the president is required to convene and notify Congress of the declaration.

17 The model of the Philippine political economy developed above has many more implications than the dozen or so listed here, which are derived and worded with an eye to the empirical observations in the following section. Explicit presentation of these implications in this section is essentially a means of organizing the assessment of the model against the historical experi-ence of the Philippine Long Distance Telephone Company.

18 Monopoly pricing may not be optimal if the ruling coalition is at all con-cerned about support from consumers, some of whom may be its own clients. For a theoretical exposition of this point see Peltzman (1976).

19 Real fixed assets are calculated by deflating the values of annual investment by the consumer price index, using the perpetual inventory model and an 8 percent depreciation rate. The base year is 1967. A reliable appraisal was made of the capital stock as of 31 December 1966. Figure 4.2 compares these accounting values with replacement cost appraisals for the years for which such data are available and an economic measure of fixed assets. The eco-nomic measure is close to the appraised values in 1980, 1983, and 1988, but overestimates the appraised value in 1975 and underestimates it in 1982. These differences are probably due to shifts in relative prices and measure-ment errors in the two variables. In any case, using the appraised values only strengthens the booms and busts in Philippine Long Distance's real fixed investment and emphasizes the seriousness of the cycles identified here. The prewar system was completely restored in five years and then growth contin-ued consistently until 1959. Between 1950 and 1959, the number of tele-phones in service grew 14.4 percent a year.

20 This point is clearly reflected in PLDT's *Annual Reports* during those years. PLDT was even spared the exchange rate tax instituted in the 1950s to effectively devalue the peso.

21 The details of the ownership transfer described here became public in 1977 as a result of investigations carried out by the U.S. Securities and Exchange Commission (U.S. SEC) and GTE management. A legal case was filed in U.S. District Court in Washington, D.C., by the U.S. SEC on 12 January 1977, against a group of Filipino businessmen controlling PLDT. The case was

settled out of court, with the defendants accepting a court injunction without admission of guilt.

22 As of 1986 the rest of PTIC shares were held by the Cojuangco family (43 percent), Yuchengco (7 percent), and Meer (4 percent). Further details of the PTIC-Prime Holdings transaction are documented by Manapat (1993, 13–14), quoting the minutes of the Special Meeting of the PTIC board of directors on 20 December 1977, and the records of President Marcos and his daughter, Imee, found in the presidential palace after their departure in 1986. These details show that the shares transferred to Prime Holdings were in three blocks. One block sold by Ramon Cojuangco was 20 percent of the total PTIC shares and was priced at P1.95 a share. Two other blocks of 13 percent were transferred by Cojuangco and Rivilla at P110 and P113 per share, respectively. The value of a PTIC share in early 1978, based on its corresponding PLDT shares, was approximately P1,500.

23 Interestingly, there was no change in PLDT's board of directors between 1977 and 1981, suggesting that the 1978 transaction was not intended to shift control of the company. The high ranking officials of the Marcos government interviewed also indicated that both before and after 1978 President Marcos had been consistently supportive of PLDT and its president, Ramon Cojuangco.

24 In the late 1960s, a $1 million increase in profits could raise the rate of return on equity by 2 percentage points.

25 However, the company's unregulated status continued after the government sold its shares at a controversial price to POTC in 1982 (Isberto 1986).

26 However, Meralco's 1971 *Annual Report* presents financing problems as the main cause of its investment restriction in those years.

27 This change had been recommended before martial law in response to the increased volume and complexity of regulatory tasks in various sectors under the commission's jurisdiction.

28 The ratio of these funds to PLDT's real economic equity reached about 5 percent in the late 1970s and surpassed 6 percent in 1983. After that, their share in total equity declined.

29 Comparing these favors with the fate of Meralco is instructive. President Marcos was wary of the ambitions of the Lopez family and after martial law managed to effectively expropriate a large part of their assets. First, the family's newspapers, which had been closed down immediately after the martial law announcement, were not allowed to reopen until they were sold to the president's relatives. Then electricity tariffs were reduced to force the sale of Meralco. When this tactic did not work, Eugenio Lopez's son was taken into custody and accused of trying to assassinate the president. Finally, Eugenio Lopez, who resided in the United States at the time, agreed to sell Meralco to the Meralco Foundation Inc., a nonstock firm set up by Marcos's brother-in-law. Later, Eugenio Lopez, Jr., escaped from prison. (See Tiglao 1989 and Manapat 1991.)

30 Government officials also tried to impose a number of obligations of PLDT, but these were inconsequential. For example, in 1975 PLDT was required to establish telephone service throughout rural Philippines. Also, along with other large corporations, PLDT was ordered to grow the rice necessary for feeding its employees and pay an extra month salary to them as bonus. These regulations were hardly enforced and PLDT only paid lip service to them.

31 In other words, in accordance with implication 9, telephone charges in 1974 must have approached monopoly prices. However, since PLDT's real tariff rates in 1974 were lower than in almost any previous year, the nominal rate adjustments could not have caused monopoly pricing by themselves. In this sense, the demand shift following the income concentration of the 1970s is an integral part of the above explanation for the evaporation of excess demand. With the demand shift, the new charge brought the telephone tariffs close to their monopoly levels and made a highly suboptimal capital stock the most profitable one.

32 According to Manapat (1993, 11–12), the "abandoned" GTE shares, which had an approximate market value of $11 million, were transferred to Ramon Cojuangco, who paid $13,500 to PTIC. Other PTIC shareholders signed letters indicating that they were not interested in purchasing any of the shares. The per share price of this transfer was exactly the same as the first (20 percent) block of shares purchased by Prime Holdings from Cojuangco a few months later.

33 RCA recently sold all its shares to Filipino investors.

34 If Retelco's assets and lines are excluded from calculation, the growth rate of capital stock declines to 18 percent and that of main lines to 5.1 percent.

35 PLDT declared some of the underreported foreign earnings later in 1986. Some of Sison's (1986) other findings were disputed by a subsequent study by Mario Locsin and Benjamin Guingona for the commission on good government. When preparing their report, Locsin and Guingona were commission representatives on PLDT's board of directors. A senior Aquino government official has suggested that the latter study was orchestrated by the Cojuangco family (Friedland 1988).

36 The committee was presented with deeds of assignment showing that in 1981 Ramon Cojuangco and Oscar Africa had attempted to buy the shares of Prime Holdings in PTIC. However, the deeds were not notarized, did not specify any payments, and were not recorded in the books of Prime Holdings (Sison 1986).

37 Jovito Salonga, commission chairman in 1986, responded to criticism about the commission's failure to pursue its investigations of PLDT by claiming that President Aquino had discouraged him by saying that "the Antonio Cojuangco family is not that bad, and is different from Danding's," her other cousin, Eduardo Cojuango, whose assets were sequestered in 1986 because of his close ties to Marcos. Aquino has confirmed the statement, but has denied discouraging her officials from pursuing any legal case (Tiglao 1993c).

38 The Philippine Consumers Foundation did attempt to challenge the automatic foreign exchange adjustment provision, but the Supreme Court dismissed the case.

39 For instance, in 1992 Antonio Cojuangco led the group of investors who took over the Philippine Airlines, which was being privatized.

40 Someone familiar with the case explained in an interview that the fundamental difference between Eastern and PhilCom may be that Eastern has been penetrated by middle-class professionals while PhilCom is still an elite-controlled firm and ostensibly maintains close ties with the PTIC group.

41 Manapat (1993, 40) quotes newspaper reports indicating that the buyer may have been a friend of the Cojuangco family.

42 The allegations are based on the opinion of David Miles Yerkes, a professor of English at Columbia University and a specialist on the authorship of

English-language texts. He was hired by Eastern Telecom to examine the text of the decision and compare it to the writing styles of Justice Gutierrez and the PLDT counsel. Justice Gutierrez, other Supreme Court members, and the PLDT counsel have denied the allegations (Tiglao 1993a).

43 Further allegations of impropriety have arisen from the fact that Mario Locsin, one of the two PCGG representatives on PLDT's board, "was appointed executive vice-president of Philippine Airlines in March [1992], when it was taken over by a consortium led by [Antonio] Cojuangco" (Tiglao, 1993c).

6. ARGENTINA: THE SEQUENCING OF PRIVATIZATION AND REGULATION

1 This is true whether the entry and tariff provisions of a regulatory regime provide for high returns or low returns. The more stable and credible the regime, the lower the risks associated with investment and the more attractive the investment.

2 This section draws heavily on McCubbins (1993).

3 The effective number of parties is a number constructed to represent the number of parties that have a chance at competing for election. This is similar to constructing the effective number of new entrants in a market. There may be many potential entrants, but none are actually observed (or many may be observed, but none are competitive).

4 While Argentina had frequently suffered from high inflation the acceleration in the rate of increase in consumer prices from 343 percent in 1988 to 3,079 percent in 1989 was unprecedented (International Monetary Fund *International Financial Statistics*).

5 One such instance would be if the deterioration in Argentina's terms of trade that has taken place since the introduction of the reform program were to be accompanied by a reversal of capital inflows.

6 ENTeL attributed the low subscription to an absolute lack of demand for lines, not a very credible interpretation given the size of the preexisting backlog. The shortfall cannot be attributed entirely to the higher price either, since calculations of price elasticities of demand for lines indicate that demand should have been higher. The most likely explanation is that customers were skeptical about whether they would actually receive the lines subscribed for and feared that their funds would be drawn out of ENTeL to finance the growing government deficit (see Abdala 1991, 51–2).

7 Government polls had shown that while Argentineans did not approve of privatization in general, they did support the privatization of ENTeL. A poll conducted by Guillermo Bravo and Pessah consultants showed that 55 to 59 percent of the interviewed ENTeL users had expressed support of the proposal to partially privatize ENTeL.

8 During the public ceremony for the executive decree establishing the terms and conditions of the sale, signing Minister of Public Works and Services Jose Roberto Dromi explained that "the Government, complying with the mandate from the people, wished to change the structure of the state in Argentina" (*La Nación*, 8 January 1990, "Se pone en marcha la privatización de ENTeL"). A 14 December 1989 article in the *Wall Street Journal*, "Will Argentina's Menem Have the Guts?" questioned whether the president would actually carry through his proposed reforms.

9 Later privatizations were implemented by laws passed by Congress rather than by decrees. While in some cases this caused delays, the delays did not have the same potential negative impact on the credibility of the reform program as delays in one of the first privatizations might have had.

10 ENTeL's assets were to be allocated among these four companies according to the services the companies were to provide. The Northern Company had an exclusive license to provide basic telephone services in the northern states of Argentina and in the northern half of Buenos Aires. The Southern Company had an exclusive license to provide basic telephone services in the southern states and in the southern half of Buenos Aires. The basic telephone service was defined as "the provision of fixed telecommunication links that form part of the public telephone network or that are connected to such network and the provision of the means for urban, interurban and international live voice telephone service" (Terms and Conditions, 5 January 1990, paragraph 8.1, contained in Decree 62/1990). All other services were deemed to be open to competition.

11 The government had considered privatizing ENTeL without granting an exclusive license, but decided that without it, there might be no bids. Exclusivity was also a necessary condition for generating the income to finance increased investment. However, by splitting the market for basic services into two exclusive geographical zones the government hoped to create a yardstick for measuring competition between the two licensee companies. In addition, by creating two companies, the government ensured that there would be at least two strong potential competitors at the end of the exclusive period.

12 Among them were the obligation to prepare accounts in sufficient detail to permit regulation of the service and to ensure that there was no cross-subsidization between services, which was prohibited; and provision for interconnection between the licensee companies and independent operators. All purchases of goods or services over US$500,000 required competitive bidding; local suppliers were given a 10 percent price preference; minimum levels of local content were set; and the import of used equipment was banned.

13 A qualified consortium had to include at least one telephone operating company that held at least 10 percent of the consortium's equity and one (or at least two) shareholder that held at least 20 percent of its shares. These requirements were designed to ensure that at least 30 percent of the consortium's equity was held by a maximum of three shareholders. These shareholders and any other shareholders holding more than 10 percent of the equity had to be able to demonstrate that at the time of the prequalification their assets exceeded $1 billion. For local firms whose membership was additional to the first 30 percent, this requirement was reduced to $300 million. All members of the consortium with shareholdings above 10 percent were required to accept joint and several obligation for the payment of the sale price. Changes in the composition of the consortium were limited. The consortium was required to delegate all management responsibilities to the operator; this management contract was subject to review by the regulatory authority.

14 *Wall Street Journal,* "Argentina Kicks Off Privatization Drive," 26 June 1990; *La Nación,* "Se adjudicó ENTeL a Bell y a Telefónica," 2 July 1990, and "Postergan la firma para la cesión de ENTeL," 13 August 1990; and *Wall Street Journal,* "Argentina Cancels Sale of Phone Unit to U.S.-Led Group," 8 October 1990.

15 Decree 2096/1990; Telecom Argentina, *Prospecto,* March 1992, p. 12; and *La Nación,* "En una tensa jornada, se ajudico al grupo stet la Zona Norte," 8 October 1990.

16 *La Prensa,* "Venden al publico el 25% de las acciones de ENTeL," 24 May 1991.

17 While value of a dollar of Argentine sovereign debt was US$0.19 on the secondary market, given the imperfections of the market, this was not necessarily the social value to Argentina of the debt repurchased. For a more detailed discussion, see Abdala (1991).

18 Decree 677/1990, 11 April 1990. The prerequisite assets levels for the operator member of the bidding consortium were increased from US$1 billion to US$1.5 billion. At the same time the minimum asset level for members of the consortium outside the principal nucleus (that included the operator and one or two additional shareholders with a minimum shareholding together of 30 percent) was reduced from US$300,000 to US$200,000 for domestic members of the consortium and from US$1 billion to US$500,000 for foreign members. Altogether the members of the consortium would have to have combined assets in excess of US$4 billion.

19 Rates were to be set prior to the presentation of offers to a level that would give ". . . an efficient operator a reasonable rate of return on the fixed assets used to offer the service" (paragraph 12.2 of the original Terms and Conditions). In the two-year transition period the licensee companies would be permitted to update their rates according to monthly changes in the consumer price index. If these adjustments did not allow the licensee companies to achieve a rate of return of 16 percent, the companies could adjust their prices to achieve this level of return. The real price of residential services would not be allowed to increase except to maintain the relative price structure that existed at the time ENTeL's assets were transferred to the licensee companies. During the five-year exclusive period following the licensee companies would not be allowed to increase the overall price of their services (net of connection charges) by more than the consumer price index minus 2 percent each year. Meeting this requirement was a prerequisite for an extension of the exclusive license for another three years. In the last three years of the license, increases in the general price level of services (net of connection charges) would be limited to the consumer price index minus 4 percent. Connection charges were limited to 50 percent of the direct cost of the line for residential services and 100 percent of the direct cost for other services. During the transition period the connection charge would be treated like a telephone tariff. After that the charge would take the form of a loan from the user to the company with a five-year term and a 7 percent interest rate. At the end of the exclusive period the regulatory agency would continue to regulate rates only in those parts of the country where there was no competition.

20 Decree 1185/1990. This decree was drafted by a joint Argentine-World Bank team.

21 *La Nación,* "Defendio Maria J. Alsogaray la privatización de ENTeL," 12 March 1990; *La Nación,* "Se modificaron los pliegos de venta de ENTeL y de Aerolineas," 2 April 1990; *Financial Times,* "Crossed Lines over Privatisation," 25 May 1990.

22 *Wall Street Journal,* "Privatization Campaign in Argentina Bogs Down," 25 October 1990 and *La Nación,* "ENTeL: el Gobierno opto por flexibilizar

valores" and "El pulso telefónico ajustado por inflación alcanzaria a Australes 293,68," 29 October 1990.

23 ENTeL, Region Norte, *Contrato de Transferencia,* section 16; ENTeL, Region Sur, *Contrato de Transferencia,* section 16; Abdala 1991, 59; Telecom Argentina, *Prospecto,* March 1992, p. 22; and Telefónica de Argentina, *US Offering Prospectus,* December 1991, p. 33.

24 Chapter 8 of the Terms and Conditions defined basic services as fixed telecommunications links that are part of (or connected to) the public telephone network and provide the means for urban, interurban and international live voice telephone services.

25 *La Prensa,* "La tarifa telefónica esta congelada, ya que es alta y remunerativa," 7 April 1991.

26 Cited in a presentation made by the Subsecretary of Communications, Dr. German Kammerrath, at the World Bank in Washington, D.C., 23 October 1992.

27 Because other economic reforms have taken place over the period, separating the increase in confidence due to improvements in regulation in the telecommunications sector and improvements due to progress in overall reform is problematic.

28 The Telefónica consortium paid US$114 million in cash and US$2,720 in Argentine sovereign debt and interest; the Telecom consortium paid US$100 million in cash and US$2,309 in debt and interest. At the time of the transaction debt traded in the secondary market at 19 U.S. cents on the dollar. Given the imperfections of the market however, $0.19 was not necessarily the social value to Argentina of the debt repurchased. For a more detailed discussion see Abdala (1991, 25–36).

29 The price for the workers' 10 percent of the companies' shares was set in late 1992, linked to the price paid for the first tranche of the privatization and therefore does not reflect changes in market perceptions.

30 As of 30 September 1992, Telefónica had paid out a cumulative US$115 million in dividends, Telecom US$51 million. These are small amounts relative to the level of investment.

31 These are the numbers reported by the companies and have not yet been verified by the National Telecommunications Commission.

32 Although in a recent appeal the executive appointed an arbitrator with expertise in the field to handle the case.

33 For a detailed discussion of the application of this methodology to the case of telecommunications in Argentina see Abdala (1991). The estimates presented in this case study are updated versions of the estimations presented in the dissertation.

34 This does ignore the effects of potential economies of scope.

35 Recall that the discount rates used in the model are 16.5 percent for 1990 and 14 percent for 1991.

References

Abdala, Manuel Angel. 1991. "Distributional Impact Evaluation of Divestiture in a High-Inflation Economy: The Case of ENTeL Argentina." Ph.D. dissertation, Boston University.

——— 1992a. "Desregulación, privatización y regulación en el sector argentino de las telecommunicaciones." *Estudiós* 63: 125–38.

——— 1992b. "Privatización y cambios en los costos sociales de la inflación: El caso de ENTeL Argentina." *Desarrollo económico* 32(127): 357–80.

Abueva, Jose V., 1972, *Complexities of Change*. Manila: U.S. Information Service.

——— 1988. "Philippine Ideologies and National Development." In Raul P. DeGuzmán and Mila A. Reforma, eds. *Government and Politics of the Philippines*. New York: Oxford University Press.

Acton, Jan Paul, and Ingo Vogelsang. 1990. *Telephone Demand over the Atlantic: Evidence from Country-Pair Data*. Santa Monica: Rand Corporation.

Agurto, Renato C. 1991. "Sector Telecomunicaciones." In Christian Laroulet, ed., *Soluciones privadas a problemas publicos*. Santiago: ILD.

Ale, Jorge. 1990. *Estado empresario y privatizacion en Chile*. Serie investigaciones 2. Santiago: Universidad Nacional Andres Bello.

Ale, Jorge. 1989. "Un nuevo esquema de regulación de monopolios naturales." *Estudiós públicos*. Santiago.

Ambrose, W., P. Hennemeyer, and J. Chapon. 1990. *Privatizing Telecommunications Systems: Business Opportunities in Developing Countries*. IFC Discussion Paper 10. Washington, D.C.: International Finance Corporation.

Arri, Raul Vicente, L. Donikian, Roberto Varone, and Vito Di Leo. 1988. *Teléfonos: De la política nacional al saqueo privatista*. Buenos Aires: Agrupación Telefónica Eva Perón.

Arriagada, Gerardo. 1984. "The Chilean Political System: An Exploration into the Future." *Estudiós Cieplan* 15.

Baglehole, K. C. 1970. *A Century of Service: A Brief History of Cable and Wireless Ltd., 1868–1968*. Welwyn Garden City: Herts.

Baldwin Robert, and Christopher McCrudden. 1987. *Regulation and Public Law*. London: Weidenfeld and Nicholson.

Banco Central de la Republica Argentina. 1992. *Indicadores económicos*. Buenos Aires.

Baron, David P. 1992. *Business and its Environment*. Englewood Cliffs, N.J.: Prentice Hall.

References

Baron, David P., and Roger Myerson. 1982. "Regulating a Monopolist with Unknown Costs." *Econometrica* 50: 911–30.

——— 1982. "Measurement Cost and the Organization of Markets." *Journal of Law and Economics* 25: 27–48.

Barzel, Yooram. 1989. *Economic Analysis of Property Rights*. Cambridge, Mass.: Harvard University Press.

Barty-King, H. 1979. *Girdle Round the Earth: The Story of Cable and Wireless and its Predecessors to Mark the Group's Jubilee, 1929–79*. London: Heinemann.

Basco, Juan, and Carlos Givogri. 1985. "Situación actual y alternativas para el reordenamiento de las telecomunicaciones en la Argentina." *Estudiós* 47.

Beesley, M. E. 1981. "Liberalisation of the Use of British Telecommunications Network." London: Her Majesty's Stationery Office.

Beesley, M. E., and B. Laidlaw. 1989. *The Future of Telecommunications*. Institute of Economic Affairs Research Monograph 42. London.

——— 1992. "The Development of Telecommunications Policy in the U.K., 1981–1991." London Business School.

Beesley, M. E., and S. Littlechild. 1989. "The Regulation of Privatized Monopolies in the United Kingdom." *Rand Journal of Economics* 20: 454–72.

Bishop, M., and J. Kay. 1988. "Does Privatization Work?" London Business School.

Bour, Enrique. 1987. *Teoría económica y reformas del estado*. In *FIEL, el fracaso del estatismo*. Buenos Aires: Editorial Planeta Sudamericana.

Bour, Enrique, and Adolfo Sutrzenegger. 1988. *Empresa pública e interés público: Rol y regulación de la empresa pública en Argentina*. Documentos de divulgación 9. Buenos Aires: SIGEP.

Boyce, James K. 1992. "The Revolving Door? External Debt and Capital Flight: A Philippine Case Study." *World Development* 20 (3): 335–49.

Bradley, K. 1992. *Phone Wars–The Story of Mercury Communications*. London: Century Business.

Bradley, I., and C. Price. 1988. "The Economic Regulation of Private Industries by Price Constraints." *Journal of Industrial Economics* 37: 99–106.

British Telecommunications. 1992. "Pricing for Choice." London (20 March).

Business Monitor International, Ltd. 1991. *Argentina 1991: Annual Report on government, Economy and Business*. London.

Bacungan, Froilan M., and Alfredo Tadiar. 1988. *Government and Politics of the Philippines*. New York: Oxford University Press.

Cabral, Luis, and Michael H. Riordan. 1989. "Incentives for Cost Reduction under Price-Cap Regulation." *Journal of Regulatory Economics*.

Cain, Bruce, John Ferejohn, and Morris Fiorina. 1987. *The Personal Vote*. Cambridge Mass.: Harvard University Press.

Calvert, R. 1992. "The Rational Choice Theory of Social Institutions: Cooperation, Coordination, and Communication." University of Rochester, New York. Mimeo.

Carsberg, Bryan. 1991. "Oftel: Competition and the Duopoly Review." In C. Veljanovski, ed., *Regulators and the Market. An Assessment of the Growth of Regulation in the UK*. London: Institute of Economic Affairs.

Cave, Martin. 1991. "Recent Developments in the Regulation of Former Nationalized Industries." Mimeo.

——— 1992. "Handout" prepared for the 20th Annual Telecommunications Policy Research Conference, Solomons Island, Maryland, 12–14 September 1992.

276

References

Clad, James. 1987a. "Tainted Watchdogs." *Far Eastern Economic Review*, 17 September.
  1987b. "Scramble for Power." *Far Eastern Economic Review*, 17 September.
Coase, Ronald H. 1960. "The Nature of Social Cost." *Journal of Law and Economics* 3: 1–44.
  1988. "R. H. Coase Lectures." *Journal of Law, Economics and Organization* 4 (Spring): 1–48.
Coloma, Fernando, and Luis Oscar Herrera. 1990. "Institutional and Economic Analysis of the Telecommunications Sector in Chile." Working Paper 125. Economics Department, Catholic University of Chile, Santiago.
Cox, G. 1987. *The Efficient Secret*. Cambridge University Press.
  1993. "The Development of Collective Responsibility in the United Kingdom." *Parliamentary History* 13: 32–47.
Crawley, Eduardo. 1984. *A House Divided: Argentina, 1880–1980*. London: C. Hurst and Company.
Danielsen, A., and D. Kamerschen. 1983. *Telecommunications in the Post-Divestiture Era*. Lexington, Kentucky: Lexington Books.
De Guzman, Raul P., and Mila A. Reforma. 1988. *Government and Politics of the Philippines*. New York: Oxford University Press.
De Luna, Noel D. 1986. "Telecoms: Interlocking Interests." *Business Day*, 14 April.
Deutsch, K. W., J. I. Dominguez, and H. Heclo. 1981. *Comparative Government: Politics of Industrialized and Developing Nations*. New York: Houghton Mifflin Company.
Dimock, M. E. 1933. *British Public Utilities and National Development*. London: George Allen and Urwin, Ltd.
Doyle, C. 1990. "British Privatization Policy and the History of British Telecom Divestiture." Paper prepared for the comparative divestiture project of the World Bank, Policy Research Department, Finance and Private Sector Development Division, Washington, D.C.
Duverger, Maurice. 1954. *Political Parties: Their Organization and Activity in the Modern State*. New York: John Wiley and Sons.
Edie, C. J. 1991. *Democracy by Default: Dependency and Clientelism in Jamaica*. Boulder: L. Rienner.
ENTeL. Various Years. *Annual Report*. Buenos Aires.
Falcoff, Mark. 1989. *Modern Chile, 1970–1989: A Critical History*. Transaction Publishers.
Fesler, James W. 1983. "The Higher Civil Service in Europe and the United States." In Bruce L. Smith, ed., *The Higher Civil Service of Europe and Canada, Lessons for the United States*. Washington, D.C.: The Brookings Institution.
Fernando, Enrique M. 1974. *Constitution of the Philippines*. Quezon City: Central Law.
Fiorina, Morris. 1983. "Legislative Choice of Regulatory Forums: Legal Process or Administrative Process?" *Public Choice* 39: 33–66.
Fontaine Talavera, Arturo. 1989. "Mapa de las corrientes políticas en las elecciones generales de 1989." *Estudiós públicos*.
Friedland, Jonathan. 1988. "PLDT's Number Change." *Far Eastern Economic Review*, 6 October.
Fundación de investigaciones económicas Latino Americas. Various Years. *Indicadores de coyuntura*. Buenos Aires.

277

References

1988. *Regulaciones y estancamiento: El caso Argentino.* Buenos Aires: Ediciones Manantial.

Furnish, Dale B. 1971. "Chilean Antitrust Law." *The American Journal of Comparative Law* 19: 464–87.

Galal, Ahmed, L. Jones, Pankaj Tandon, and Ingo Vogelsang. 1992. "Questions and Approaches to Answers." Paper presented at World Bank Conference on the Welfare Consequences of Selling Public Enterprises, June.

1994. *Welfare Consequences of Selling Public Enterprises: An Empirical Analysis.* Washington, D.C.: World Bank. New York: Oxford University Press.

Gavino, Jacinto. 1992. "A Critical Study of the Regulation of the Telephone Utility: Some Options for Policy Development." Ph.D. dissertation, College of Public Administration, the University of the Philippines.

Gely, Rafael, and Pablo T. Spiller. 1990. "A Rational Choice Theory of Supreme Court Statutory Decisions, with Applications to the *State Farm and Grove City* Cases." *Journal of Law, Economics and Organization* 6: 263–301.

General Telephone and Electronics Corporation. 1976. *Notice of 1976 Annual Meeting and Proxy Statement.* Stamford, Conn.

Gerchunoff, P., and Alfredo Guadagni. "Elementos para un programa de reformación económica del estado." 5ta Convención de Bancos Privados Nacionales desregulación y crecimiento. Buenos Aires.

Gerchunoff, P., and Alfredo Visintini. 1990. "Privatizaciones en un contexto de inflación e incertidumbre." In A. Porto, ed., *Economía de las empresas públicas.* Buenos Aires: Editorial Tesis.

Gilbert, R., and D. Newbery. 1990. "Regulatory Constitutions." University of California, Berkeley.

Givogri, Carlos. 1985. "Estudio de un programa para la expansión del servicio de telecomunicaciones, 1985–2005." *Estudiós* 47.

Glaister, S. 1987. "Regulation Through Output Related Profits Tax." *Journal of Industrial Economics* 35: 281–96.

Goldberg, V. 1976. "Regulation and Administered Contracts." *Bell Journal of Economics and Management Science* 7: 426–52.

Gonzaga, Leo. 1982. "Philippines Modernizes Telephone System." *Far Eastern Economic Review*, 8 April.

Greenwald, Bruce, and William Sharkey. 1989. "The Economies of Deregulation of Local Exchange Telecommunications." *Journal of Regulatory Economics* 1 (December): 319–39.

Grieve-Smith, J., ed. 1984. *Strategic Planning in Nationalised Industries.* London: Macmillan.

Guadagni, Alieto. 1976. "Análisis económico del financiamiento de las empresas del estado." *Desarrollo económico* 15 (60): 549–64.

Hawes, Gary. 1987. *The Philippine State and the Marcos Regime: The Politics of Export.* Ithaca: Cornell University Press.

Hazlewood, A. 1953. "The Origins of the State Telephone Service in Britain." *Oxford Economic Papers* 5: 13–25.

Heald, D. 1980. "The Economic and Financial Control of UK Nationalized Industries." *Economic Journal* 90: 243–65.

Heclo, H. 1977. *A Government of Strangers.* Washington, D.C.: The Brookings Institution.

Herrera, Alejandra. 1989. *La revolución tecnológica y la telefonía Argentina.* Buenos Aires: Editorial Legasa.

278

References

1992. "Del cuasi monopolio estatal al oligopolio privado: La privatización de la telefonía Argentina." *Revista de la Cepal*. Buenos Aires.

Hormell, Orren C. 1928. "Electricity in Great Britain: A Study in Administration." *National Municipal Review* 17 (6).

Huber, Peter W., Michael K. Kellogg, and James Thorne. 1992. *The Geodesic Network II: 1993 Report on Competition in the Telephone Industry*. Washington, D.C.: The Geodesic Company.

Instituto Argentino para el desararrollo económico. Realidad Economica, 1992–3. Buenos Aires.

Instituto de estudiós económicos sobre de realidad Argentina y Latino Americana. 1987. "Informe de diagnóstico. Empresa Nacional de Telcomunicaciones." Córdoba.

IEERAL. 1989. "La asociación de ENTeL con Telefónica de España." Programa de asistencia al poder legislativo 18. Córdoba.

Isberto, Ramon R. 1986. "The Philcomsat Story." *Business Day*, 19 August.

Jacobson, Gary C. 1990. *The Electoral Origins of Divided Government: Competition in the U.S. House Elections, 1946–1988*. Boulder: Westview Press.

Jamaica Telephone Company. 1969–87. *Annual Report*. Kingston.
    Balance Sheets. Kingston.

Jamaica International Telecommunications Ltd. 1973–87. *Annual Report*. Kingston.
    1988–91. Balance Sheets. Kingston.

Johnson, L. L. 1989. "Price Caps in Telecommunications Regulatory Reform." Rand Note N-2894-MF/RC. Rand Corporation, Santa Monica.

Jones, Leroy, Pankaj Tandon, and Ingo Vogelsang. 1990. *Selling Public Enterprises: A Cost–Benefit Methodology*. Cambridge, Mass., MIT Press.

Joskow, Paul L. 1972. "The Determination of the Allowed Rate of Return in a Formal Regulatory Proceeding." *Bell Journal of Economics and Management Science* 3: 632–44.

    1973. "Pricing Decisions of Regulated Firms: A Behavioral Approach." *Bell Journal of Economics and Management Science* 4: 118–40.

    1974. "Inflation and Environmental Concern: Structural Change in the Process of Public Utility Price Regulation." *Journal of Law and Economics* 17: 291–328.

Joskow, Paul, and Roger G. Noll. 1981. "Regulation in Theory and Practice: An Overview." In G. Fromm, ed., *Studies in Public Regulation*. Cambridge, Mass.: MIT Press.

Joskow, Paul, and Richard Schmalensee. *Markets for Power*. Cambridge, Mass.: MIT Press.

Joskow, P. L., and P. McAvoy. 1975. "Regulation and Franchise Conditions of the Electric Power Companies in the 1970s." *American Economic Review* 65: 295–311.

Kahn, A. 1988. *The Economics of Regulation: Principles and Institutions*. 2nd ed. New York: John Wiley and Sons.

Kay, J., C. Mayer, and D. Thompson. 1986. *Privatization and Regulation: The U.K. Experience*. Oxford: Clarendon Press.

Keen, F. N. 1925. *The Law Relating to Public Service Undertakings*. London: P. S. King and Sons, Ltd.

Kerry, M. 1983. "Administrative Law and the Administrator." *Management in Government* 38 (3).

References

Knieps, Günter, and Pablo T. Spiller. 1983. "Regulating by Partial Deregulation: The Case of Telecommunications." *Administrative Law Review* 35: 391–422.

Laffont, Jean Jacques, and Jean Tirole. 1986. "Using Cost Observation to Regulate Firms." *Journal of Political Economy* 94: 614–41.

———. 1993. *A Theory of Incentives in Procurement and Regulation.* Cambridge, Mass.: MIT Press.

Levy, Brian, and Pablo Spiller. 1991. "Regulation, Institutions and Economic Efficiency: Promoting Regulatory Reform and Private Sector Participation in Developing Countries: A Proposal." World Bank and University of Illinois, Urbana, Economics Department.

Lewis, Paul H. 1990. *The Crisis of Argentine Capitalism.* Chapel Hill: University of North Carolina Press.

Littlechild, S. 1979. *Elements of Telecommunications Economics.* London: Institute of Electrical Engineering.

———. 1983. *Regulation of British Telecommunications Profitability.* London: Her Majesty's Stationary Office.

Llach, Juan. 1990. "La nueva economía institucional y la desestatización de empresas públicas." In A. Porto, ed., *Economía de las empresas públicas.* Buenos Aires: Editorial Tesis.

Loeb, Martin, and Wesley Magat. 1979. "A Decentralized Method of Utility Regulation." *Journal of Law and Economics* 22: 399–404.

Luders, Rolf. 1988. "Aspects of Privatization: The Case of Argentine 1976–81." World Bank Discussion Paper 16. Washington, D.C.

Lyon, T. P. 1991. "Regulation with 20-20 Hindsight: 'Heads I Win, Tails You Lose'?" *Rand Journal of Economics* 22: 581–95.

McCubbins, Mathew D. 1993. "Prospects for Stability in Argentine Politics." Department of Political Economy, University of California, San Diego.

McCubbins, Mathew D., Roger G. Noll, and Barry R. Weingast. 1987. "Administrative Procedures as Instruments of Political Control." *Journal of Law, Economics, and Organization* 3: 243–77.

———. 1989. "Structure and Process, Politics and Policy: Administrative Arrangements and the Political Control of Agencies." *Virginia Law Review* 75: 431–82.

Manapat, Ricardo. 1991. *Some Are Smarter than Others: The History of Marcos Crony Capitalism.* New York: Aletheia Publications.

———. 1993. *Wrong Number: The PLDT Telephone Monopoly.* The Animal Farm Series Pamphlet, Manila.

Marino, Geraldina. 1991. "La privatización de ENTeL-Empresa Nacional de Telecomunicaciones." Boletín informativo techint 265. Buenos Aires.

Mathios, Alan, and Roberto Rogers. 1989. "The Impact of Alternative Forms of State Regulation of AT&T on Direct Dial, Long Distance Telephone Rates." *The Rand Journal of Economics* 20: 437–53.

Matthews, R. 1986. "The Economics of Institutions and the Sources of Growth." *Economic Journal* 96 (December): 903–18.

Meek, K. 1988. *Telecommunications Price Control in the U.K.* London: International Institute of Communications.

Melo, Jose Ricardo. 1992. "Panorama de las telecomunicaciones en Chile." Universidad de Chile, Santiago. Mimeo.

Mendez, Roberto. 1990. "La opinion publica y la eleccion presidencial de 1989." *Estudiós públicos.*

References

Miller, Charles. 1985. *Lobbying Government: Understanding and Influencing the Corridors of Power.* Oxford: Basil Blackwell, Ltd.

Mills, C. E. 1981. "Public Policy and Private Enterprise in Commonwealth Caribbean Countries." *Social and Economic Studies* 23 (2): 216–37.

Montero, Cecilia. 1990. "The Evolution of the Chilean Entrepreneur: The Rise of a New Actor." *Estudiós Cieplan* 30: 91–122.

Moore, J. 1986. "The Success of Privatization." In J. Kay, C. Mayer, and D. Thompson, eds., *Privatization and Regulation: The U.K. Experience.* Oxford: Clarendon Press.

Mueller, M. 1993. "Comments on Interconnection for European Telecommunications." Paper presented at the 21st Annual Telecommunications Policy Research Conference, Solomon Islands, Maryland, October.

Newman, K. 1986. *The Selling of British Telecom.* London: Holt, Rinehart and Winston.

North, Douglass C. 1981. *Structure and Change in Economic History.* New York: Norton.

———. 1990. *Institutions, Institutional Change, and Economic Performance.* Cambridge, Mass.: Harvard University Press.

North, Douglass C., and Robert P. Thomas. 1973. *The Rise of the Western World: A New Economic History.* Cambridge, Mass.: Harvard University Press.

Nuñez Miñana, Hugo, and Alberto Porto. 1976. "Análisis de la evolución de precios de empresas públicas en Argentina." *Desarrollo económico* 16 (63): 307–32.

Office of Water Services. 1991. *The Cost of Capital-Consultation Paper.* Birmingham.

Oftel (Office of Telecommunications) 1985. *"British Telecom's Price Changes November 1985."* Statement issued by the Director General of Telecommunications. London.

———. 1986. *Review of British Telecom's Tariff Changes.* Statement issued by the Director General of Telecommunications, November. London.

———. 1988b. "Response to Oftel's Consultative Document on the Future Regulation of British Telecom's Prices." London.

———. 1988a. "The Control of British Telecom's Prices." Statement issued by the Director General of Telecommunications, 7 July. London.

Palmer, M. S. R. 1992. "The Economics of Organization and Ministerial Responsibility: Towards a Framework of Analysis for Westminster Government." Mimeo.

Panaligan, Rey G. 1993. "Justice Gutierrez Retires from High Court." *Manila Bulletin,* 2 February.

Panzoni, E. 1983. "Background, Nature and Problems of the Public Sector in Argentina Economy." *Annals of Public and Co-operative Economy* 54 (4): 377–85.

Paredes, Ricardo. 1987. "Análisis de la ley antimonopolios en Chile." Working Paper 15. Universidad de Chile, Santiago.

Parris, C. D. 1981. "Joint Venture I; The Trinidad-Tobago Telephone Company 1968–1972." *Social and Economic Studies* 30 (1): 108–26.

Payne, A. J. 1988. *Politics in Jamaica.* London: C. Hurst and Company.

Peltzman, Sam. 1976. "Toward a More General Theory of Regulation." *Journal of Law and Economics* 19 (2): 211–40.

Redwood, J., and J. Hatch. 1982. *Controlling Public Industries.* Oxford: Basil Blackwell.

281

References

Riker, William H. 1967. *The Theory of Political Coalitions*. New Haven: Yale University Press.

Riordan, Michael H. 1992. "Revelance of the New Regulatory Economics for Telecommunications." Washington, D.C., The World Bank. Mimeo.

Ronquillo, Bernardino. 1963. "Profile of Manila." *Far Eastern Economic Review*, 12 September.

——— 1965. "Philippines: Election Issues." *Far Eastern Economic Review*, 22 April.

Rosenblatt, Robert A. 1977. "GT&E Accused of Giving Big Loans for Pact." *Los Angeles Times*, 13 January.

Salzberg, E. M. 1990. "The Judges of the English Court of Appeal. Decision-making Characteristics and Promotion to the House of Lords." University of California at Berkeley. Mimeo.

——— 1991. "The Delegation of Legislative Powers to the Courts and the Independence of the Judiciary." University of California at Berkeley. Mimeo.

Schwartz, Edward, Pablo T. Spiller, and Santiago Urbiztondo. 1993. "A Positive Theory of Legislative Intent." *Law and Contemporary Problems* 57: 51–86.

Scobie, James R. 1971. *Argentina: A City and a Nation*. 2nd ed. London: Oxford University Press.

Select Committee on the Treasury and Civil Service. 1981. *Report on the Financing of the Nationalized Industries*. HC 378. London: George Allen and Unwin Ltd.

Shepsle, Kenneth, and Barry R. Weingast. 1981. "Structure-Induced Equlibrium and Legislative Choice. *Public Choice* 37: 503–19.

——— 1987a. "Institutionalizing Majority Rule: A Social Theory with Policy Implications." *AEA Papers and Proceedings*: 367–71.

——— 1987b. "The Institutional Foundations of Committee Power." *American Political Science Review* 81: 85–105.

——— 1989. "Penultimate Power: Conference Committees and the Legislative Process." Hoover Institution Working Paper P-89-7. Stanford University.

Shin, Richard T., and John S. Ying. 1992. "Unnatural Monopolies in Local Telephone." *Rand Journal of Economics* 23: 171–83.

Shugart, M. S., and J. M. Carey. 1992. *Presidents and Assemblies*. Cambridge University Press.

Sindicatura Gengra de Empresas Publicas. Various years. "Estados contables de los principales empresas publicas, 1980–7." Buenos Aires.

Sison, Luis F. 1986. "Report of PLDT Supervisory Committee, Presidential Commission on Good Government." Manila.

Spiller, Pablo T. 1988. "La Economía política de regulaciones a las industrias: Un informe con implicaciones para estudiós de Regulaciones en paises en desarrollo." *Estudiós de Economía* 15 (3): 419–70, December 1988.

——— 1993. "Institutions and Regulatory Commitment in Utilities' Privatization." *Industrial and Corporate Change* 2: 387–450.

Spiller, Pablo T., and Rafael Gely. 1990. "A Rational Choice Theory of Supreme Court Statutory Decisions, with Applications to the *State Farm* and *Grove City* Cases." *Journal of Law, Economics and Organization* 6: 263–301.

——— 1992. "Congressional Control or Judicial Interpretation: The Determinants of U.S. Supreme Court Labor Decisions: 1949–1988." *Rand Journal of Economics* 23: 463–92.

——— 1993. "Notes on Public Utility Regulation in the UK: 1850–1950." University of Illinois, Urbana. Mimeo.

References

Spiller, Pablo T., and Santiago Urbiztondo. 1994. "Political Appointees vs. Career Civil Servants: A Multiple Principals Theory of Political Bureaucracies." *European Journal of Political Economy.*

Spiller, Pablo T., and Luis Viana. 1992. "How Not to Do It: Electricity Regulation in Argentina, Brazil, Chile, and Uruguay." University of California, Berkeley. Mimeo.

Spiller, P. T., and I. Vogelsang. 1992. "Regulation without Commitment: Price Regulation of UK Utilities (with Special Emphasis on Telecommunications)." University of Illinois, Urbana. Mimeo.

Spulber, Daniel. 1989. *Regulation and Markets.* Cambridge, Mass.: MIT Press.

Stone, C. 1981. "Party Voting in Jamaica (1959–1976)." In C. Stone and A. Brown, eds., *Perspectives on Jamaica.* Kingston: Jamaica Publishing House.

———. 1986. *Class, State and Democracy in Jamaica.* New York: Praeger.

———. 1992. "Putting Public Enterprises to Work: A Study of Privatization in Jamaica." National Investment Bank of Jamaica, Kingston, Jamaica.

Swaby, R. A. 1974a. "The Rationale for State Ownership of Public Utilities in Jamaica." *Social and Economic Studies* 30 (1): 75:b2107.

Swaby, R. A. 1974b. "Some Problems of Public Utility Regulation by a Statutory Board in Jamaica: The Jamaica Omnibus Services Case." *Social and Economic Studies* 23 (2): 242–63.

Taagepera, Rein, and Matthew S. Shugart. 1993. "Predicting the Number of Parties: A Quantitative Model of Duverger Mechanical Effect." *American Political Science Review* 87: 455–64.

Tancangco, Luzviminda G. 1988. "The Electoral System and Political Parties in the Philippines." In R. P. De Guzman and M. A. Reforma, eds., *Government and Politics of the Philippines.* New York: Oxford University Press.

Taylor, Alan M. 1992. "External Dependence, Demographic Burdens, and Argentine Economic Decline after the Belle Epoque." *Journal of Economic History* 52 (4): 907–35.

Taylor, Lesley. 1980. *Telecommunications Demand: A Survey and Critique.* Cambridge: Ballinger Publishing Company.

Telecommunications of Jamaica. 1988–91. *Annual Report.* Kingston.

Telefónica de Argentina. 1991. *Annual Report.* Buenos Aires.

———. 1991. *Prospectus for Public Offer Sale.* Buenos Aires.

Tiglao, Rigoberto D. 1988. "The Consolidation of Dictatorship." In Aurora Javate-De Dios, Petronilo Bn. Daroy, Lorna Kalaw-Tirol, *Dictatorship and Revolution.* Manila: Conspectus Foundation Inc.

———. 1989. "Lopez Power Revolt." *Far Eastern Economic Review,* 20 March.

———. 1993a. "Into a Corner: Philippine Phone Monopoly Assailed by Critics." *Far Eastern Economic Review,* 11 February.

———. 1993b. "Open Lines: Philippine Phone Firm Faces Challenges." *Far Eastern Economic Review,* 25 February.

———. 1993c. "On the Hook: Ramos Moves Against Philippine Phone Firm." *Far Eastern Economic Review,* 25 March.

Ugalde, Alberto. J. 1984. *Las empresas públicas en Argentina.* Buenos Aires: Ediciones El Cronista Comercial.

U.S. SEC (U.S. Securities and Exchange Commission). 1977. "SEC vs. PLDT, Civil Action No. 77-0067." United States District Court, District of Columbia, 12 January. Quoted in Manapat (1991) and in *Los Angeles Times, New York Times, Wall Street Journal,* 13 January.

References

Velijanovski, Cento. 1991. "The Regulation Game." In C. Velijanovski, ed., *Regulators and the Market: An Assessment of the Growth of Regulation in the U.K.* London: Institute of Economic Affairs.

——— 1992. *The Future of Industry Regulation in the U.K.: A Report of an Independent Inquiry.* London: Lexecon Ltd.

Vickers, J., and G. Yarrow. 1986. "Telecommunications: Liberalisation and the Privatization of British Telecom." In. J. Kay, C. Mayer, and D. Thompson, eds., *Privatization and Regulation: The U.K. Experience.* Oxford: Clarendon Press.

——— 1988. *Privatization: An Economic Analysis.* Cambridge, Mass.: MIT Press.

Vogelsang, I. 1989. "Price Cap Regulation of Telecommunications Services: A Long-Run Approach." In. M. A. Crew, ed., *Deregulation and Diversification of Utilities.* Boston: Kluwer Academic Publishers.

Vogelsang, Ingo, Leroy Jones, Pankaj Tandon, with Manuel Abdala, and Christopher Doyle. 1992. "The Divestiture of British Telecom: A Cost-Benefit Case Study." World Bank, Washington, D.C.

Wall Street Journal. 1977. "New Details on GTE Philippine Payments Disclosed in SEC Suit against 3 Concerns," 13 January.

Waisman, Carlos H. 1987. *Reversal of Development in Argentina: Postwar Counterrevolutionary Policies and Their Structural Consequences.* Princeton: Princeton University Press.

Warren M., and J. Lis. 1992. "Regulatory Standstill: Analysis of the 1993 Budget." Occasional Paper 105, Washington University, St. Louis.

Water Services Association, Water Companies Association. 1991. *The Cost of Capital in the Water Industry.* London.

Weingast, Barry R. 1984. "The Congressional-Bureaucratic System: A Principal Agent Perspective." *Public Choice* 44: 147–92.

——— 1993. "The Economic Role of Political Institutions." Stanford University. Mimeo.

Weingast, Barry R., and M. Moran. 1983. "Bureaucratic Discretion or Congressional Control: Regulatory Policy Making by the Federal Trade Commission." *Journal of Political Economy* 91: 765–800.

Williamson, Oliver E. 1975. *Markets and Hierarchies: Analysis and Antitrust Implications.* New York: Free Press.

——— 1976. "Franchise Bidding for Natural Monopolies: In General and With Respect to CATV." *Bell Journal of Economics and Management Science* 7: 73–104.

——— 1979. "Transaction-Cost Economics: The Governance of Contractual Relations." *Journal of Law and Economics* 22: 3–61.

——— 1985. *The Economic Institutions of Capitalism.* New York: Free Press.

——— 1988. "The Logic of Economic Organization." *Journal of Law, Economics and Organization* 4: 65–93.

——— 1991. "Comparative Economic Organization: The Analysis of Discrete Structural Alternative." *Administrative Science Quarterly* 36: 269–96.

——— 1993. "Public and Private Bureaus: A Transaction Costs Economics Assessment." University of California, Berkeley. Mimeo.

World Bank. 1992. "Bolivia: Restructuring for Growth, Part One: The Main Report." Washington, D.C.

Wurfel, David. 1988. *Filipino Politics: Development and Decay.* Ithaca: Cornell University Press.

References

Wynia, Gary W. 1978. *Argentina in the Postwar Era: Politics and Economic Policy Making in a Divided Society*. Albuquerque: University of New Mexico Press.

Young, H. 1985. "Judges and the Exercise of Power." *The Guardian*, 31 October.

Zupan, Mark. 1989. "Cable Franchise Renewals: Do Incumbent Firms Behave Opportunistically?" *Rand Journal of Economics* 20: 473–82.

Index

Index